A Social Work Approach to The Tea Plantation Labour in India

Dr. D. John Paul

ATLANTIC

PUBLISHERS & DISTRIBUTORS (P) LTD

Published by

ATLANTIC

PUBLISHERS & DISTRIBUTORS (P) LTD

7/22, Ansari Road, Darya Ganj, New Delhi-110002
Phones : +91-11-40775252, 40775214, 23273880, 23275880
Fax: +91-11-23285873
Web: www.atlanticbooks.com
E-mail: orders@atlanticbooks.com

Printed & bound in India by Atlantic Print Services

Foreword

Social work profession is facing lots of challenges, and the greatest challenge is the non-availability or lack of accessibility of micro details in some sectors. The challenges in the professional practice need more of theoretical and analytical knowledge base for decision, mainly by the practitioners.

The book, *A Social Work Approach to the Tea Plantation Labour in India* by Dr. D. John Paul is expected to meet the needs of HR/Welfare officials of corporate, cooperative, government and small tea plantations to assess the problems faced by the plantation workers and arrive at remedial measures.

I was part of Dr. D. John Paul's venture from his Ph.D. stage to the publication of this work. A number of references have gone into the book.

"What is written without efforts is generally read without pleasure", said Samual Johnson.

I am confident that for the efforts Dr. D. John Paul has made to finalize this book, he would get good readership from social work institutions, tea plantation management and related stakeholders.

The book gives a detailed profile of the tea plantation labour in India, Sri Lanka, Bolivia and Brazil.

Dr. John Paul has used these references to project a comparative picture of the tea plantation workers of the Tamil Nadu Tea Plantation Corporation Limited (TANTEA) which forms the basis of his Ph.D.

This book will be of immense use for the readers, especially the social work students, and stakeholders connected to the tea industries. This is a rare collection on tea plantation labourers' status and would attract more readership in the public, institutional, corporate and college libraries.

Dr. C.J. Paul
Senior Development Consultant,
Chennai

Preface

The socio-economic and working conditions of the tea plantation workers in India require immediate attention. The employment in the tea plantations depends purely on the use of 'master-servant relationship'. This is a clear reminder that the labour force often consists of the descendants of the migrant workers whose rights are few, working conditions frequently grim, education minimal, and health poor—in many instances worse than that of similar workers outside the plantations. Though the number of tea gardens has been reduced, the number of workers and their dependants has increased manifold. This has led to innumerable socio-economic and political problems in the tea plantation states.

The book entitled *A Social Work Approach to the Tea Plantation Labour in India* presents a panoramic view of the tea plantation labour scene in contemporary India. Employment relations and working conditions in the tea plantation sector are examined in the context of the existing legal provisions to protect the workers' interests in this largely exploitative system. Based on social work and other social sciences' intervention, it throws new light on the possibilities and limitations of popular participation in the development of tea plantation labour in India. Critical issues of agrarian reforms and living and working conditions of the poor tea plantation workers are seen against the background of existing provisions and inability of the labour force to access the benefits of reforms.

Though not claiming to deal with all aspects of the labour scene in India, the book does provide a fresh perspective of critical labour issues of today and tomorrow. To that extent it should stimulate further discussion among policy-makers, administrators, employer organizations, trade union federations, scholars, international NGOs, and others concerned with labour problems. The recent starvation deaths in North Bengal tea plantations support my work.

Finally, this book is written in order to bring out the poor plight of the tea plantation workers and various problems faced by them, including the occupational risks and health problems. Not many people know that tea is the product of enormous hardships by a worker who has slogged it out in a far away plantation. The book brings to light the fact that the tea which relaxes us is the fruit of cumulative toil of the poor labourers who work hard round the clock and produce this "black diamond"—the most common beverage of the world. It will be useful for all those concerned with the labour aspect of tea plantations in India.

Dr. D. John Paul M.A., M.Phil., Ph.D.
Assistant Professor, P.G. & Research
Department of Social Work,
Loyola College (Autonomous),
(College of Excellence)
Nungambakkam, Chennai-600034

Acknowledgements

I express my sincere thanks to all my faculty colleagues and staff members of P.G. & Research Department of Social Work, Loyola College (Autonomous)—College of Excellence, Chennai for their support to complete the work well in time. I am happy to have received positive response from the management of the college, especially Rev. Fr. Rector, Rev. Fr. Principal, Rev. Fr. Secretary and the Head of the Department, when I expressed my desire to write this book.

I wish to acknowledge my deep appreciation and debt of gratitude to Dr. C.J. Paul for writing the Foreword. He helped me a lot in my doctoral studies and guided me well to handle the Ph.D. thesis. My sincere thanks go to Dr. Thilakavathi Subramanian, Scientist, Deputy Director (Senior Grade) & Head, Division of Social and Behavioural Research, National Institute of Epidemiology, I.C.M.R., Ayapakkam, Chennai for encouraging and guiding me to come up with this publication. My sincere thanks are due to Dr. Udaya Mahadevan, Professor Emeritus in Social Work, Loyola College (Autonomous), Chennai, for her valuable suggestions and feedback while editing some of the chapters at the pre-manuscript stage.

I express my sincere thanks to Mr. Harjeet, Atlantic Publishers & Distributors (P) Ltd., New Delhi for encouraging and reminding me to complete the typescript well in time. I also thank the editorial and production team for publishing the book in a record time. My sincere thanks to Dr. K.T. Dilli, Librarian, Loyola College (Autonomous), Chennai, for providing me relevant material for completing the book.

My special thanks to my wife, Mrs. D. Bagia Sangeetha, for encouraging and providing support to complete the study and also partly typing the manuscript. Without her help it would not have been possible to publish this book. I am also indebted to my beloved sons, J. Fulton Joseph Sheen, J. Faber Francis Xavier and J. Ferdinand Dominic Savio as I could not attend to them while being busy with this work. I must also express my sincere thanks to my brothers and sister for constantly supporting me in accomplishing this work.

Dr. D. John Paul, M.A., M.Phil., Ph.D.

Contents

1

A Social Work Approach to the Tea Plantation Labour in India

Assam found a significant place in the global map due to tea plantation. The colonial powers brought immigrant labourers from Bihar (mainly from Chhotanagpur), Uttar Pradesh, Madhya Pradesh, Odisha and Andhra Pradesh to cater the needs of the agro-based tea industry in Assam (Purnendu Kumar, 2006; Pranab Kumar Das Gupta, Iar Ali Khan, 1983). The local labourers thought to be sufficient at the initial stage, but were found inefficient, lazy, irregular and disinterested in plantation work. They considered plantation job below their status and dignity. As such a large number of labourers on contract basis were brought from outside Assam. However, they stayed back even after the expiry of contract period and settled permanently in the tea estates of Assam. At present, the descendants of the immigrants have become part and parcel of Assam; for all practical purposes they have made it their permanent abode.

It is a fact that the labourers were starved, illiterate, innocent and exploited people in their place of origin. They were allured by the agents touring them to this inhospitable and inaccessible tea plantation area. Bribery, coercion, deceit, false promises were the tactics applied by the agents to bring them here. In course of their journey through steamer, boat and later on by train, they suffered immensely and many men, women and children died due to various diseases (cholera, dysentery, etc.), hunger and congestion.

Those who survived were sent to the tea gardens of Assam (including Cachar Valley) like animals. They were kept in barracks without caring for the privacy of women. Subsequently, plantation life began and gradually better plantation environment appeared. Divergent ethnic groups, living together made many compromises, sacrificed their tradition, mother-tongue and cultural values. However, they helped establishing edifice of the tea industry in Assam (Purnendu Kumar, 2006). They left no stone unturned to make the industry viable and prosperous. The study covers three districts of Barak Valley —Cachar, Karimganj and Hailakandi where more than 15% of the total population is constituted by the tea garden and ex-tea garden labourers settled from many generations in the vicinity of the tea gardens (Rajani Kanta Das, 1931). Many labourers having subsistence agricultural background escaped from the rigorous plantation life and settled in nearby vacant land. They adopted agriculture as their mainstay. Similarly, after expiry of contract, many labourers voluntarily left the plantation work and settled in those vacant lands and started cultivation. These groups of labourers were branded as ex-tea garden labourers; they are now settled in many villages/*bastees* of their own.

Tea garden labourers including ex-tea garden constitute an important segment of the total population of Cachar. They are part and parcel of socio-economic and political life of Cachar. Their socio-cultural interaction with other linguistic and cultural groups remained closed in the past but now, the doors have been opened and as such there has been acculturation among the immigrant labourers with the local culture (Purnendu Kumar, 2006). Besides, the emergence of the urge for political identity along with the spread of education, political awareness, trade union activities among the tea garden labourers highlighting unemployment and various other demands have ushered in an era of assertions and identity.

A few studies were undertaken on the following key areas on a micro level:

(i) Main causes of poverty, ignorance, illiteracy and socio-economic backwardness of tea garden and ex-tea garden labourers of Cachar.

(ii) Working conditions, income and relationship with other workers, living condition at home, main problems of these labourers and the role of the family in their habitat.

(iii) Extent of socio and economic exploitation, atrocities perpetrated on the tea garden labourers of Cachar.

(iv) Acculturation process of the tea garden labourers of Cachar.

(v) Political perception of the tea garden labourers including ex-tea garden labourers of Cachar and their role in local, regional and state politics.

(vi) Attitude of the tea garden labourers on different societal aspects—social, economic and political.

The study on the tea plantation workers is most significant in present-day context, considering the rising trends of labour unrest and sporadic disturbances arising out of increasing unemployment, extreme poverty and illiteracy among the tea garden labourers. The rising frustration and step-motherly treatment of the management and partial neglect by the government machinery result in strikes, lockout, violence and sometimes brutal killings of managerial staff. These developments naturally draw attention to social scientists and scholars of various disciplines to make in-depth study of the situation (Iar Ali Khan, 1983).

The immigrant plantation workers of Cachar like other parts of Assam have also added new dimension to ethnic turmoil of Cachar (Umananda Phukam, 1983). The sociological and anthropological aspects of study in the changing national scenario are another significant aspect of the study. The focus of such studies centers round the historical antecedents, the socio-economic and political life of the tea garden workers who contribute a major share in the economic advancement of the state and the country as a whole through foreign exchange by the tea export. Such a study further exposes the exploitation and harassment of the workers by the management and indifferent attitude of the proprietors. The role of trade unions and other NGOs also comes under the purview of such studies (Purnendu

Kumar, 2006; Elizabeth Kaniampady, 2003). From empirical study of a sample tea garden, namely Kashipur, relevant data and other materials have been collected. The general study of all other tea gardens of Assam, or Tarai and Doars regions of West Bengal, the hierarchy in plantation, process of recruitment, wage pattern, job opportunities are same all over the tea estates of Assam. One particular study has been carried out in detail by Dr. Purendhar Kumar in the state of Assam which is worth while to be considered in these aspects.

The data and other materials have been collected from both published, and unpublished sources as well as field study of different tea gardens of Barak Valley and Assam Valley (Brahmaputra Valley). During the period, many valuable materials were collected from these institutions and organisations. The technique of research is data oriented, based on field works. For primary information a questionnaire method was used followed by extensive sample (118 houses) survey of households (workers) belonging to different ethnic groups and other castes engaged in plantation work. The information collected from interview and case study were supplemented by data collected through personal observations. Besides, some managerial staff, seasoned trade union leaders and activists having special knowledge of tea plantation had been interviewed.

In fact, no work has so far been done on socio-economic and political life of tea garden workers of Assam. P. Griffith, in his work *The History of Indian Tea Industry* (1967) and E. Gait, in his work *The History of Assam* (1935) have made passing reference to the historical background and development of tea industry. However, they did not mention any socio-economic and political aspect of plantation workers' life. J.B. Bhattacharjee, in his book *Cachar under British Rule in North East India* (1977) has simply made a casual reference to the tea garden labourers of Cachar. R.C. Awasthi's work on *Economics of Tea Industry in India* (1975) and Amalendu Guha's book *Planters Raj to Swaraj* (1977) have analysed the economic part as well as historical and political part of the tea industry workers in general but no specific study on Cachar have been made. S.S. Harlalkar, in his work *Socio-Economic Study of Tea Garden Labourers of Assam* (1973) has thrown some light on socio-economic life of the Tea Workers of Assam in general but no in-depth study has been stressed upon in respect of Barak Valley. *S.* Bhowmik, in his work *Class Formation in the Plantation System* (1981) and S.K. Bose. in his book *Capital and Labour in Indian Tea Industry* (1954) have taken the thread of Marxist ideology and coloured the socio-economic aspect of the tea plantation workers of India in their own way. Many other scholars and researchers in their unpublished work have also studied various features of tea garden workers of various plantation districts of Assam, which are considered incomplete in many respects. Thus, the present study is necessitated to draw a vivid picture of the socio-economic and political life of the tea workers (tea garden labourers including ex-tea garden labourers) of the whole district of Cachar (south Assam), which remained unexplored till today.

A Brief Introduction about the Tea Plantations in Northern and South Assam

Eighteenth century English poet William Cowper's view "the cup that cheers but not inebriates" still holds good in the modern civilized society. Nowadays, tea has become one of the cheapest universal beverages in the world. People, right from the intellectuals, down to the ordinary manual workers in different fields of activities feel pleasure while sipping "tea, and get relief, relaxed and refreshed". Earlier, the Europeans, particularly the British and Americans were habituated of taking tea regularly (Elizabeth Kaniampady, 2003). The Asiatic countries followed the taste of tea much later in 19th century. Gradually, it became universal and people from every walk of life enjoy the pleasure of tea. Tea is regarded as a stimulant and it contains important ingredients like caffeine, protein, vitamins, etc. It reduces mental tension and gives little rest to mind. Tea plantation in India is virtually a gift of the British colonial administration. The history of the tea plantation as elaborately discussed (Piya Chatterjee, 2001) in subsequent chapters reveals that strenuous efforts were made to develop plantation in North East India, particularly in the Assam Valley and its success encouraged European planters and entrepreneurs to expand the plantation throughout the region which was favoured by the geographical factors. In the Surma Valley also the first tea plantation was started in 1855-56 by the Williamson and Co. near Barsangan (near present Kathal Bagan) and its success opened the eyes of many planters and adventurous capitalists and entrepreneurs who applied for grant of land in Cachar. The early administrators of Cachar like Capt. T. Fishers, Lt. G. Verner and R. Stewart also took initiative to promote tea plantation in Cachar. The 'wild rush' of the planters led to liberal grants of land, on easy terms under the patronage of the colonial administrators for tea plantation, and within a short time many gardens were opened in Barak Valley. Before 1861, it was less than 50 but in 1869 it increased to 71 with 8600 acres. Later by 1895, it reached up to 199 covering an area of 280172 acres. At present, Cachar is the seventh leading district in India in respect of production of tea.

The tea plantation has developed along the Brahmaputra River in northern Assam and along Surma River (now Barak, the upper part of the same river which remained in India after partition) in South Assam (Cachar). For convenience sake, the northern part is called Assam Valley and southern part, the Barak Valley or Cachar. The Assam Valley includes Lakhimpur. Darrang, Sibsagar, Jorhat, Golaghat, Kamrup, Sonitpur, Goalpara districts. The Barak Valley includes Cachar, Karimganj and Hailakandi districts.

Table 1.1: Top Ten Tea Producing Districts

Ten Producing Districts	1992	1993
Dibrugarh (Assam)	139.38	142.73
Dooars (West Bengal)	118.94	129.9
Sibsagar (Assam)	91.93	96.88
Darrang (Assam)	78.08	81.85
Nilgiris (Tamil Nadu)	69.97	77.03
Idukki (Kerala)	40.84	51.04
Cachar (Assam)	43.69	42.44
Nilgiris (Tamil Nadu)	21.43	27.27
Idukki (Kerala)	25.01	26.25
Cachar (Assam)	9.87	10.85

The number of workers accordingly went on increasing and immigration of labour increased (Purnendu Kumar, 2006). Tea plantation labour-oriented work which requires large number of labours. The local labourers initially engaged did not meet the requirements; hence, the importation of labourers from outside Assam was thought and action taken immediately. Within a short time, the entire Assam tea plantation area was covered by immigrant labourers. At present the number of gardens though reduced, yet line number of tea garden labour and their dependants has increased manifold. This has opened the gate of innumerable socio-economic and political problems within the State. Keeping these important points in view, the study begins with the description of historical and geographical features of the district which favours tea plantation.

A Short History of Cachar

The province of Cachar, formerly called Hirimba, was informally attached to British dominion on 13 June 1830 following the death of the last king Govinda Chandra who was without any heir. The province was subsequently annexed by the British on 14 August 1832.

The original district of Cachar with Hailakandi and Silcruir sub-division was known in older times as 'Hirimba Desha' named after the demons Hirimba who married Bhimsena, the second Pandava of Mahabharata and gave birth to Ghatotkacha. Till 16th century, the rulers of Cachar used to be known as Hirimbeswar (Mahendra P. Lama, 1986).

The 13th century Barak Valley was ruled by Tipperah—a section of Bodos and the capital was at Khalangshi now known as Rajghat on the bank of the River Rukni in Cachar. The Tipperns moved eastwards and with Tulsidwaj as the reigning Prince, an independent kingdom was established in 15th century AD. In the beginning of the 16th century, Cachar was annexed to Tripura. The authority of Tripura in Cachar came to an end when Koch rulers defeated the Raja of Tripura at Longai now in Karimganj district and the Koch general Chilarai left a contigent of Koch soldiers at Brahmapur now known as Khaspur near Udharbond in Cachar. Later, Cachar came under Hirimba kingdom.

The kingdom of Hirimba once extended to a vast area covering a part of the present Nowgong district and western portion of Sibsagar as well as the entire belt of Cachar, North Cachar and Karbi Anglong district but during the reign of Raja Govinda Chandra it began to shrink gradually. After the annexation of the plain portion of Cachar by the British on August 14, 1832 by the proclamation of Governor-in-Council, Capt. T. Fisher was appointed Superintendent of Cachar who administered the district from Cherapunji and subsequently shifted to Doodhpatil from where the headquarters were finally shifted to Silchar. The official nomenclature of Cachar appeared on the administrative map of Assam in September 1835 and the old name of Hirimba was wiped out from the age-old map of Cachari kingdom (Piya Chatterjee, 2001).

North-West Province, Awadh and Panjab which helped migration of hungry and starved people to the districts of Assam. The British planters exploited the opportunity and recruited a large number of labourers through their agents called 'Arkattis'. Thus, labourers from famine and poverty-stricken areas of Bihar (Chhotanagpur, Ranchi, Hazaribagh, Dumka, Buxur, Gaya, Palamu, Bhagalpur, Mongher, Chapra and Patna), Odisha (Ganjan, Kalahandi), Madhya Pradesh (Raipur/Bastar, Bilaspu, Raigarh), Uttar Pradesh (Deoria, Balia, Basti, Mirzapur, Gazipur, Azamgarh, Gorakhpur), Bengal (Medinepur, Purulia, Bakura, Burdwan) were recruited by the agents under contract system. Though the climate was favourable of tea plantation, it was not favourable for the planters. The high temperature, extreme humid climate, diseases like malaria, cholera, kalazar, small pox, dysentery, and typhoid were widespread (Umananda Phukam, 1983). All these negative factors hampered the pioneering work. However, frantic efforts were made by the adventurous European planters despite unsuitable and inhospitable climate for them to develop tea plantation in Assam by appointing 'Arkattis'. They were the agents of the planters who infiltrated into the remotest villages wherever a suitable opportunity occurred. They resorted to nefarious and fraudulent practices for tempting or forcing men and women in the country side for agreement, i.e. a contract to serve for at least a period of three years to be made by the starved people. This was in reality a trap for reducing them to slavery. They were kept in a closely guarded depot pending their despatch to the tea gardens in Assam.

While on journey for more than a month indentured labourers were given limited quantity of dry ration and were forced to embark the country boat beyond its capacity. They were virtually packed up in the boat-like animals and no human consideration was even thought of regarding the privacy of women. Due to long journey and bad climate, many labourers and their children who were poor and ill-nourished, deluded by the 'Arakattis', died en route because they were unable to withstand the hostile climate of North-East India (Purnendu Kumar, 2006).

One of the methods of recruitment of labour was through licensed contractors who themselves employed licensed recruiters known as Arkattis (Arkattis literally means pilots). The dead bodies were thrown into the river water like beasts. Nowhere in annals of mankind was such a great dishonour shown to the dead as was meted out to the newly-recruit tea garden labourers dying under trying circumstances. Those who survived reached their destination in Cachar in psychologically-depressed mood and most frustrating appearance. They were at first put in the concentration camp at Katigorah or Silchar from where they were sent to different tea gardens. The moment the uprooted men put their feet on the soil of Cachar, their hopes and aspirations were shattered by the blow of misfortune. They were disheartened and perplexed to find a typical geographical environment. As a matter of fact, they were not accustomed to such an environment. They were asked to clear the jungle first and to make huts or common barracks for their dormitory-living. In case of any refusal to work, boots and kicks of the European planters were the only reply. Migrants were subjected to round the clock surveillance of the garden chowkidar. After detection, they were whipped mercilessly by the managers and in fact, cane was indispensable accompaniment of the garden manager. The out-raging of the women's modesty was also not rare in the garden world. They were treated as the object of 'hire and fire' at par with men (Uday Kumar Varma, M.M. Rehman, 2005).

The planters enjoyed extra-authoritarian power over the labourers. They were not only the masters of the labour but also magistrates to decide disputes, arrest and punish them for breach of contract. They arbitrarily exploited the labourers and beat mercilessly whenever they tried to escape from the garden. The labourers were discriminated and had to suffer injustice from them because the planters treated them of inferior breed. They were treated as 'beast in a menagerie'. Sometimes Saheb called them as black feather to be used for their selfish end. The sorrowful and heart burning feeling forced the labour to shun their tears in the isolated and most secluded part of the tea garden. The folklore of the tea garden women workers of the garden reflects the feelings of the workers.

"Hai re nirmohi shyam Faki din anlo Assam"

("O Cruel God, agents brought us to Assam by bluff")

Instances are numerous when the women labourers were occasionally tied up to a tree and their clothes lifted up to the waist and were beaten on bare buttocks with leather strips or boots (Elizabeth Kaniampady, 2003). For sexual atrocities committed upon the female workers of both immigrants and local tribes, many victims even committed suicide to escape such torture. Lamenting upon such inhuman behaviour of the planters has been remarked:

> It is very painful to contemplate that those who call themselves Christian even by name should so far forget the most solemn injunction of the Bible. That they should not feel the least compunction to tempt away by the glitters of gold, a class of ignorant and simple-hearted women and rob them of a treasure which is even more precious than the richest diamond that may adorn a throne.

Such inhuman treatment and sexual exploitation of the tea garden women workers have been highlighted by social activists and many trade union leaders (Piya Chatterjee, 2001). It is indeed a well-known fact that the tea gardens were managed by the European managers during the British days. They were vested with powers to arrest and imprison the labour living in the estates for many wrongful acts. This power was misutilised for creating a terror and doing 'oppression'. Women living in the estates were often utterly dishonoured and demoralised by having illicit sexual relationship. At one stage, the increasing number of illegitimate Eurasian children, reflecting the slur on Indians posed a serious problem that drew the attention of Mahatma Gandhi who wrote in *Young India* his serious concern and warned both Indian and European Managers of the tea gardens to refrain from dishonouring womanhood.

The sensational Khoreal shooting case during April 1921 in which Reginald William Read, Assistant Manager of the Garden wanted a labour girl named Hira to live with him and on being refused Mr. Read shoot down her father Gangadhar and her brother Nepal. This is a heinous crime and inhuman treatment meted out to labour. Similarly, one Mr. Dowson, Manager of Badarpur Tea Estate (who served Esabeel TE also) used to dance with female workers in his bungalow in naked condition. On being refused, he used to punish them and harass them economically too. The Baladan Murder case 1892 is also the story of European manager's atrocities on women workers. The manger was a man of bad character who used to exploit the chastity of the innocent female workers, although in most cases, the incidents were given different colours and many innocent persons were falsely implicated (Purnendu Kumar, 2006).

The present occupational pattern and acute poverty of the labour community is the result of existing pattern of employment as well as exploitative measure adopted by the planters. Further, illiteracy among the tea garden workers and lack of awareness among them due to less contact with the outside world, have put them, in such a position of perpetual slavery. Prolonged poverty of the workers, regular indebtedness, and frustration due to unemployment of the sons and daughters always burdened their spirit.

Area-wise Distribution of Tea Plantation in Cachar

The labourers are identified everywhere in the garden with torn cloths, lacerated faces, dusty shoes, frustrated and exhausted look and above all dark complexion. These are the typical characteristics of the tea garden labourers. They were treated by the British planters not as human beings but as animals. This feudal outlook has not changed and continues to influence the minds of the Indian planters even today (Arul Sarma, 2012). The tea garden workers have become socially and culturally acclimatized in the soil of the tea garden of Assam. They have been for all practical purpose become part and parcel of Assam. Their ancestral places have been forgotten by more than 20% of the labour. A sizeable per centage of them simply know their ancestral places but have not visited the places any time. They consider the garden as their permanent abode and treat the place as temple of love, affection as well as the temple of bread and butter. Whenever tea tree grows, the place is sacred whether it exists on the mountain, slope or on the plain field.

Of all the problems confronted by the labourers, the problem of wage and fringe benefits is most pressing and persistent (R.L. Sarkar, Mahendra P. Lama, 1986). There is still discrimination in their daily wages and wages offered to the workers are much lower than the wages prevailing in other sectors of the country.

The Labour Commission, 1868 Opines:

> The most garden, especially in Assam, labourers earn very much below the minimum wage. During 1881 the tea garden workers used to get ₹ 3-50 whereas an ordinary worker in Bombay during 1860-62 got ₹ 7-50. Even at present a tea garden worker gets ₹ 35-30 per day whereas outside the garden the same labour gets ₹ 50-70 per day. (Pranab Kumar Das Gupta, Iar Ali Khan, 1983)

This discrimination had a great impact on the economic activities leading to stagnant economic status of the workers. The housing problems faced by the tea garden labourers are also acute and painful. They are living in isolated and solitary jungles of labour line. Their accommodation even from Indian standard is horrifying. The Plantation Labour Act, 1951 has not been fully implemented. As such most of the workers live in thatched houses partly mud-built and partly bamboo plastered with mud and cow dung. The ground is damp and infected with white ant. The report of the Royal Commission on Labour in India in 1931 observes:

> ...the average number of persons per room is four which, judged even by Indian standard of city life must be called bad...thirty-three per cent of the population live in rooms occupied by more than five persons at a time and 1% in room occupied by over 20 persons at a time. The number of persons living in rooms containing from 6 to 9 persons which is more than 50% of the labour line.

Historical Background of the Tea Plantations in India

The tea drinking habit of the local people in Assam was very primitive. The tribal population of the province, particularly those living in upper Assam (Singphos) of Sadiya used it as a medicinal drink known as 'Finap'. In 1815 one Col. Latter noticed the tea drinking habit of the people of upper Assam which appeared to be the starting point East India Company to venture for tea plantation in India. There have been many divergent views which transpire from the report published by Col. Keatings, the Chief Commissioner of Assam regarding the inventor of tea plants in Assam (Rajani Kanta Das, 1931). Many opine that Robert Bruce was the first among the British to know about the existence of tea plants in Assam in 1823.

He is acclaimed, to have pioneering role towards commercial cultivation of tea in Assam. During his travel, Robert Bruce developed friendship with Bessgaum, Singpho Chief in Assam, who gave him some indigenous tea plants and seeds in 1823. This incident is thought to be the discovery of tea in India. But Robert Bruce's brother Charles Alexander Bruce who was working for East India Company, regarded himself as 'the man of destiny' who first penetrated into the forests and visited the tracts in British Sadiya. H.K. Barpujari opines that Major Jenkins was not slow to avail himself of this opportunity. The investigation which carried out in collaboration with Lt. A. Charlton, officer-in-charge of Sadiya, revealed in early 1835 the existence of tea plant from Sadiya and Beesa to the Chinese frontier province of Yunan where the shrub was cultivated for its leaves. The Agro-

Horticulture Society, Calcutta awarded its own medal to Capt. Andrew Charlton and Major Francis Jenkins for their work in the discovery of the indigenous tea plants.

A second story regarding the discovery of tea is narrated in China (Purnendu Kumar, 2006). It is said that in 2737 BC. Emperor Sheh Nung found that a few leaves which fell into boiling water gave a delightful flavour. He named the resultant brew 'tay' or 'cha'. According to Japanese legend, the Buddhist sage Parma dedicated seven years to sleepless meditation. In order to keep awake he cut off his eye lids. They sprouted into tea bushes where leaves would come to be used by others who wanted to ward off sleep.

Tea is a word derived from 'Te', a Chinese Fukien dialect. China is the country which gave the name and beverage to the world. 'Te' means Tea in Malayan, Danish, Italian, Spanish, Norwegian, Swedish, Hungarian and Czechoslovakian. The word 'cha' in Chinese Fukien dialect means Tea pronounced 'chah'.

However, it is difficult to trace out the exact period when tea was first used as beverage after proper treatment of leaves and became a palatable drink. Tea had its genesis in China untold centuries ago but its real history is lost in the obscurity of China's venerable antiquity and foremost part is traditional.

Tea, according to Chinese legends, as a beverage was known in the country as early as in 1937 BC. But the first recorded reference about tea is found in a classical compilation by Confucius about 500 BC. In China, tea has not only been used as a beverage but it has been a part of the social history. The *Encyclopedia of Britannica* highlights:

> Tea originated in China about 700 BC possibly because of the need of boiling water for health purposes. Tea cultivation developed in Japan about AD 800. It spread to other Asiatic country, later and by the first half of 18th century tea became a popular beverage in Holland, England and the American colonies. In some Asiatic countries, the leaves are consumed as a vegetable called Leppet in Burma and Miarig in Thailand.

There are many stories regarding the origin of tea plant which came to China from India. Samuel Baildon, a well-known authority and expert on tea history opines that tea was indigenous only to India and no other country of the world. He holds the opinion that tea plant was introduced in China and Japan from India. There was only one species of tea—the Indian and the inferior quality of tea leaves of China type were the results of uncongenial and unfavourable conditions of soil and treatment of plant. (Purnendu Kumar, 2006)

Role of East India Company

The East India Company was the pioneer in the development of tea trade and later tea plantation in India which led to flourishing tea industry in India. It had complex control of tea export trade from China which continued up to 1833 (Umananda Phukam, 1983).

The company was buying tea and silk from China in exchange of Silver and Bullion. The trade agreement of 20 years was over in 1833 and the Chinese Government refused to renew the agreement granting the East India Company the right of British trade monopoly with China. Consequently, the East India Company had to take initiative vigorously to establish a source of supply from India. Accordingly, the then Governor-General Lord William Bentinck appointed a Tea Committee in 1834 with Dr. Wallich as the Secretary to study a plan for introduction of tea culture in India and for its superintendence of execution.

While constituting Tea Committee, Lord William Bentinck had political as well as commercial interest/aim behind this initiative. The province of Assam, nearest region of India to the Chinese tea districts was then a wild land, misgoverned and scantly populated. The government wanted it to be placed as a settled, prosperous looking and was prepared to cultivate its waste spaces.

Labour Immigration

Tea plantation is a labour-oriented enterprise as it is agro-based. It requires huge labour at every stage of its work right from clearance of jungle, making the land suitable for plantation, work for the nursery, giving manure both in the nursery and in the plantation area, spraying of pesticides, drain cutting, path making, plucking, manufacturing and finally despatching to different destinations. Without labour not a single tea plant can survive as no baby can survive without mother (Uday Kumar Varma, 2005).

Local labourers were found lazy and remained absent for longer duration on simple pretext of festivals, *puja*, marriage, *shradha*, etc. which hampered the ongoing work of plantation. Regular complaints started coming from the planters and the district authority was compelled to think in terms of importing labour from other areas.

As in Assam Valley, the local people were mostly reluctant to work in the garden and considered it derogatory and below dignity to work in the garden which transpires from a folk song (Bihu):

Angrszor chakri na lage karibo
Na iage ghatibo dhan
Gharote bohibo ramayan paribo
Take suni thakibar man
(We don't like to serve under British
we need not require wealth
Sitting at home, we shall recite Ramayana
And keep our mind happy after hearing the same.)

The local Bengalis and tribals were not willing to work sincerely in the tea plantation. This put the planters and district administrators in mental strain. The district administration finally agreed to import labour from outside which would bring much benefit to the country.

The craze for enlarging the tea plantation in N.E. India was also augmented by the political factor (Rajani Kanta Das, 1931). The entire India, particularly, the Northern and Western part was burning under fire due to Sepoy Mutiny in 1857 and the British were mentally perturbed. Europeans from outside Assam preferred to invest in this region which was least affected and thus they wanted to settle and invest money in Assam despite shortage of labour.

Tea is cultivated in more than 45 countries spread over all the continents except North America within the longitudinal range of 40°N and 35°S. Tea culture is agro-based, labour-intensive and renewable natural resources. It makes use of waste land also which are otherwise not very productive for other crops. Indian tea industry is now 160 years old and has contributed immensely to the economic development of the nation. At present, its contribution to the GNP is over ₹ 30 billion and foreign exchange earning amounts to over ₹ 17.3 billion.

All the development in the field of tea plantation in Cachar is the result of pioneering enterprising skill of European planters who helped in bringing dynamic changes in the socio-economic and political scenario of Cachar. The real assessment and analysis in subsequent chapters would expose the economic development of Cachar. Thus, it paved the way for large-scale expansion of tea plantation in Cachar for which immigrant labourers needed to cope with the work. The Government of Bengal took initiative, to import labour from outside Assam.

Situating Labour in the Context of the Present Crisis of the Tea Plantations in India

The tea industry in India is said to be going through a crisis since the early 1990s, primarily because of a fall in tea auction prices. Other manifestations of the crisis include decline in exports, closure and abandonment of tea gardens, increasing labour unrest at times leading to violent protests and confrontations, non-payment and curtailment of wages and other statutory benefits of workers, declining living standards and worsening human security in the tea gardens. There is, however, divergence of opinion regarding the precise nature of the 'crisis'. For example, it has been pointed out that the focus of discussions on the tea sector is on the marketing front and not so much on production. Tea production in India is not only enough to meet the domestic demand but also export around two lakh tones a year. From the producers' point of view, the major question is securing a remunerative price for tea, particularly after the opening up of imports under the WTO Agreement (*The Hindu*, 2010). Although imports for domestic consumption are still negligible, this cannot be a ground for much compliancy as the fairly high prevalent import tariff could be reduced gradually to the global level of 3 to 4 per cent in course of time (Ramadurai, 2002). Tea gardens in India experienced closures and abandonment especially during the years 2002-04 in the Dooars region of West Bengal, in Ponmudi, Trivandum district and Peermade, Idukki district of Kerala with a lesser magnitude in Assam and Tamil Nadu. At present, there are reports of continuous closures in some of the tea gardens in West Bengal and Kerala (Talwar et al., 2005).

There have been reports of strikes, unrest and even cases of violent confrontations between workers and management personnel. The crisis in the tea sector, particularly in Assam, has led to labour unrest and apprehensions regarding the future prospects of the sector as well as the workers depending upon the sector (Lahiri, 2000; Misra, 2003). In Dibrugarh districts, a tea garden manager was hacked to death by agitation workers. This event was far from an aberration; rather it was an extreme manifestation of a much deeper crisis affecting the sector (Misra, 2003). The relation between tea garden employees and laborers has deteriorated over the past decades, aggravated by the crisis in the tea industry. However, there appears to be a larger dimension to this tension.

Attacks on Tea Garden Labourers

On 24 November 2007, when 6000 Adivasis from the tea gardens of Assam gathered at a protest rally in Guwahati to demand ST status, their rally was attacked by local muslim shopkeepers and youth in retaliation to violent attacks by some of the agitators. A report in *Outlook* magazine describes the incidents as follows: "In a retaliation of a sort never seen on the streets of Guwahati before, the shopkeepers and local residents came down heavily on the adivasis. Within less than an hour of the frenzy, a 46 year old adivasi protester lady dead, 250 others were wounded." In the meelee, an adivasi girl was stripped naked and pursued by miscreants. She was rescued by an elderly man, who gave her his shirt and she reached the safety of a nearby police station. Also nursing her wounds at the hospital was Marconi Soren, an 18-year-old adivasi girl from Mornai Tea

Estate, in the western Kokrajhar district. "Someday, we shall get justice," she said.

The labourers in the tea garden (Biswas et al., 2005; Lines 2006) were subjected to frequent brutality and harassment. *The Guardian*, for example, in one of its reports claimed that in West Bengal alone at least 700 Indian tea workers have died from diseases linked to malnutrition in the last year after 16 estates were closed (*The Guardian*, 2007). The Centre for Education and Communication (CEC), New Delhi, organized a fact-finding visit by the independent experts to investigate the conditions of workers in the tea gardens of West Bengal in 2003. The findings of the team confirmed the non-payment of wages, and in some cases reduction of wages and increase in work load, non-deposit of provident fund and severe curtailment of health and housing facilities (Banerjee et al., 2003).

Tea estates are enclave economies in which the workers are provided with subsided ration, drinking water, housing, health, and other basic facilities by the management. With the closure and abandoning of the tea estates, the living conditions of the workers have been drastically affected. So far as housing and sanitation are concerned, the conditions were already poor and have simply deteriorated further. A rather alarming report mentions, "while the children have stopped going to school, the women are migrating to cities in search of illusive jobs. Some others survive by crushing stones or by collecting wild fruits and vegetables. In some cases, impoverished women are forced to sell their bodies as means of survival". These problems have compounded with existing social problems, particularly non-compliance to labour legislation that already characterizes the industry. There have been reports of malaria epidemics and worsening health conditions and even starvation deaths from the tea gardens (Biswas et al., 2005). Poor food and water has allegedly led to the deaths of over 350 people in four tea estates of Dooars region in six months in the year 2003. Similarly, there are more than 12 cases of starvation deaths and suicides reported from Kerala. Since all the estate hospitals have closed down, there is no medical help available to the workers.

Faced with the decline in job opportunities, worsening living conditions and lose of livelihoods, the tea garden workers have started to look for work outside the tea gardens (Deepak K. Mishra, Vandana Upadhyay and Arul Sarma, 2012). It is the casual labour force that bears the brunt of downsizing in the gardens. They are the first to face evictions from the tea gardens and for them alternative sources of livelihood are difficult to come by. These casual workers are not covered under The Plantations Labour Act, 1951 or the State Plantation Rules of the respective tea-producing states and therefore face severe employment insecurity. Their predicament is all the more severe, as they get work only for five to six months during peak plucking season, after which they are forced to look for employment outside the plantations. As such there has been a gradual process of land alienation from the tea garden labour community, and given their low levels of education, skills and exposure, they find it difficult to get jobs outside the garden.

The tea garden labourers outside the garden are also called Adivasis, tea-tribes or sometimes mistaken as ex-tea garden labour community. Politically-loaded statements of self-identification, particularly in Assam, or forces the plantation workers to migrate to new areas such as Arunachal Pradesh or rest of the north-eastern states. The tea gardens, on the other hand, are severely downsizing and hence the only option for the tea garden labourers is to join the agricultural labour market at abysmally low wages (Mahendra P. Lama, 1986). Low levels of literacy, high drop-out rates among the children and alcoholism further aggravates their plight. Because of their low-fall back positions and lower access to institutional support from the government and non-government agencies, the tea garden labour community is at times disproportionately affected by natural disasters like floods. Natural disasters have "amplified the livelihood crisis which these communities face in Assam" (Mishra, 2005). Chhotanagpur region of Jharkhand, and the neighbouring tribal belts of Odisha, Madhya Pradesh and Chhattisgarh, eroded the communal property rights of the tribal populations over land, water and forests.

Plantation Labour in India

It is thus seen that extensive territories variegated topography, diverse climate, and rich soil fertility give India a great advantage for the development of plantation industries and for the production of tropical and sub-tropical commodities for which there is a great demand both in foreign and domestic markets. Of 980 tea gardens in Assam in 1928, 641 plantations were located in the northern part of the province, called the Assam or Brahmaputra valley and 339 gardens in the southern part called the Surma valley. In the former, the leading districts of tea cultivation are Lakhimpur and Sibsagar having respectively 223 and 196 gardens in 1928. Among the others regions, the most important centres of production are districts of Nilgris and Travancore, which had 192 and 116 gardens respectively (Rajani Kanta Das, 1931). The importance and growth of tea industry may be indicated by the increase in the investment of capital. The total amount of capital invested by joint stock companies both in England and in India increased from ₹ 17 crores in 1902 to ₹ 48 crores in 1928 while the latter consisting of ₹ 36 crores in the United Kingdom.

The rise of Plantation Workers in India

Being akin to agriculture, plantations are more congenial to women than other organised industries such as factories and mines. In the second phase, the very fact that the labourers not only work but also generally live on plantations or in the vicinity give women a chance to work on them. In the third place, the system of labour contracts based on the principle of utilising very able-bodied person in the family for labour and of fixing the wages rates accordingly compelled women to seek employment in order to balance the family budget. The contract system has been practically abolished but the system of wages rates and the custom of cheap women's labour still remain. Most of the children have to live on plantations with their parents either one or both of whom may be employed on tea gardens. The lack of educational facilities in India is one fundamental reason for a large number of children being employed in all occupations and plantation labour is no exception. The nature of plantations work also makes child labour profitable to planters. Moreover, the extreme poverty of the people and the low wages of adult labour easily induce the parents to take advantage of the wages of their children.

Labour Recruitment in Tea Plantation Sector in Ancient India

A Brief Introduction

Unlike sugar plantation, the tea plantation requires constant working force to be readily available at every stage of the work. The growth of population had been stopped in Assam during the Ahom rule. The Burmese War caused a steep fall, about 75% by 1835. Cholera, in all epidemic form in 1839, 1847 and 1852 and small pox further reduced the population. Moreover, due to high rate of opium consumption, the common Assamese did not want to undertake hard labour with only exception of Cacharis. The Assamese were too indolent or too well-off to accept regular employment (Purnendu Kumar, 2006).

Causes of Migration

The craze for enlarging the tea plantation in the N.E. Region was one of the fall out of the Sepoy Mutiny of 1857. There was widespread anti-White feeling in the entire country. Europeans from outside Assam thought that Assam is safe and less affected. They, therefore, decided to put entire weight on the tea plantation activities in Assam (Deepak K. Mishra, 2012). The European capitalists had already come to invest in indigo in Gangetic plains between 1830s and 1840s. Many of them shifted to Assam and started tea plantation with missionary zeal. Consequently, extra labour was to be urgently imported from outside. The cry of more labour came not only from speculators but also from the real tea cultivators during the continuance of tea mania.

In the neighboring provinces of UP, Bihar and Central Provinces, social anarchy and economic pressure in those days were undoubtedly the main reasons for migration of poor and weaker section of the society. Migration of peasant is totally absent where the subsistence form of economy prevails. Even an agricultural worker would be unwilling to migrate from their native village as their peasant masters who utilise their services for the cultivation of land is able to and willing to support them in times of distress while the tenant farmers under the Zamindari system did not enjoy such protection. This has been established from the descendants of the immigrants of the tea gardens in Cachar that the travails of Zamindars and other forms of landlordism imposed on them were one of the causes of migration to the tea plantation in Assam. Excessive exploitation and economic harassment of the ordinary farmers and landless workers belonging to lower castes by the feudal lords and Zamindars led to the early immigration to Assam like the colonial immigration. Those who came in the early part of the plantation belonged to poor and downtrodden community particularly the tribal and lower caste people who were held victims of exploitation.

Notwithstanding the subsistence character of Indian economy, a large number of people, however, migrated to the plantation in the tropical islands like Malaysia, Sri Lanka since middle of 19th century (Elizabeth Kaniampady, 2003). Sometimes, the failure of subsistence economy, in meeting the limited wants of the people due to frequent occurrence of natural calamities like drought and floods followed by epidemics also caused migration. The inhabitants of both hills and plains, who live by unskilled labour were in a wretched condition, ill-fed and ill-clad, with no resources to with stand such calamity were forced to move elsewhere. The Colonial Government knew the nature and aptitude of the docile tribal of Chhotanagpur and simple and plain people of Bihar, UP who had proved themselves very successful in sugar plantation in Mauritius and West Indies. Therefore, the same British colonial administrators started importing labourers to the N.E. India from the same regions. It is further admitted that there were frequent famines in Bihar in 1866, 1874, 1896 and the British policy concentrated on the development ethos and neglected the relief measures or other crash programmes. Migration was a common means of survival for poor peasantry, both men and women, and was not confined only to famine years. At one time almost 10% of the adult population of Siwart and Gopalganj (Bihar) migrated.

Cruel behaviour of the Zamindars towards the poor peasants also led to migration to Assam. The peasant unrest in Bihar and Bengal also might have accelerated large-scale emigration. The failure of Rent Act, 1859 and the Bengal Tenancy Act, 1885 made the life of ordinary peasants miserable. The period of 1960-80 was the period of unrest in many parts of Bihar and Bengal. British indifference to the tenants might often led to the agrarian tension in rural areas and frequent agrarian uprising might have led to emigration.

It was also known that the tribals had suffered much in the recurrent unrest in the Chhotanagpur plateau. The 'Sardari Larai', 'Birsa Movement' and 'Tana Bhagat Movement' in Chhotanagpur division and the 'Kharwar Movement' in Santhal Pargana created a great turmoil. There were some bloody uprisings and left a trail of destruction of men and crop which ultimately brought miseries to the people (Pranab Kumar Das Gupta, 1983).

The 'push' and 'pull' factor had also been the important factor in the labour emigration. The unfortunate simple tribals were neglected by the new master, oppressed by the aliens and deprived of the means they had formerly possessed in obtaining redress through their own chief. To escape from social and economic oppression at home, the innocent tribal had no other alternative than to accept tea plantation work. Under such circumstances, the pull factor became operational for better prospects and induced the people to migrate. In some villages, the tribals had completely lost their proprietary rights. Under the 'Kamiauni' system, they almost became slave for life. Sometimes even their children had to serve for the debt they had not cleared. In Bihar, Kamiauni system is prevalent under which a bonded labour is engaged for one year in exchange of money and a "small plot of land". Next year, he may return the money and would be free (Mahendra P. Lama, 1986).

In such a deplorable situation, emigration was a good way to escape from the claws of the Mahajan (moneylenders). The social and economic oppression of the lower castes at the hands of upper caste and the Zamindars (landlords) and Nawabs (Muslim landlord) also led to emigration; Sometimes one push factor sufficed to cause emigration, for example, famine, earthquake, epidemics. Similarly, the pull factors may be strong enough like gold lust or discovery of oil in some areas. There are examples of rushing to South America or to West Indies to shake the proverbial pagoda tree.

The competition from colonial emigration department and jute and the mining industries also came in the way of labour recruitment for tea plantation in Assam. Since tribals died in large number during their voyage to the colonies, they preferred the tea garden in Assam. Mostly the tribals—Kol, Gonds, Pannika, etc. emigrated from Raipur and Bilaspur. But much more than that was contributed by Ranchi and other districts of Tribal Bihar in the first decade of the 20th century. From the Ranchi district alone in around 1906 as many as 91000 labourers immigrated to Assam. The Dhangers (Oraons) were the most liked coolie by the tea estates. Many tea estates avoided men from the Gangetic plains (Balia, Gazipur, Azamgarh, Gorakhpur and Basti) of UP and Bihar (Arrah and Chhapara) because only the tribal could stand the rigorous jungle life. In fact, the change in the climate, mode of living and diet and deviation from the familiar milieu had a depressing influence on their psyche. The health of the tribals from Chhotanagpur generally suited well in the changed climatic conditions in Assam.

Indenture System

The indenture system was originally a method under which Chinese workers were recruited to the plantation in South America and Cuba from Portuguese Colony of Macao. When the slavery was abolished from the British Empire in 1834, the indenture system was adopted for importing labour mainly from India to the plantations in tropical colonies. The migrants under the system were bound by the contract to serve in the plantation for a few years under the terms and conditions which were in no way better than slavery. The system was finally abolished in 1920 following public clamour against it in India. A slightly modified version of the same known as 'Kangani system' was in vogue for the import of labour to Sri Lanka and Malaya.

Family migration of labour to the tea plantation was generally preferred (Purnendu Kumar, 2006). So, both husband and wife along with children were encouraged to migrate to the tea gardens. This was done to make the labour stable and settle permanently in the tea estates.

Methods of Recruitment

Before the Amendment of the Act, 1915, there were two important methods of recruitment of labour in Assam tea plantation,

(i) Contractors System, 1859-1915

(ii) Garden Sardars System, 1870-1959

Free Contractors System

A contractor was a person licensed for specific area to supply labour in the tea gardens of Assam. He was also allowed to employ sub-contractors who were also to be licensed. From 1841 to 1863, recruitment to the tea gardens in Assam was entirely in the hands of contractors known as Calcutta contractors. Individual tea planters had contacts with recruiters in Calcutta who brought labourers from Bihar, Orissa, Madhya Pradesh, Bengal and sometimes also from Bombay, Madras and Rajasthan. Calcutta contractors were known by the native term 'Arkatti'. The rapid growth of the industry created a class of contractors who were spread like locust in neighbouring states and there were cut-throat competition among them to recruit labour from the villages. Obviously, in such a sordid work they employed all sorts of tactics to seduce the labourers. This system of free contractors system brought havoc in the system of recruitment (Umananda Phukam, 1983). The Government of Bengal appointed a committee of enquire into the system under which emigration of labour was conducted. The planters always took recourse of the 1859 Act of Workmen's Breach of Contract Law, which enabled them to prosecute the labourers according to contract papers. The Committee of Inquiry, 1861 of the Bengal Government enquired into the emigration of labour to Brahmaputra Valley and Barak Valley. The committee felt the necessity of control over emigration of labourers to the plantation in Assam, and suggested passing of the first Inland Emigration Act (Bengal Act of 1863).

Licensed Contractor's System

According to the provision of the Act III of 1863, all recruiters were required by law to be licensed. The recruitment under this Act was known as licensed contractor's system. But in actual practice, procurement of licenses by a few contractors was enough to run the affairs. There were many sub-contractors who were not licensed and they operated the work in the name of licensed contractors. Thus, the Act of 1863 did not bring about any significant change in the nature of recruitment except that time-expired labour could legally re-engaged under contract by planters who also continued to take advantage of the 1859 Act of Workmen's Breach of Contract Law (Purnendu Kumar, 2006).

Dhubri System of Recruitment

The Bengal Act of 1882 is virtually known as the Dhubri System of Recruitment. It was made to facilitate free recruitment to Assam. However, in actual practice, it reinforced the contractors system. Goalpara became a labour district, i.e. place for recruitment to the tea districts. The legal contract could be executed here.

Sardari System

The conditions prevalent during the free contracts system did not improve after passing of the Act of 1863. This necessitated the passing of the Act of 1865 which empowered the tea garden managers to arrest absconding labourers without warrants, and also made indolence and desertion punishable by law. It simply reduced the period of contract from five years to three years, made the contract voidable in case of unhealthy tea garden, gave fixed monthly rate of wages (Uday Kumar Varma, 2005).

It also gave many powers to the garden managers to keep the recruited labour under control. Thus, some basic problems and abuses regarding misrepresentation, mortality in transit and unhealthy recruitment led another Commission of Inquiry in 1868. Consequently, the new Act of 1870 by the Bengal Government was made to legalise recruitment by garden sardars.

The Sardari system was in practice, particularly, in Cachar against the provisions of the Act III of 1863. The planters used to send their trusted labour to pursue people to come to the tea garden for livelihood. But this Sardari system was recognised and was regulated in 1870. The recruitment made by the garden sardar proved to be non-satisfactory than the 'Arkattis' recruited labour. The managers used to send some selected settled members of their gardens to their respective home districts to recruit people of their own class. The Arkattis were virtually concerned with their inflated commission. The sardars who took care of the labourers brought by him because they were living with them in the same labour line. Both shared pleasure and pain and thereby reposing confidence on each other. Thus, Sardari system of recruitment became indispensable to the tea industry in the early half of the 20th century. The Royal Commission Report on Labour in India (RCL), 1931 did not criticise the Sardari system, but simply recommended the end of its monopoly in recruitment. Assam accepted many recommendations of RCL and the tea garden labourers were sought to be made free from the strict control of planters. As a result, there developed a greater confidence among workers and with more freedom of movement, they began to opt for a longer stay in Assam (Piya Chatterjee, 2001). Thus, a stable labour force came into existence in most of the gardens.

Free Recruitment and Emigration

In the introduction of Act VII of 1873, in January 1874 free recruitment and emigration gave satisfactory result to the planters. Among the free emigrants, there was a considerable number of famine-stricken people of Bihar (Saran District) who could not afford steamer fare from Goalunda to Dhubri. They proceeded on foot and with great difficulty used to cross the River Brahmaputra and made their way to garden of Brahmaputra Valley. They had with them family including minors and infants. It was a long strenuous journey and they had neither money to purchase food nor strength to move on foot. Recruitment of labour at different centres were not the end of drama (Rajani Kanta Das 1931). It was followed by their quick transportation to the destined places in Assam, distance of 800 km without any rail or road link.

Transport of Labour

The rapid growth of tea plantation in the entire Assam Valley and the Surma Valley resulted in a pro-active government machinery. It was realised that the inland emigration could not be governed by the laws passed for colonial immigration. The immigrants were ignorant and easily bluffed. Moreover, the tedious journey caused sickness, overcrowding and mortality.

To avoid complication on various points, a central depot for the emigrants was set up at Calcutta. The depot established by the contractors for the purpose of accommodation of immigrants recruited on behalf of the licensed recruiters were situated at Entally and Sealdah which were very near to Eastern Bengal Railway Station from where the emigrants were forwarded by train to Goalundo from where the labour can move to Assam by steamer and to Cachar by boat (Iar Ali Khan, 1983). In Cachar usually labourers were despatched in boats in small batches of 25 under the supervision of an Indian commander known as Native Doctors and a Chaprasi engaged by the recruiting contractors on whom alone the tea company relied for safe despatch of the labour to their destination.

The planters, by and large, preferred getting their labourers by country boats in small batches for the sake of health of human cargo. Their journey was more comfortable and they looked more cheerful and good at the time of disembarkment. It was the custom to provide clothing, medicine along with other necessary arrangements to all the recruits to reach the destination at the expense of the recruiters. But instances were not rare when the whole provisions exhausted before the boat reached only half the journey. Consequently, difficulties came on the way in despatching the labourers by country boat up to Cachar. Neither sanitary nor adequate medical facilities were provided during the journey. Before the journey from Calcutta to Cachar, they were kept for several days in filthy depots of the private recruiters. The steamer route through Sunderban could not be the ground for heavy mortality during voyage as the steamer was to pass through the area during the day of journey. Until the early 1890, all the depots were located in

Calcutta, Dhubri and Goalundo. It was also located in far-off places in Purulia in Bengal and Bilaspur and Jabalpur in Central Province (Rajani Kanta Das, 1931).

Recruiting Associations

It is a known fact that recruitment of labour and their despatch to the tea gardens in Assam was the most gigantic task in those days. For smooth running of the business, a few associations sprang up. In 1859, a Planters Association in Calcutta and after sometimes many more associations were formed. There were Longai Valley Employers Association, The General Coolie Recruiting Association, The Assam Labour Association and many recruiting firms. In 1892, the Bengal Chamber of Commerce took initiative to unite together which led to the formation of Tea Districts Labour Supply Association. Some independent agencies were also operating this business. In 1917, the Assam Labour Association and the Tea Districts Labour Supply Association merged together and formed Tea Districts Labour Association (Vandana Upadhyay, 2012). This organisation was the only organisation concerned with supervision of recruiting. This association was liquidated in 1960.

Recruitment of Labour within Assam

The tea Garden workers are Generally categorised as (i) labour, (ii) staff, and (iii) artisan. The labour includes all manual workers employed in various works of the field and the factory which include peons, chowkidars, sardars, malis, jugali, ordinary-leaf pluckers. The plantation labour is also categorised into the following groups keeping in view the nature of employment.

Permanent Resident Labourer

A labourer is considered to be permanent resident if he or she resides in the garden and has completed the probation period. The employee is deriving benefits of PF and bonus, free house and other fringe benefits.

Temporary Labourer

A temporary labourer is one who is engaged for a limited period and is terminated after the expiry of the work. A temporary worker is deprived of many benefits like housing, PF and bonus. The temporary worker is on probation for six months and during this period, his performance is assessed, if found satisfactory, during the temporary period, his appointment is made permanent and then he is entitled to get all other benefits (Rajani Kanta Das, 1931).

Casual Labourer

In case of additional requirements, the management employs labour from outside the garden. Local villagers or bastiwallas are also engaged in the work of the garden when shortage of labour is found.

Royal Commission on Labour, 1931

The recommendations of the Royal Commission are as follows:

(i) Migration to Assam be encouraged for great majority of immigrants the change is for the better.

(ii) The Commissioner recognised the system of recruitment of family (wife and children) rather than individuals.

(iii) Practice of granting land for spare time cultivation be encouraged. It would justify that the life of tea garden labour resembled with the life of villagers and avoid the worst feature of urban life as in case of textile workers.

(iv) The Commission was impressed with the fact that over six lakhs ex-tea garden labour had been able to settle on government land and their frank admission despite minor unsatisfactory criticism, they regarded migration to Assam an avenue of escape from destitution and even servitude.

(v) Repatriation of labour whether coming from free-recruiting area or not should be entitled to repatriation at his employer's expense after three years' work.

The Commission also proposed that the Assam Labour Board which is concerned with the recruiting labour and their forwarding should be replaced by a Controller of Emigrant

Labour, who would also take up welfare measures besides normal work (Uday Kumar Varma, M.M. Rehman, 2005).

On the basis of the Royal Commission's recommendations, the Tea Districts Emigrant Labour Act was passed in 1932 (XXII of 1932) which came into effect on 1 October 1933. The Act repealed the Assam Labour and Emigration Act, 1901 and thus removed the last vestige of penal contract from the statute book.

The Act of 1932 followed the general scheme of the Commission's recommendation and provided three types of recruiting areas—controlled, restricted and uncontrolled. The Act provided for the first time the statutory rights of all immigrant labour to be repatriated from Assam after three years.

Staff Pattern

Tea plantation, like any well-organised industry, has an organisation of work and a hierarchy of staff. The organisation of work includes distribution of works among the various categories of staff, both technical and non-technical, either monthly rated or daily wages (Arul Sarma, 2012). The staff pattern in tea gardens of the Nilgiris' District, Tamil Nadu is almost the same in each and every garden. However, the number of categories is increased or decreased depending upon the size and capacity of the garden. Keeping this view in mind the general staff pattern in a standard garden of the Nilgiris District, Tamil Nadu is given below:

- *Executive post*: Managing Director, Joint Managing Director, General Manager, Manager, Divisional Manager, Deputy Manager, Commercial Manager, Factory Manager, Tea Maker, Medical Officer, Assistant Manager and Welfare Officer.
- *Office staff*: Head clerk, Provident Fund clerk, Cashier, Accountant, Excise clerk, Dispatch clerk, Computer clerk.
- Medical staff: Pharmacist, Compounder, Auxiliary midwife, Dresser, Medical Carrier.
- *Factory staff*: Worker, Electrician, Fitter, Turner, Tea Tester, Shorter, Trough House Controller and Mechanics.

- *Field Staff*: Assistant Manager, Field Conductor, Assistant Field Conductor and workers (labour/coolie).
- *Sub-staff*: Supervisor, Waterman, Plumber, Carpenter, Cook and Driver to carry green leaf (tractor, truck, small vehicle).

Wages

The system of payment of wages in tea plantations in Tamil Nadu like other states is based on the employment of family. Earlier wages were fixed by the planter themselves so that the family could survive on their pooled income. It was arranged not with a view to improving the standard of living. But in actual practice the workers were employed on family basis simply for earning bare necessity of life and not to talk of decencies, luxuries and savings. The family basis employment also does not reflect the generosity of the planters in respect of social welfare or national economy.

Wage payment in cash and kind in the tea industry is another example of the difference from other organised industries. The planters justify this as most benevolent to workers in times of scarcity and high prices (Piya Chatterjee, 2001). But, in reality, they receive barely minimum wages to ensure physical survival and in times of scarcity of rice or atta consequent upon the high price the cash and kind system help the workers.

Labour Organisation in the Plantation Sector

In contrast with the employers, the labourers on plantation are nothing but incoherent and unorganised masses. They have no knowledge of the place and nature of their work nor do they understand their relationship with their employers. They have been quite unable to take organised action for promoting their common interest. There are several hindrances to organised activities on the part of the workers.

- They are illiterate and ignorant and are unable to organise themselves into trade union for concerted action.
- The very much composition of plantation workers makes such combinations rather remote. They are

mostly recruited from the poorest and most ignorant classes of the people. It is their helpless condition rather than any spirit of adventure that leads them to emigrate. Moreover, most of the labourers are recruited during a time famine or scarcity and when they arrive in the garden they are often in debt and in a helpless condition.

- The very nature of plantation industry is detrimental to labour organisation. Plantations are scattered over a large area, giving scarcely any opportunity to the labourers in one garden to come into contact with those of others.
- The condition of living is still another detriment. Most of the workers live on the plantations and any strike on their part means eviction with their families.
- The remoteness of the plantations from cultural centres including the places of industrial and political activities and the difficulty of labour leaders and political workers in entering plantations are also among the important reasons for the absence of sufficient activity on the part of plantation labour.
- In spite of all these difficulties, the feeling of cohesion and consciousness of class interest have been growing among the workers on various plantations, as indicated by the rising disputes between planters and workers, especially during recent years.

Work Organization and Labour Forces

In a tea plantation, not many skilled workers are required as bulk of the work is associated with plucking of tea leaves from the garden and pluckers constitute about nine-tenth of the total workforce. They are known as labourers. They are daily-rated workers and get wage according to the piece rate, i.e. volume of work done. Above them are a few monthly paid staff consisting of manager, assistant manager, senior staff (clerical and medical personnel) and sub-staff (various categories attached to garden and factory).

The garden labourers both men and women are said to be very much addicted to liquor, and this habit is said to be the prime cause of their deterioting health (Pranab Kumar Das Gupta, Iar Ali Khan, 1983). The food should be cooked in metal utensils while some in old earthen pots. It is said that other ethnic groups accept food and water from the caste Hindus even if the food is cooked in their households. This higher social status of the caste Hindus is perhaps due to their numerical strength in the locality. The priest is usually a brahmin and vegetables or fruits are offered on the occasion. In each settlement, there is a sacred spot under a tree having some sacred stones and flags planted, where the worship is performed. Dancing and singing in a limited scale are also a part of these festivals. Most interesting feature of these festivals and community worships is that each labour settlement manifest some integration on these occasions which is comparable to a village solidarity. All the communities living in the settlement donated for the community worships and participate in the functions. The Hindu employees of garden organize the worship of Hindu goddesses near the staff quarters and all the employees of the garden including other reglious groups subscribe.

The general health condition of the labourers does not appear to be good. The areas of tea garden were infested with malaria and viral infections (Elizabeth Kaniampady, 2003). The general disease of the labourers are high or low blood pleasure, menarchial trouble, gastric and tuberculoses, etc. The health workers ascribe bad food habit of the plantation workers to be the root cause of their poor health condition. The labourers had sometimes consumed rotten food and frequently consumed country liquor in the market.

Economic Organization of the Labour Force

About nine-tenth of the workforce in a tea industry is attached to the gardens. Their work concern preparation of the nursery bed, transplanting, pruning, cleaning and clearing, drainage, loosening of the soil, etc. and the most important work of plucking of tea leaves. All the works which require spade-work is done by men. Pruning is done both by men and women.

Cutting away of dead woods and unnecessary twigs is done by women mainly with the help of small knives. Weeding is also women's job during transplantation. Plucking is done mainly by women but men also works as pluckers. Plucking continues almost throughout the year. Plucking is done for about eight hours a day. It starts at 8.00 a.m. and continues up to 12.00 noon. Then there is lunch break for one and half hours. Work is resumed at 1.30 p.m. and lasts up to 5.30 p.m. The leaves are deposited in front of the factory gate twice a day, once after the first session of plucking and then labourers carry the leaf load in gunny cloth on their heads while some carry the same on their back with the help of a carrying strap passing over the forehead (M.M. Rehman, 2005).

If there is no extra hand in the family, a woman labourer gets up at 4 a.m. in the morning, attends nature's call, plasters the courtyard with cow dung and earth solution and then sits in her kitchen. She cooks, rice and vegetables. She takes and serves the breakfast to her family members which consists of rice, a little vegetable and tea. Then with sound of the factory siren, she proceeds to the garden for plucking. She returns home at about 12.30 noon, takes bath and then eats rice and vegetable already prepared in the morning. Then again she goes for plucking and returns in the evening. She cooks again rice and vegetables for dinner. She goes to bed about 8 p.m after finishing dinner. Women go through more physical strain compared to men as they work in the garden as well as look after domestic work and cooking. Lactating mothers carry their babies to the garden and keep them under the shed of the tree. While mother is busy in plucking, the babies are looked after by the old ladies called patti-ma or baby nurse. The mothers feed the babies at intervals. Drinking water is carried to the gardens where plucking is in progress in tractor vehicle and is supplied to the labourers by the watermen or water suppliers.

There is a fixed quota of leaves which a labourer should pluck in a day. It is 25 kgs for a male and he receives ₹ 137 in return. The quota for a female labourer is equally the same. And the remuneration is also the same. For every additional kg. of leaves plucked, an incentive of one rupee and fifty paise above the normal rate is given. The income of a labourer fluctuates according to the leaf position in a garden. A labourer does not get any wage on the weekly holidays and monthly income of a male worker ranges from ₹ 3500 to ₹ 4000. The income of a female labourer is little less. But the overall family income is not very low as a number of members from each family work in the garden (Umananda Phukam, 1983).

During peak plucking season which runs between May and September, temporary hands are employed to complete the plucking in appropriate time. Leaves are to be plucked at certain stage of its growth. Plucking from a plant is done at an interval of seven or eight days which allows new shoots to grow and the operation should be completed in time, otherwise the quality of tea will deteriorate. The women pluckers sing, chat and cut jokes while plucking, and no sign of boredom is noticed during work. It is known to all that the women have unbound love for flowers.

Other economic benefits which a worker derives from the company are gratuity and contributory provident fund. Each worker and his/her two dependants get weekly ration in rice and wheat/flour at subsidized rates. The company also supplies fuel free of cost to the labourers and provides free quarters and offers medical aid, though the medical part is denied by the labour force.

Work Organization

C.T.E. maintains 39 monthly-paid staff in various categories in both the sector, i.e. the garden and the factory. All of them are men expect only one woman who works as dai or midwife attached to the dispensary. There are only 11 members in the monthly—paid staff who belong to scheduled tribes and six of them are munda. All the top positions are held by Bengalee Hindus (Elizabeth Kaniampady, 2003).

Total member of permanent weekly-paid staff is 195 which include 85 women. There are nine jogali sirdars (all men) in this permanent staff. A jogali sirdar is the head of a group of workers who maintains attendance, etc. Of the workers and receives a lump remuneration of ₹ 100 per year besides his regular wage. Majority of the permanent weekly-paid staff are tribes and six of them are jogali sirdars. Expecting the monthly-paid staff all the workers including the permanent weekly-paid staff get for six days a week (on Monday no work and no pay).

Work and Wages

The chawalas of the factory are daily-rated workers (i.e, the wage is ₹ 3.77 per day) but they get pay for full month and paid once a month. The sirdars of the garden and the factory enjoy a scale of pay like that of monthly-paid staff. Sirdars of both garden and factory and the chowkidars enjoy the scale of ₹ 100-150 with ₹ 2.50 as annual increment. Besides they get D.A. @ 14.5% and variable D.A. @ 25.5%.

The difference of benefits provided to the permanent and temporary labourers is in the ration, fuel, gratuity and provident fund. The provident fund is contributory and is 12% of the total wage and is deducted at source from all monthly-paid workers and they are entitled to all the statutory welfare measures according to the provisions of The Tamil Nadu Plantation Labour Rules, 1955 and subsequent amendments made to the Act.

All permanent workers including their dependants get ration which is much lower than the market price. Temporary workers also get ration at a subsidized rate but they have to pay more and no ration is provided for their dependants.

Managerial and supervisory staff get free fuel for their kitchen. Other monthly-paid and permanent workers are paid some fuel allowance which varies according to the category of workers.

Monthly-paid and permanent workers get gratuity to the tune of 15 day's wages for every year of service with the maximum of twenty month's gratuity. The amount of gratuity is calculated taking into account the wages (excluding servant allowance, bonus, leave wage, overtime or any other special grant) as payable on the date of retirement.

Workers of all categories are entitled to have maximum bonus of 20 per cent of annual wages.

Socio-Economic Profile of the Tea Plantation Labour in the Niligiris' District, Tamil Nadu

A Brief Introduction

Gunner Myrdal opines that the ideas of economic development, being the determinant of socio-cultural development is implicit in the Marxian literature. The indentured tea garden labourers under the Kangani system came back to this state not as invaders but as befooled captives. They were allured by false promises and were brought by the European planters duly co-helped by the British for furthering their own interest. They went to Sri Lanka on contract basis for maximum period of five years in the beginning, later on reduced to four years and lastly to three years, but practically no one was sent back to their original places (Pranab Kumar Das Gupta, 1983). They were rather forced to stay in the precincts of the tea estates and ultimately made this place as their permanent abode. They completely forgot their ancestral places and accepted this place as their permanent place of habitation. They also adopted the language culture and norms of life of the indigenous people. Finally, they were brought back to the Niligiris' District, Tamil Nadu under the rehabilitation scheme of the GoI to benefit the Estate Tamils.

Dravidian Group

One of the categories of labour barring Tamils who arrived in different tea gardens of the Nilgiris' District, Tamil Nadu belonged to Dravidian group who were brought from undivided Madras Presidency (Telugu-speaking districts of Godavari, Vijoywara, Vishakhapatnam or Telanga region). They belonged to Malulu, Kapulu and Naidu community. They speak in their own language in some gardens only. In other tea estates where they are in minority, they have forgotten their mother tongue and speak in the language of the majority of the labourers working in the tea estates (Umananda Phukam, 1983).

Maintenance of Ethnic Boundary

Three major cultural attributes by which the ethnic groups maintain their ethnic boundary in the social contacts of a tea garden are commensality, connubial and language. Other social cultural parameters are either dysfunctional or redundant in such a heterogeneous ethnic situation (Vandana Upadhyay, 2012). No single ethnic group enjoys a decisive and numerical dominance and spatial and socio-political hold for nurturing and sustaining its ethnic boundary. Each group has to communicate and interact face-to-face with a number of other groups involved in the same economic activities. Even in the sphere of commensality, connubiun and language, they had to evolve a compromise formula and an attitude of tolerance.

In marriage feasts, different ethnic groups do not dine together. Rice, meat, oil, spices, etc. are divided between the invitees from different ethnic groups. Each group cooks and dines separately on the occasion.

Marriage alliance is another factor in boundary maintenance. Though inter-ethnic marriages occur and are tolerated, choices of spouse is usually restricted to one zone ethnic group. On this occasion, relatives and friends living in other labour settlements of the garden or neighboring garden are invited.

While discussing about the mechanism of ethnic boundary, maintenance, it must be clearly focused that there is an overriding inter-ethnic solidarity particularly in the level of labour settlement which is reflected on the occasions of marriage, funeral, religious practice, etc. In a labour settlement, members of different ethnic group address each other with some kinship terms according to age group. Anna, ayya, amma, patti, thatha and thambi are few examples of such kinship terms.

Religion and Belief System

Drastic change and attenuation have taken place in the religious life of the people. Tea garden does not provide for celebrations and festivals in full length (Purnendu Kumar, 2006). Living side by side with a number of ethnic groups having different cultural traditions, the tea garden labourers had to find out a compromise formula to cater the need of all ethnic groups so far as the religious practices and belief system are concerned. While limiting the performance of traditional rites like ancestor and household worship and rites associated with traditional festivals to the family level, all the ethnic groups living in a labour settlement unite and involve themselves in a joint worship known as gram puja for welfare of the people of the settlement. Such community worship is held in each labour settlement when all the ethnic groups of settlement cooperate. In this matter, a labour settlement operates as a village unit and even the Christians families subscribe. The ethnic component of the priest and his assistants varies from settlement to settlement and there is no barrier for religion or caste. However, a few Christians churches were located near the tea garden. There are both protestant and Roman Catholic churches and followers from different labour settlement attend the same (Purnendu Kumar, 2006).

It has been mentioned before that the gram puja is the only community worship when all the ethnic groups in labour settlement participate. The priest and the assistant may belong to any ethnic group. The priest utters incantations in his own mother tongue. In a number of labour settlement listed below, the ethnicity of the priest and his assistant is as follows:

> Gram puja performed at the foot of a banyan or a jack fruit tree having a little open space in front where the members can assemble and take Prasad, the sacrificial meat and rice. Religious paraphernalia include tulse, mango and wood apple leaf, beetle nut and beetle leaf, coconut, banana, molasses, incense and a lamp. Fouls, pigeons, ducks and goats are sacrificed. Three flags of white, red and black colours with sticks are planted in the ground in front of the shrine. The white and black flags are meant for sun god and kali or mother goddess respectively, where is there red one for other deities of jungle, water, etc. when the worship is over, sacrificial meat and rice are prepared on the spot by assistant and consumed by all assembled there. No rules of commensality operate on this occasion. (Rajani Kanta Das, 1931)

There is one Amman temple in Naduvattam, about 22 kms. away from Ooty. A Brahmin priest officiates there and people including dalits from far of places visit his temple, offer fruits, vegetables and sweets and sacrifice goat, pigeon, etc.

The staff members of Samraj Tea Estate organize annual temple puja which is the main festive occasion in the garden when all the staff and labourers irrespective of religious and ethnic affiliation subscribe and participate. The company donates ₹ 10000 for the puja fund and declares a holiday with full pay. The priest is the refuge Tamil Brahmin who comes from neighboring village. On this occasion, cinema shows and street plays are organised and all the labourers take keen interest in these functions. The company donates ₹ 8000 from the labour recreation fund for arranging such function. The celebration of puja has become the main festive occasion for the baduga laboures also. They wait eagerly for this occasion; do over time and save money for purchasing new clothes on this occasion (Umananda Phukam, 1983). Data on indebtedness show that though the baduga laboures, in general, are free from this vice, on the occasion of annual temple puja, they take some new clothes on loan from the merchants, majority of whom were Chettiars, known for their money lending activities at exorbitant rate of interest and exploiting the poor tea plantation workers who used to pay in installments.

Belief in evil spirits causing some harm and illness and dependence on a magician to get rid of such calamities has not dead down among the labourers of a tea garden. Though the labourers receive free medicals aid from the hospital run by the company, they quite often consult a magician to get rid of the wrath of an evil spirit. These magicians in this garden belonged to various ethnic groups but mostly from Kerala. They claimed to detect the case of any calamity in their own way by spreading sun-dried rice on a banyan leaf and then prescribe the remedy.

Religion is the most important cementing factor in human life. It binds together and brings to the common platform to think and lead a harmonious relationship between different ethnic or linguistic groups. The tea garden labourers though transplanted in new social environment of tea plantation followed the same religion of their ancestors. A majority of the tea garden labour fell under the great umbrella of Hinduism. They practiced their religious rites, festivals, puja and worshipped with great sanctity. In each garden, there was a temple of Kali, Lord Shiva, or Amman where daily Kirtan, Bhajan is arranged. During the British days, the European planters and managers, though Christians did not try to interfere in religious matters. They could have easily converted them into Christian, fold but in fact, this did not come to their mind. They did not ask the caste Hindus to bring beef from the nearby markets. They enjoyed Hindu festivals with great joy and helped the labourers financially also.

A considerable section of the total labour force belonged to Christian faith and they were in great numbers in the tea estates located in Kotagiri, Coonoor and Naduvattam. They have constructed church in the labour line areas. Muslims in the labour group were very less. On the whole, there was communal harmony in the gardens in matters of religious functions and everyone irrespective of religious denominations enjoyed the occasions.

Important Festivals

Tamil Nadu is the land of fairs and festivals. The state has been frequently referred by residents of other states to be the safe custodian of the life and property of non-Tamilians as well. It is the home of colourful festivals projecting religious belief, passion, heritage and creative urges. There are occasions when people of every section irrespective of caste, creed and belief celebrate the festival with pomp and gaiety (Purnendu Kumar, 2006). It is the fairs and festivals which enable them to come into close contact with the people of various religious faiths who despite all differences make life meaningful. To many others, it bridges the gap of their cultural differences, and carries the messages of love, peace, understanding and brotherhood.

Cultural and Religious Festivals of the Tea Plantation Labour in Tamil Nadu

Pongal, Deepavali and Christmas

Lakshmi Puja and Saraswati Puja are also very popular in these hilly regions of Tamil Nadu. It is due to the impact of Brahminian culture. Other groups of people also participate in these festivals. Every festival in the tea garden is accompanied with dance and music. Music by flute or drums is associated with these dances. The dance and music centre round the nature and life. It provides happiness and relieves hardship, mental agony and worries.

Social Life

The social lives of the tea garden, workers are circumscribed by social taboos, dogma and orthodox views. This is perhaps due to less exposure, less social interaction of the tea garden labourers belonging to different ethnic groups with neighbouring villagers. The society, in which the labourers are living is caste ridden. This feeling has divided the entire society into groups and sections such as higher caste, lower caste, touchable; and untouchable. The higher caste, though in minority, dominates the lower caste including the baduga groups. In the gardens 'Panichal system' existed. It means that water touched by lower caste people will not be taken by other caste people like Goala, Koeri. The lower caste non-Panichal group cannot fetch water if higher-castes or 'Panichal groups are fetching water from a well. This orthodox feeling is still a ruling force in some of the tea gardens maintained by the private companies the employers of which belonged to the so-called upper castes. 'Panichal' is customary rule of the garden in which water is served by only a few recognised castes. The Muslim labourers are also included in 'non-Panichal group'. The tribals, in general, are branded as 'non-Panichal' group (Purnendu Kumar, 2006).

Marriage System

Normally, marriage of boys and girls of the tea garden labourers is arranged within their own castes, own gotra or tribe. Inter-caste marriage is looked down upon and considered an unholy alliance. But such marriages have taken place in past. Even if it takes place, the marriage is accepted by their own clan or group on certain conditions. A panchayat of caste sits together, decides the matter, imposes fine and a community feast is arranged to clear the hurdles. In the past, when the plantation started in Tamil Nadu, labourers were pressed into services in different gardens.

The uneven sex ratio among the recruited compelled the labour to marry ignoring the caste hierarchy. A typical example of inter-caste marriage in a tragic circumstance is presented here.

While coming to tea garden, both husband and wife boarded two different ships at Kili Nochi to reach Tiger Hills, Coonoor. After reaching Madras (now called Chennai) both entrained separately and forgot each other. Ultimately, the husband selected a new partner of life and settled in Glendale tea garden. Social customs, rituals and customary rules and tradition are in their ancestral places.

Food Habit

Normally, the food habit of any person is adjusted according to the climate, crop grown in the area, and physical condition of the human being. Some social stigma also prohibits man from taking anything according to taste (Piya Chatterjee, 2001). Certain communities among Tamils have distinct social characteristics and way of life. Their food habit differs from others. Some locals claiming to be the sons of the soil told that they even consumed snake, frog, and jackals while majority of the workers did not touch these things. For others they had pigs and hens and ate the same.

Types of Family

The households are broadly classified into nuclear and joint family. The nuclear family normally consists of husband, wife and unmarried children. All others include joint or extended families. When big families in which all brothers and father's brother are living together with married sons and daughters are called joint or extended family.

Games

Football is the most popular and young men belonging to all ethnic groups play together. Hockey is played in a limited scale mainly by the local youths. They play with bamboo-made possess proper hockey sticks. Cricket is also played in summer. Play of badminton and golf is limited to the officers and staff.

Commitment of the Tea Plantation Labourers

If the rate of absenteeism is taken as an objective indicator of the level of commitment, then the tea garden labourers are not that committed to their work. But the rate of absenteeism is not comparatively high if we take into account the general rate of absenteeism in the industrial sector of India (Elizabeth Kaniampady, 2003).

In a tea garden, the rate of absenteeism varies between the temporary and permanent labourers and also between the garden and factory labourers. There is not much difference between the men and women labourers. Absenteeism among the permanent men garden labourers and permanent women garden labourers is about 24%, whereas the rate of absenteeism among the temporary women garden labourers stands at 28%. Absenteeism among the temporary factory labourers is 8% and the same is a little less among the permanent factory labourers. A composition between the factory labourers and the garden labourers shows that the former are a little better in attendance (Uday Kumar Varma, 2005). It has been reported both by the management and the labourers that the nature of the work in the garden, i.e. plucking, earth-cutting, pruning, transplanting, etc. is more laborious than that in the factory and that is the main reason of different in the rate of absenteeism.

If we consider the length of service of tea garden labourers, we find that a labourer enters in service at young age and retires when old. His/her sons or relatives fill up the vacancy. Children being born and brought up in a tea garden acquaint themselves with the nature of job and it is not difficult for them to take up the work in appropriate time. Changing job from one garden to another by labourers is not frequent.

Political Organization

The supervisors of tea garden hold responsible position. They not only supervise the work of the labourers under him but also are responsible in maintaining discipline and solidarity of the labourers and peace in the labour settlements. Under each supervisor, there is a group of labourers who usually belong to same ethnic sgroup and live in one labour settlement. To maintain the solidarity of the labourers, a supervisor is supposed to entertain them once in a year on the day of annual temple festival or on the occasion of the local festival with meat and liquor or rice-beer. After the death of a supervisor, one of his sons takes up the position (Elizabeth Kaniampady, 2003).

Role of Trade Union in the Life of Tea Plantation Labourers

Before the formation of trade union in the garden, the supervisors were responsible in resolving disputes between the labourers within a settlement. If the dispute was between members of two settlements then supervisor from both of the settlements used to sit for judgement along with some elder members of the settlements belonging to different ethnic groups. They could impose some fine to the offender and the amount used to be spent in rice-beer.

Nowadays, minor disputes are settled by the supervisor. A case which the supervisor cannot resolve or it is of complicated nature is referred to the trade union. If the trade union also fails then the manager of the garden intervenes. Criminal cases are referred to the trade union. Union imposes fine to the offender and the amount is deposited in the union fund. Union may also drive away a labourer from the garden for serious offence or for violating the verdict of the union. There is no separate political organization for each ethnic group (Vandana Upadhyay, 2012). But usually each trade union is backed by a political party.

Social offences like inter-ethnic marriage, etc. are tolerated and ignored nowadays. But in olden days when the ethnic boundaries were strong, a number of inter-ethnic disputes used to occur. An example could be cited here to illustrate how strong the ethnic sentiment was. It happened in the year 1978. A dalit boy fell in love with a upper-caste girl and one day he took the girl to his house. The caste Hindus became furious and the father of the girl got very angry, though was persuaded to be calm. After three days, father of the girl invited his daughter and son-in-law to his house apparently showing that he was now prepared to accept them socially. A feast was arranged and dancing and singing were organized. At night the boy and the girl were offered an apartment to sleep. At dead of night, the father of the girl took vengeance, murdered the dalit boy with an axe and then surrendered to the labour agent of the garden. Police came and arrested him. In the court, the man confessed boldly that he murdered the boy to save their prestige of their community.

Incidence of divorce is very rare in the garden. Since the wife is also an earning member of the family, she is considered as an economic asset (Rajani Kanta Das, 1931). This leads to maintaining harmonious relationship between husband and wife. But there are a few cases when married women fled away with their lovers to other gardens. Such inter-garden disputes are also settled by the supervisor and elderly members of the gardens and the case is resolved after the offender pays compensation money to the aggrieved husband. A fine example could be presented here. A Keralite man from Samraj Tea Estate married a girl of the same community living in nearby tea estate. In the year 1969, the wife fled away to Glendale Tea Estate with a Tamilian. The husband and his relatives demanded money from the Tamilian boy. He paid ₹ 350 and the case was resolved.

Living side by side for more than a hundred years, ethnic groups in tea gardens have grown the attitude of tolerance towards other groups and it is reflected not only in the sphere of political organization, but also in many other social interactions during marriage, funeral, etc.

Living Conditions: Housing and Sanitation

A eighty-one year old Gurusamy, a former labourer of Hooker Tea Estate informed the researcher that his grandfather Govindarajan who came to this garden, had to clear the jungle around line to build huts with mud wall and thatched roofs. The labour lines were scattered over a wide area to avoid epidemics (R.L. Sarkar, Mahendra P. Lama, 1986). Further, barrack lines were made with tin roofs and brick walls and these huge sheds were divided by bamboo partition. There was much congestion in these lines and sometimes each person had less than 25 ft. of space. The women workers were critical of it because of lack of privacy. This state of affairs continued for many decades.

After independence, the Plantation Labour Act, 1951 was implemented and accordingly the accommodation problem to a great extend was solved.

Living Conditions

The general health of the workers in the tea gardens of Tamil Nadu unlike those of Assam valley or Terai region is very poor. The tropical climate with heavy rainfall, high temperature and abundance of swamps and jungle are singled out by many observers. But the under-fed and malnutrition of the tea garden labourers are the main problems even today which is responsible for poor out-turn. They are undernourished. Hence, they lack vitality and they live in most unhygienic condition. Consequently, they have weak physique having no glamour on their faces. Even in youth, they lose their vitality. Their living condition is very poor. In a small house of two rooms, the entire family with dependants (total eight members) is housed together. An ordinary cot, without any furniture, minimum utensils and limited necessary things are the common features of labour sheds (Deepak K. Mishra, 2012). The general standard of living is still pitiable. Sometimes, the labourers remain starved at night due to non-availability of food materials. They are unable to purchase minimum clothes needed to cover their body, particularly during winter nights, their pitiable condition can move any civilized person. The labourers reply in course of personal interview is that their forefathers did not think to amass wealth due to the fact that they had come for temporary period and were determined to leave the place. So, the tradition of uncertain future kept them in these pitiable conditions (Rajani Kanta Das, 1931).

Land

Early emigrants in the tea gardens were lured to get sufficient land to grow vegetables in the Niligiris' District, Tamil Nadu. The topography of land favoured the workers to get small plot of cultivable land in the garden. During spare time, the workers could keep themselves busy in vegetable cultivation which could minimise economic pressure. The psychological satisfaction and feeling of contentment was on the face of every worker having a small piece of land. This benefit was encouraged by the planters to make them loyal and stable work force. The planters used it a safety valve during conditions of depression in the industry.

A retrenched worker could always lean back on his land so long as one member of his family continued to be employed in the garden.

Literacy

As discussed earlier, the general condition before the advent of the Britishers in the Nilgiris' District, Madras Presidency was most horrible (Purnendu Kumar, 2006). The general education in the district was depicted by the British Planters in 1834:

> There does not exist any provision either public or private in any part of this hilly area for the instruction of the people nor does it appear that anything of the kind ever did, at least in a permanent way.

This sad state of affairs continued for long period in the majority of the tea estates of Ooty Valley which were completely detached and isolated from the general stream of life of the rural and urban centres. They further observed:

> The means of instruction would indeed be a boon and gratefully received as such by the inhabitants of the Nilgiris' District where education of any sort is wholly unknown but I fear the resources.

Education was very poor among the tea plantation labourers in Tamil Nadu. There were some inhabitants who knew how to read and write. Most of the early settlers were of lower classes and were all tillers of the soil up to 1850. There were no schools in the tea estates for a long period. No record is available to show when and where the first primary school was opened in the tea garden (Purnendu Kumar, 2006). Poor communication, isolated plantation environment, lack of initiative by the planters to open primary schools in the garden, non-availability of teachers to teach in garden school, lack of awareness among the early recruited labourers to give priority to education to their wards resulted into total 11 literates before 1900. In Gudalur town, the first primary school was opened in 1920s. Hence, the first two generations of labour remained completely illiterate. However, there were some Brahmins working in the office of the tea gardens who had link with original places, knew Hindi and through that they could have good relationship with the civil authorities. Some of the labourers also were literate who used to teach the next generation in common place at night. One 96-year-old Nanjundan (formerly a tea labourer) of High Field Tea Garden informed the researcher that he used to get 4 annas for writing a letter on behalf of the illiterate labourers to their homes in southern parts of Tamil Nadu and in some cases to Vavunya or Matta Kilappu in Sri Lanka (Elizabeth Kaniampady, 2003).

Educational Standard

Out of total literates just literate are 13.99% (20), primary standard 33.57% (48), middle school 27.27% (39) and high school 17.48% (25) and matriculate and above 7.69% (11). Among the eleven post-matriculates, three are post-graduate degree holders. This reveals that the per centage in higher education in relation to the total population in the sample is really meager (Piya Chatterjee, 2001).

The analysis further reflects that there is growing urge for education among the low-caste labourers, but at the same time the level of education was found to be lacking among the business classes such as Nadars and Chettiars. There are two panchayat schools, one middle and one high school within the jurisdiction of Chamraj Tea Estate which are within easy reach of everyone working in this tea garden. However, the labourers were not very conscious of the value of education. This may be due to the financial instability among the labourers. It is further noted that the younger generation is very much interested in education and their per centage is fairly increasing (Rajani Kanta Das, 1931).

Economic Organisation and Status

The economic status of TANTEA Tea Estate labourers has been broadly classified into workers and non-workers. The women shoulder the burden of the household affairs, though they are in most cases equal partner in earning.

In tea plantation normally, there are two types of workers such as daily-rated and monthly-rated (salaried) workers. The tea pluckers and unskilled labourers employed in the field are given wages on daily basis for six working days only. But the practice was such that the wages to the tea plantation workers were disbursed at the end of the every month. No payment has been given on holiday. The wages vary from time to time. At present, the daily wages for unskilled labour has been enhanced from to ₹ 137 besides other fringe benefits. The drivers, supervisors, mechanics, electricians, turners, etc. are given wages on monthly basis. All the monthly-rated workers get a little higher monthly wages and consider themselves superior to others.

The plantation workers have agricultural background. Unlike industrial workers of textile industry, the tea industry workers are inferior due to their rural and rustic characteristics. Such industrial workers occupy higher or superior status than the tea workers who live in an isolated or semi-isolated island of tea estates. The industrial workers are not family-based employees like tea workers who keep residential quarters from generation to generation (Umananda Phukam, 1983).

In the tea plantation, there are different sources of income. Besides, daily wages, a worker earns from agriculture also. The garden labourers in private tea estates have small size of operational holdings. The workers get regular vegetables which minimises daily expenditure. Some vegetables are also grown in the home yards which fetch some amount from sale in the daily bazar of the garden. The households include some other productive animals. Milk procured from cows and buffaloes is sold in the market. A good amount of money comes from the sale of goats, draught animals, pigs and poultry birds. But pig and poultry birds are not reared by all the workers of the garden due to social stigma and caste consideration. Unemployed members of garden households go outside the garden and work as daily labour in villages or in urban area, in Public Works Department's road work, Border Road Task Force work, works in tea stalls, grocery shops, rickshaw pullers, cleaner in workshop, brick works or as helper in building construction. By doing such works, the unemployed workers manage two square meals. Minor girls also work as part time maid servants in urban families (Uday Kumar Varma, M.M. Rehman, 2005).

Distribution of Income

A previously conducted minor study by the United Planters' Association of South India, Coonoor, Tamil Nadu highlights the following statistics on the distribution of total income of the tea plantation workers. Besides daily wages as the primary source of income, some extra income is also accrued from other sources. The income groups of the garden clearly reflect that 95.76% of the households is below the annual income-level of ₹ 2500. The households, consuming 85.96% of their income in meeting basic needs, are in fact the poorest of the poor. Another 3.38% of the households was in the income group of ₹ 2500 to ₹ 3500 and they shared 8.31% of the total income. Only 0.85% of the households was above the income level of ₹ 8500 and they share 5.73% of the total income.

The income inequality among the tea garden population can not be of higher magnitude because of the fact that earnings of worker both in self-employment and wage earners were almost similar. The economic resource at their disposal was also low. The same minor study (Purnendu Kumar, 2006) also presents the following statistics on the distribution of total income of the tea plantation workers: Eighty-nine households out of 118 sampled households falling within the income group of five hundred to one thousand five hundred which constitute 64.24% of the total income group.

Table 1.2: Distribution of Households and Total Income by Income Groups in the Nilgiris' District, T.N.

Income Groups	Households		Total Income (₹)	
	Number	Per centage	Income (₹)	Per centage
1-500	9	7.63	3684	2.56
500-1000	48	40.68	39212	27.23
1000-1500	41	34.75	53294	37.01
1500-2000	11	9.32	18697	12.98
2000-2500	04	3.39	8902	6.18
2500-3000	02	1.69	5481	3.81
3000-3500	02	1.69	6478	4.50
3500-4000	-	-	-	-
4000-4500	-	-	-	-
4500-5000	-	-	-	-

Income Groups	Households		Total Income (₹)	
	Number	Per centage	Income (₹)	Per centage
5000-5500	-	-	-	-
5500-6000	-	-	-	-
6000-6500	-	-	-	-
6500-7000	-	-	-	-
7000-7500	-	-	-	-
7500-8000	-	-'	-	-
8000-8500	01	0.85	8245	5.73
Total	**118**	**100.00**	**143993**	**100.00**

Source: United Planters' Association of South India, Coonoor, Tamil Nadu (1988).

Expenditure

The total household expenditure and per centage distribution on each item which includes food items, i.e. cereals, other food materials (pulse, mustard oil, salt, vegetables, etc.) constitute 54.17% of the total expenditure. Cereals alone constitute 32.73% of the total expenditure. The labourers also get rice and Atta at subsidised rate but that do not meet their total requirement. Rice is the staple food of the labourers.

Intoxicants occupy 16.20% of the total expenditure. Only a few tea plantation labourers did not spend any amount on liquor. However, they spend a petty amount on betel and pan, mava, sniff powder, raw tobacco, etc.

Expenditure on dress comes to the tune of 7.42% arid average expense per households is ₹ 47.33 only. In fact, the socio-economic backwardness and acute financial constraints do not allow the poor labourers and their families to spend more on dress. The bare minimum set is purchased in eleven monthly instalments from the known cloth merchants (majority of them were 'Chettiars') who squeeze double the amount of the actual price due to their lack of knowledge of price of cloth.

Table 1.3: Expenditure Pattern of Households of the Plantation Workers in the Nilgiris' District, T.N.

Items	Total Expenditure (₹)	%	Average Expenditure (₹)	No. of Household which do not Spend on it
Cereals	24623	32.73	208.74	-
Other food materials	16136	21.44	136.74	3
Fuel, oil, candle	5621	7.47	47.63	-
Intoxicants	12194	16.20	103.33	40
Simple comfort	2672	3.56	22.64	03
Dress	5585	7.42	47.33	-
Education	2365	3.14	24.04	50
Medical	1135	1.50	9.61	-
Entertainment	1187	1.58	10.05	-
Travelling	2245	2.99	19.02	18
Interest on loan	1042	1.39	8.83	15
Misc.	435	0.58	3.68	115
Total	**75249.00**	**100.00**	**641.64**	**– 244**

Source: United Planters' Association of South India, Coonoor, Tamil Nadu (1988).

Expenditure on education is incurred by 68 households and the average per households' expenditure among them was ₹ 24.04%. This is due to the fact that the younger generation is studying in primary and middle schools. In some cases, high school where no tuition fee is charged, a small amount of ₹ 34.04 meets the need of paper, books and pencil of their children.

Young boys and girls are very much fond of amusement and entertainment programmes (Purnendu Kumar, 2006). They press their guardians for radio, TV and musical instruments. But financial problems and difficulties do not allow such facilities. However, 40 households have radio and 15 households have TV sets. Only 1.58% of the expenditure is on entertainment.

The expenditure pattern on the whole reveals very low standard of living. Their standard of living is so poor that they have become a social parasite. At every stage, their ignorance, illiteracy, laziness is reflected. Their dirty habits, nasty dealings and filthy talks are the symptoms of their low level of living standard. There has been no change in the style of living even after independence. If there is lockout in the factory, the labourers will have to go without food from the very third day. They purchase everything on credit and after weekly payment they clear all the dues. But, in fact, they had to pay more. The local grocery dealers take more than the actual price. Consequently, they always remain in debt. Sometimes, they borrow money from the local people or from moneylenders and pay interest monthly. On many occasions, it become overdue and accumulation leads to sale of land or part of it, to outsiders (Rajani Kanta Das, 1931).

Habit of thrift is practically absent in tea plantation labour circle. Ignorance of market price, lack of bargaining capacity as well as living in an isolated society quite different from urban and rural atmosphere are some of the factors behind the deplorable economic and social condition of the tea garden labourers. Under such situation, the businessmen and moneylenders exploit them by selling goods of low quality at an exorbitant price.

Occupational Distribution of Grandfathers

Among the grandfathers of the current workers in the tea gardens of six top tea producing states, nearly 44% were permanent tea garden workers and there was virtually little diversification in that generation. Studies showed that nearly 92% of the grandfathers were in the tea gardens. Nearly 6.4% were cultivators. Among the grandfathers of the workers outside the gardens 21.5% were permanent tea garden workers. Excluding such cases of non-reporting, nearly 33% of the grandfathers of current workers outside the gardens were cultivators and 12% were agricultural labourers. Vertical mobility presupposes a hierarchical ordering of occupations. Terms of income, social status, and distance ordered occupations (*source*: Tea Board of India Calcutta,West Bengal, 2006).

Management of Tea Industry in India

Albert Einstein, the world famous scientist, once told his friend while sipping tea, "Look, when I lift the cup, I am reminded of the toil of the potter that he has brought to it. This tea is the product of the enormous hardship by a worker who might have slogged it out in a far away plantation. When I visualise their labour, I cannot afford the luxury of leisure". This observation clearly reflects that the tea which relaxes us is the fruit of cumulative toil of the poor labourers, supervisory and the managerial staff and the proprietors who work hard round the clock and produce this 'black diamond'—the most common beverage of the world (Pranab Kumar Das Gupta, 1983).

Tea is an agro-based industry, the management of which is a gigantic task beginning with the cultivation of tea bushes whose tender leaves (two leaves and a bud) are processed to make made-tea. In between the cultivation of tea bushes and final despatch of made tea, a large number of men (immigrant labour), materials (machinery, tools, fertilisers, weedicides and other insecticides) are required. The garden management is a labyrinthine affair in which every one is actor right from an ordinary unskilled labour to the top executive officer. Tea plantation has multi-dimensional characteristics—agriculture, industry, commerce and man-management. It has been remarked:

> Although a plantation uses land and is concerned with production, grown on land, in its scale and methods of operation it is more analogous to a modern factory than to an owned or rented family farm worked by unpaid family labour or occasionally hired labour (Arul Sarma, 2012). The spread of plantation culture must be viewed as a spread of industrialised agriculture. The most striking difference between the modern factory industry and tea industry lies in the structure of work organisation.

Land procurement for tea plantation is a very important part of the history of tea industry. After the discovery of tea in Assam in 1823, it was the policy of the government to encourage the opening of the sparsely populated tracts of the state by offering land on favourable terms. The first Special Grants Rules was enacted on 6 March 1838 (related to Assam proper only). No grant was to be made of a less than 100 acres and not more than 10,000 acres. The next rules were those of leasehold grants of 23 October 1854 commonly called the old Assam Rules. Accordingly, one-fourth of the grant was exempted from assessment in perpetuity and remaining 3/4 were granted revenue free for 15 years to be assessed thereafter at three annas per acre for ten years and at six annas per acre for 74 years more, making the whole term of 99 years after which the grant was to be subject to resurvey and settlement.

The following classes of land were held:

- Fee sample grants
- Redeemed grants
- 99 years lease rule grants
- New lease rules for 30 years for special cultivation
- Periodic leases for special cultivation
- Periodic leases for ordinary cultivation
- Annual leases

Grants in fee simple were issued for the first time in the year 1862 according to the Fee Simple Grant Rule of 1861. But rule 19 thereof the grantees of previously existing Rules in Cachar only that of 1854 being extended in 1856, the grantees could redeem the future land revenue. The grantee will be treated for the purpose of the Rules as if the lands were permanently settled. The language used in one such contract with the secretary of State for India in Council on 4 July 1864 mentions together with all rights of forest pasturage, mines, fisheries, and all other proprietary right of the said secretary of state for India in Council (Umananda Phukam, October 1983). Rule of 1862 was repressed by the Revised Fee Simple Grant Rules of 1874 which reserved the right of the government to levy royalty on mines.

During the initial period, the planters mostly Europeans showed great enterprising skill to develop tea plantation in Cachar Valley. The Cachar Superintendents, namely T. Fisher, G. Vernar, and J.W. Edgar took interest in the development of tea plantation and encouraged the planters to come forward. They also extended all administrative helps in procurement of labour from outside Assam. With the help of indentured labourers, the jungles within the district were cleared, tillah lands were made clean, bunds were constructed to tame natural water, reservoirs were made, grass and reed lands were cleared for tea plantation as well as for human settlement.

All the land grants received from the government to grow tea were surveyed. It was also planned to establish factory in suitable central location having other facilities within its reach; every section of tea planted, labour lines, bungalow, staff quarters—all were thoroughly planned and discussed by the planters with the experts on the basis of survey report (Rajani Kanta Das, 1931). For a profitable tea plantation, it requires proper land planning, drainage survey including outlets, prior to starting plantation. This was meticulously done by the planters in Cachar. As a result within a short time the picture of the district was changed both geographically and economically.

Category of Tea Estates in Tamil Nadu, India

- The estates which are owned by proprietors or partnership firms those where only cultivation (green crops) is carried on and, where both cultivation and manufacturing are undertaken.
- Estates owned by limited companies registered in India with rupee capital (controlled by Board of Directors) whether Indian or non-Indian. This is further sub-divided into public limited or private limited companies.
- Estates owned by limited liability companies with rupee capital managed by managing agents (having a mixed Board of Management, Indian and non Indian and mixed shareholders by Indian and non-Indian).
- Tea estates managed by corporation. Estates owned by limited liability companies registered in UK with sterling capital.
- Tea estates managed by the state corporation, i.e. Tamil Nadu Tea Plantation Corporation Ltd. (TANTEA).

Manager of Tea Industry in Tamil Nadu, India

The management of a tea garden depends directly on the manager of the estate who is the main actor of the garden. The manager is appointed by the proprietor of the company on either fixed salary or on the basis of commission (Piya Chatterjee, 2001). It depends upon the condition of the garden and the role played by the manager in improving the production of tea (both quality and quantity). The services of the manager depends upon the sweet will of the company and may be terminated any moment after one month's notice or one month's advance pay.

The manager is the pivot around which the entire machinery of the garden revolves. He is, in fact, the eyes and ears of administration upon which the prospect and prosperity of garden depends. The manager is a seasoned planter and experienced bureaucrat of the garden. The sick gardens, down-rated gardens, economically unviable and doomed gardens can bloom with bright future, if the manager is hardworking, experienced, honest, and diligent and man of scientific approach to tackle the situation.

Supreme authority of the garden is vested in the manager who is the immediate uncrowned king of the tea estate. Under the patronage of the government, the European managers were the ambassadors of the estates and the frontier sentinels of the colonial empire (Mahendra P. Lama, 1986). In the beginning of the tea plantation up to the first quarter of the 20th century, the European managers were the captain of the ship of the tea estates. As a captain of the ship of the tea estate, they looked after the safety of the property of the estate and maximum utilisation of the existing resources with minimum cost of production along with maximum concession and benefits to the labourers. The European planters from the scratch, they gave tears and blood, and sometimes lost their lives even in giving sound economic base in the last part of the 19th century.

Field Management

The progress and prosperity of the garden depend upon the sound field management. The factory depends upon the raw materials (green leaves). The production would be maximum if green crop is higher per acre. The higher yield of green leaves depends upon efficient labour, good condition of the tea bushes, their scientific management and proper application of fertilizers, insecticides, weedicides, etc.

It is the customary duty of the tea garden manager to make regular visit to different sections of the plantation. This is called 'supervision' work which starts from 9 o'clock in the morning after breakfast. Before this, he goes to office at 7 o'clock in the morning, checks up all routine works, register of yesterday and passes order for today (outgoing letters, dak, etc. to different offices including head office). He thoroughly checks the statistical information sent to government offices. The subordinate staff gives information regarding number of persons engaged in a particular section in the sick ling, spraying of pesticides, plucking, factory work and office work. He gives direction to Divisional Manager/Assistant Manager and other field staff attached to headquarters. Then he goes to the factory where he checks the work done on previous day. Petty problems, complaints by the labour, general grievances of group or individual through Panchayat are also sorted by him (Piya Chatterjee, 2001).

The main purpose of supervisory role is to keep the workers alert and attentive during work. The manager looks after every section of the garden, their physical condition and keeps in mind any deficiency, improper plucking, requirements of manuring, pesticide, spraying of weedicides and other chemicals in particular section topographical damage due to soil erosion, drainage, fencing, cutting of unwanted grass (sick ling).

From a distance, he marks the negligence of workers. The managers give direction to the tea pluckers not to take coarse leaves. Fine plucking takes its rotation within seven to ten days and normal rotation between 13 and 15 days. The managerial and supervisory staff keep in mind that quick transportation of plucked leaves to be sent to factory without any sun exposure or injury to leaves for further processing. The divisional manager/ assistant manager also watches alertness and discipline of the field conductor/A.F.C., supervisors and other subordinate staff during operation of works and sometimes warns them to improve their efficiency. Cattle trespass and free movement of cattle in the section spreads various types of plant diseases. The line supervisors were given direction to prevent cattle trespass in the section. From regular surveillance work, the manager returns to office and factory, gives round to the factory work and checks or gives direction to the factory workers and then moves to the Bungalow for lunch.

In the evening, he again comes to factory for supervision work, gives direction to factory in-charge, factory supervisor, factory assistant, excise clerks. Besides, he also tastes tea and notes down the freshness, briskness, flavour including aroma of the tea. The manager again goes out for field supervision and makes sure that the F.C., A.F.C. and assistant managers and other supervisory staff are on duty.

In the evening, either in office or at his residence he makes assessment of the work or progress made head wise and reviews the works done earlier.

Office Work

The manager is the custodian of company's accounts (Umananda Phukam, 1983). All the financial transactions are operated by him. He is given power of attorney by the proprietors or the Board of directors which authorises him legal status on all financial dealings of the tea estate on company's behalf.

The manager scrutinises all the financial bills and passes the same if it is within his limit or refers to the head office for sanction. He keeps watch on garden cash book and other books of account. Before spending any amount he thinks thrice whether the expenditure is absolutely necessary for the development of the garden. The expenditure on development work and extension of new plantation sometimes exceeds the annual budget. The manager always keeps his grip tight and explains the genuineness of the expenditure in view of increasing green leaf production.

The best management of the garden depends upon four factors: Behavioural, Economic, Strategic and Technical. The behavioural dimension of management is concerned with dealing

of 'man-management'. The manager of the garden applies his skill of motivation to motivate all his employees to accomplish their allotted duties. For that, the manager is also to reciprocate their welfare. The economic dimension deals with the financial aspects of decision making for cost control with utilisation of high level of productivity, improvement techniques on long-term basis. The strategic dimension of management means forward looking approaches on long-term basis (Purnendu Kumar, 2006). The main purpose is development of the garden on all fronts. Within the limited resources, the managers have to proceed cautiously step by step. The manager is the real executive officer of the garden who presides over the destiny of thousand labourers and their dependants. The manager is a lion who creates panic and terror inside the garden. His very presence in the field, factory and office causes fear in the minds of the workers at all levels. He is still loved with great reverence as guardian of workers like the British counterparts in early days. Further, it is the broad mindedness and fine noble character of the manager which energises every illiterate worker (Uday Kumar Varma, M.M. Rehman, 2005).

Management of Tea Gardens in the Nilgiris' District, Tamil Nadu, India

Land

The land selected for planting is cleaned in the beginning of the dry season. Preparation of land prior to planting is most important aspect of the planting programme. The whole area is surveyed properly to make ready for layout of roads, drains before plantation begins. The soil is tested to determine any deficiency. Normally, soil having pH value between 4.5 and 5.5 is suitable for tea plantation. Higher pH value leads to alkalinity and lower to acidity. For replanting after proper uprooting and removal of roots of both tea and shade trees, the land is kept under green crop (mulching grass) for couple of years. On the tillah, according to rainfall and per centage of slopes and type of soil, contour drains are dug at certain distance of vertical drop (R.L. Sarkar, 1986). These drains are at least 45 cm deep each. On the flats, it is essential to dig wide and deep drains (about 90 cm deep each) around the base of tillah and rest of the drains on the contours to take away the excess of rain water.

Planting

The young bushes uprooted from the nursery are planted in plateau, tillah and flat land with different methods and spacing according to the suitability of soil and environment. The success of planting and survival of the young plants depend upon proper and timely planting. On tillah land chances of success are always higher. The best timing for planting on tillah commences after the first good rainfall during late March or early April and is completed by mid-June whereas on the flat land planting begins from mid-September onward even up to end of December or early January which has proved to be successful.

Bringing Up of Young Tea

Young tea area is always kept spotlessly clean so that tea bushes do not have to compete with fast growing weeds. For tillah once the bushes are established, i.e. approximately 4-6 weeks after planting, thumb pruning (at a height of about 22 cm) is done (Elizabeth Kaniampady, 2003). This encourages the plants to throw out lateral shoots and with split doze of manure about four times with an interval of six weeks helps quick growth of the laterals. When the laterals are grown, knife is used judiciously to remove thumb/nail pruned portion.

It has been observed that bushes grown under above process are tipped at the height of 40-45 cm from end of August or early September. These bushes are kept unpruned next year and are tipped after a margin of approximate 5 cm and one 0-2 years, knife is used judiciously to take out centre or cross branches and bushes are levelled off at 45 cm and then tipped and plucked with 20 cm margin.

Pruning

Tea plants have been pruned under different systems as given below:

- Orthodox pruning (only centering)
- Pegging

- Thumb/nail pruning (once the branches are out, centering followed by pegging)
- Centering and pegging
- Tipping
- Conservative tipping (orthodox type of high tipping)
- Low tipping and step up
- Medium tipping.

Mulching

Mulching is very important part of tea plantation (Purnendu Kumar, 2006). Young tea areas mulched with any green materials from October onward. Thicker the mulch, better will be the result which can be top dressed with a sprinkle of urea so that the mulch rots quickly. This not only improves the quality of the soil but also reduces the requirement of irrigation and suppresses the growth of weeds. Thus, it reduces weedicides consumption also. Mulching is a process of covering the soil with soft and sappy plant leaves to conserve the soil moisture. Mulching conserves soil moisture by reducing evaporation loss. It protects soil from direct sun and wind and suppresses weeds' growth. It reduces erosion and increases soil fertility through decomposition. It also keeps the soil warmer in winter and promotes quick growth.

Irrigation

Irrigation is essential for young planted area, failing which the drains on the flat is blocked and water is retained to keep the ground moist as far as possible. This work commences immediately after September-October. Irrigation is ideal for young tea either on tillah or on flat land, but due to economic reasons it may not be very practicable nowadays. In flat area, the drains are blocked in good time and thus the enough moisture is retained.

Manuring

Depending on the growth of the bushes in the first three years manuring is applied for quick growth (Purnendu Kumar, 2006).

Drainage

Tillahs are given contour drainage according to soil conditions. Flat lands have also contour drain as well as straight drains according to drop and soil conditions. Flat land has always been a problem in hilly areas as such the flats are affected by the back pressure from the main outlets which are beyond the individual or the collective efforts of the garden.

Shade Tree

Shade is an important part of tea plantation. It is called the life blood of the tea bush ('two leaves and a bud'). It is the shade which ensures natural resistance against pests and infections and also reduces transpiration and evaporation rate. Perhaps poor shade is one of the reasons why the plantation in the Nilgiris' District, Tamil Nadu suffers on account of wilting due to drought during the first flush harvest of the crop. There are three important stages of shade status co-related with the growth stages of tea plantation in Cachar. This crop stage, temporary shade status stage and finally the permanent shade tree stage. To avoid soil wash and degradation due to exposure when tillahs are cleared off jungle cover to provide shade in hot sides and to retain moisture for the growth of tea and to allow primary cover against hail and direct sunlight shade tree is needed. The important plants for shade are *Indigo ferra teysmanii*, *Bocaine*, *Derris robusta* and *Albizzia molucana*, *Melia azedarach* (Ghora neem) and Su-babul.

The quality of tea depends upon the age of leaves. The terminal buds are most valued in the trade and commonly referred to as golden tips. The smallest leaf forms orange-pekoe, the second leaf, pekoe, the third leaf pekoe-souchong, the fourth leaf souchong and the fifth leaf congou grade of tea.

Process of Tea Plantation at the Factory of TANTEA

The green leaves have to pass through various stages of final product (i.e. made-tea) which pass through the following stages.

Withering

The actual operation in the factory starts when the green leaves (golden buds, two leaves and a bud) are plucked from the tea bush and brought to the factory either directly in the basket by the individual pluckers or collected at certain points and then brought to factory under garden authority's arrangement (Rajani Kanta Das, 1931). The tea 'flush' contains 75-80% water which is reduced to 60-70% through withering. Withering plays an important role in producing quality tea. During withering loss of moisture and turgidity, break down of carbohydrates to carbon dioxide, increase of caffeine and development of flavour volatile from terpenoides, etc. take place. Withering is divided into three categories—light or soft withering, medium withering, and hard withering.

Rolling

Rolling stage is very crucial one where the leaves are broken physically by a mechanical process (orthodox or CTC method). The object of rolling is to twist the withered leaves and rupture the cells wall of the leaves for oxidation of polyphenol. In the process, juice is liberated which is responsible for bloom of CTC tea, golden tip colour of orthodox tea and also for liquor properties. Rollers are charged correctly and rolled properly otherwise unwanted flat leaf is produced. Flat leaf does not undergo oxidation and thus adversely affect liquor.

Fermentation

The third stage is the fermentation stage in which the rolled tea leaves, physically nurtured, are allowed to ferment in the air for one to three hours. Earlier it was kept on the floor in layers for oxidation but now in thick layers with a forced air supply.

During fermentation, the polyphenolic flavanols (or catchiness) in green tea are oxidised by the oxygen in the air to form around constituents and higher molecular weight polyphenolics—especially the theaflavins which gives the tea brew its red coloration and the dark thearubigins responsible for much of the mouthful of tea. This oxidation comes about through the catalytic action of an enzyme called polyphenol oxidise. The aroma components strongly affect the flavour of a cup of tea through our sense of smell. However, the taste or mouthful, of the tea brew derives mainly from the various tea polyphenolics modified by caffeine. During fermentation, green colour changes into brown, coppery, grassy flavour gradually disappear, typical tea flavour starts appearing.

Firing or Drying

Firing is the fourth stage of the tea manufacturing. The object of drying is to arrest oxidation and removal of water from the processed moist tea leaves particles. In course of drying changes that take place are loss of moisture, activation of enzymes, development of black/brown appearance, and breakdown of chlorophylls to pheophytins (blackish in appearance) and development of some aroma components, possibility from sugar to amino acid. The Nilgiris planters in the beginning began by firing according to Chinese practice. The rolled tea was first placed in an iron pan over a fire—a process, known as panning and then dried in trays above an open charcoal brazier. In the beginning of 1870s, an European planter named McMeekin invented a refined process of firing which became very popular and widely used in the Nilgiris' District, Tamil Nadu.

Sorting or Grading

The tea discharged from the drier is a mixture of long and fine tea leaf which requires sorting and grading. The tea is taken out to the shifting room for this purpose. The sifting room is chosen to be a large one, well let and constructed in such a way that the fluff and dust from selfters do not find their way into other parts of the factory.

The sorting machines are mechanically vibrated sieves or tables which sift the teas and separate them into particles of different sizes. The larger particles are broken into smaller bits with the help of cutting machine before grading.

The important grades are: (i) Orange Pekoe, (OP), (ii) Pekoe, (iii) Pekoe Souchong, (iv) Broken Orange Pekoe, (v) Broken Pekoe (BP), (vi) Broken Pekoe Souchong, (vii) Broken Orange Pekoe Fanning, (viii) Broken Pekoe Souchong Fanning, (ix) Dust, and (x) Flowery Broken Orange Pekoe (FBOP).

Production of Top Quality Tea

The factory must be airy and clean because even a slight infection of bacteria is sufficient to reduce the brightness or liquor and adversely affect the value of tea (Piya Chatterjee, 2001). Thus, every precaution is taken to eradicate bacteria.

Packing

As soon as grading and sorting of tea is completed, proper packing either in plywood tea chest with aluminium foil lining or in gunny bags with trade mark is done and stored in a godown from where the whole lot is sent to auction centre or to a party.

Quality of the Made-Tea

The distinctive character of tea is mainly due to three principal constituents—essential oil, alkaloidal fraction and polyphenol. The aroma and flavour of tea is due to the presence of etharnal oil, theol, the stimulatory and refreshing properties due to caffeine, alkaloid and the bitterness and astringency due to polyphenols (tannins). Chemically, tea consists of theine (2.5%), polyphenols (13-18%) and essential oils. In addition, it contains several B complex vitamins and nicotin acid. It is astringent, stimulant diuretic and nervine.

The quality of tea is the summation of the desirable attributes comprising internal and external like aroma, flavour, strength, colour, briskness. The quality of tea varies from garden to garden and also from time to time, although the quality of second flush tea is still the best. However, the quality cannot be made best overnight. The fine plucking, quick transportation to the factory in undamaged condition, no sun exposure, immediate spread in withering trough, proper rolling and fermentation and firing timely are the prerequisites of good quality tea. Besides, processing three important factors are taken into consideration, i.e. genetic, environmental and cultural. Tea quality is primarily determined by the genetic properties of tea plant and those of tea bushes in particular. Both climate and soil (environmental factor) influence the quality of the tea. Temperature, humidity, sunshine, duration, rainfall are the determining factors. Thirdly, field operations like pruning, fertilising, shading, plucking rounds and plucking standard also play important role in determining the quality of tea. Judicious plucking policy, balanced pruning cycle and blending of quality, standard clones in planting programme are important points in quality improvement scheme.

In fact, there are four categories of tea, black or fermented tea, green or unfermented tea, oolong or semi-fermented tea and lastly brick tea. Black is commercially the most important and it is produced mostly in India and Sri Lanka, Indonesia and East Africa, fermented tea is known as Green Tea. For manufacturing of green tea immediately after plucking, instead of proceeding to wither, cool and fermentation the fresh green leaf is subject to heat treatment by steaming and roasting. This heat treatment destroys the enzymes and prevents fermentation. The green leaf after heat treatment is rolled and during the process being repeated till the desired degree of dryness is obtained. Where the green tea is manufactured in substantial quantities the rolling and drying machine are similar to those used for the manufacture of black tea. For initial steaming, separate equipment is used (Purnendu Kumar, 2006).

Process of Tea Production

The tea plant is raised from seed which is sown in nurseries in November and December. Germination takes place in a month or six weeks and, when about a year old, the seedlings are transplanted in rows, the distance between the plants averaging from 4 feet by 4 feet to 6 feet by 6 feet. Transplanting is done either in May-June or rainy season or in autumn during October-November. The plants attain full maturity in fifth or sixth year but become fit for light plucking in the third year. Tea plants may survive 100 years but the economic life of a plant is estimated to be 50 years. The first pruning or *kalam* of young plants is done a year after planting, and each successive year they are allowed to grow a little higher until they produce thick bushes branching from the ground and grow about three feet high.

Mature plants are also pruned every year during December-January. Besides pruning some other operations like *khulni* or cutting away of dead wood and unnecessary twigs, *thalli* or clearing of weeds, *farua* or loosening of the soil, etc. are also done during winter. Plucking season begins in March or April and continues till about the middle of December; the peak period being May-September. Two leaves and a bud is the general rule for plucking, and the operation is done by hands. The green leaves collected are then transferred to withering sheds where the leaves are rolled and then sift in sifters, and the processed leaves are spread one inch thick on the floor of a cold room. They are kept there for about two hours and 15 minutes for fermentation. Next operation is called drying or firing. The fermented leaves are put in the chamber of a drier and hot air is passed in the chamber. The temperature within the drier is maintained at 200-210 F then the leaves are placed in a second drier when the temperature is 180 F. This completes the drying process and the dried material is allowed to pass through a breaking machine for reducing the size of the larger leaves. Then the leaves are sift in a series of five sieves having different size of nets and are separated into different grades. This completes the process of production of tea (Purnendu Kumar, 2006). The finished tea is then carried to the packing section where it is packed in wooden boxes and made ready for delivery.

Social Security Schemes in Tea Plantation Sector in India (with Special Reference to Tamil Nadu)

Tea garden workers, earlier called 'coolies' that acquired derogatory meaning had sorrowful days in the beginning. They had no voice to raise against European planters who were looked by the workers as their 'Big Boss'. They worked hard, spent their sweat and blood and made the tea plantation most prosperous. But they got nothing after their retirement except tears and misfortune of life. During the British days and even after independence, there was no provision of social security. Even the introduction of the Minimum Wage Act, 1948, Employees State Insurance Act, 1948, Workmen's Compensation Act, 1923 was practically not extended to tea plantation workers.

The Plantation Labour Act, 1951 tried to improve the condition of the workers remarkably. Credit goes to late Omeo Kumar Das, Labour Minister who is regarded as the real doyen of social security movement in Assam. He watched the miserable and deplorable economic condition of the tea garden labour society. The workers were guardianless and no one looked upon them to ameliorate the economic hardship of tea workers. He opined:

> The desperate and miserable condition of the tea labourers after retirement is beyond description. The labourers had little to fall back upon on retirement and indeed could not look forward any hope in their old age. Implementation of the Plantation Labour Act, 1951 will go a long way to raise the standard of living to the workers.

The tea garden labourers after years of service could scarcely look forward to any savings to fall back upon in their old age and were often forced to become object of charity. It was the generosity of the employers to provide them with paltry pension or to engage them into light jobs. A happy and contented labour force is the greatest asset to the industry and no employer will grudge this little burden.

Habit of thrift is practically absent in tea plantation labour circles. Ignorance of market price, lack of bargaining capacity as well as living in an isolated society quite different from urban and rural atmosphere are some of the factors behind the deplorable economic and social conditions of the tea garden labourers (Elizabeth Kaniampady, 2003). Taking the opportunity of such an advantageous situation, the businessmen and moneylenders have been exploiting them by selling goods of very low quality at exorbitant rates and by realising money on the very weekly payment days. Crores of rupees are drained out of their hands to enrich traders, moneylenders and shopkeepers. One cannot but feels pity at the plight of the workers who go to begging when the money is exhausted. Keeping in view the provisions laid down in the Constitution under Articles 38-39, 41 of the Directive Principles of State Policy, the Government of India and other federal states thought upon making law for the social security provisions for the workers in various industries. Following the Employees' Provident Fund Act, 1952, the Government of Assam passed the Assam Tea Plantations Provident Fund and Insurance Fund Scheme Act, 1955 in order to improve the socio-economic conditions of the workers employed in tea plantation of Assam. The Government of Tamil Nadu came out with the Tamil Nadu Plantation Labour Rules, 1954 to safeguard the employment rights and working condition of the tea plantation workers employed in the State of Tamil Nadu (Umananda Phukam, 1983).

Initially, it was for the resident labourers but subsequently amended to cover all non-resident workers and all office staff and technical staff drawing a salary or total emolument, less than one thousand.

Provident Fund Scheme for tea plantation workers is a landmark in the history of our social welfare legislation. This legislation was a leap forward in the implementation of labour welfare, which is first of its kind in India. The scheme includes:

(a) Provident Fund Scheme (1955)
(b) Life Insurance Scheme (1963)
(c) Pension-cum-Family Pension Scheme (1967)
(d) Deposit Linked Insurance Scheme (1984)
(e) The Assam Tea Garden Employees Gratuity Fund Scheme Act, 1972
(f) Tamil Nadu Plantation Labour Rules, 1954

The Provident Fund Organisation is administered by a Board of Trustees in which the workers' representatives, employers' representatives and government's representatives are included. The Board consists of 15 members in total. The chairman of the Board is nominated by the government. Generally, the position goes to the Labour Minister of the respective tea producing states. The main principle behind the composition of the Board is the sense of participation in the management of organisation. No employee should feel that his/her voice is not honoured in the administration of the organisation.

In fact, Provident Fund and Pension Fund Scheme is the bed-rock on which the edifice of social security is erected. It is the first step to provide social security to the labourers. Each labour contributes 12% of the basic pay and the same amount is paid by the employers. Thus, 24% makes a big fund which is deposited by the Board in government security.

Table 1.4: Provident Fund Deposits—Board of Trustees, ATPPF Scheme (Regional Office, Silchar) 1999-2000

District	Gardens Covered	Number of Member	Amount Collected (₹)
Cachar Assam	101	Permanent 52866	10,82,33,343.39 12,678,008,599.20
	824	Temporary 9180	

Source: Regional Office, Board of Trustees and Assam Tea Plantations Provident Fund Scheme, Silchar.

Social security measures have manifold significance for the developing countries. These measures reduce absenteeism and labour unrest and help in the formation of stable and efficient labour force. Social security is often used to augment national savings and to promote capital formation (Purnendu Kumar, 2006). If the national economy is to expand in real terms, there must not be any brake on investment but if investment is restricted, the national economy may shrink.

Table 1.5: Pension Amount in Cachar Area

Item	Workers	Amount
PF settled		
Payment of family pension paid	2285	5,39,08,018.02
Payment of family pension advance for marriage and *shradha*, etc.	1511	93,41,956.48
Payment of insurance benefits		3,20,40,061.00
Advance	12,74,662.00	
Recovery	92,025.77	
Total family pension income from late deposit (15% interest)		

Source: Regional Office, Board of Trustees and Pension Scheme, Silchar.

So far as Tamil Nadu is concerned, a considerable portion of economy of the state depends mainly on the tea industry and it may be recalled that the tea industry contributes considerable amount of Excise Duty to the Govt. of India. Besides, the industry contributes a sizeable amount of the government revenue from export, income tax and it earns valuable foreign exchange also. Tamil Nadu contributes over 1/3rd of the total tea export from the country.

Industrial Relations and Labour Welfare

Role of the Stakeholders in the Development of Tea Plantation Sector in India

Government Control

Gone are the days when the European managers were the uncrowned king of the tea estates. Their words were laws, not to be challenged by their subordinates. They were the managers and magistrates. They committed mistakes after mistakes, violated the chastity of women without any fear and none dared to protest. Many workers were expelled from the gardens without any fault. The tea garden labourers (coolies, a derogatory word in the beginning and now replaced by the Sramik or labour or workers) looked at them awfully. They called them as their 'Maa-Baap' (reverence given to authorities). The labourers used to fold umbrella when European planters passed through the section. They also did not put on shoes in presence of European planters. The government officials including Deputy Commissioner had to take permission from the European manager to enter into the garden. There was no labour union in those days to organise labour and encourage them to stop the work in case of denial of welfare measures. Even the government rules and regulations were rare and the planters did not care for them. This was mainly due to fact that they were the sentinels of British Empire. They were enjoying the patronage of the British Government. Even after independence, colonial hangover did not vanish easily. The managers were very powerful men enjoying vast powers over the labour and the tea-related staff and agencies. However, their hands had been chained by various enactments and they could not override them easily and were liable to face ill consequences if the implementation of the provisions enshrined in Acts or Rules framed by government delayed or denied.

After 1920 many Acts were made to ameliorate the labour conditions. The Workmen Compensation Act, 1923, Trade Union Act, 1926, Industrial Disputes Act, 1947, gradually spread their arms to the far-flung garden also and these became headache for the planters and the managers (Umananda Phukam, 1983).

The management of tea factory comes under the purview of the Factory Act, 1948 (Act of Parliament) and the Assam Factory Rules, 1950 for the safety, health and welfare of the workers engaged inside the factory. Under the provision, the Chief Inspector of Factories has power to inspect the factory and before giving licence to install a new plant he stresses upon the proper spacing of the machine for movement of the workers freely, proper light arrangement, sufficient ventilation, temperature control system, dust and fume clearance.

The government keeps watch on the proper health and hygiene of the workers inside the factory. The workers should not suffer from noise pollution, dust exhaust and high temperature. The workers should be given mask, earplug and must have regular medical check-up. Work inside the factory is different from the work outside the factory. Any minor neglect or carelessness of the workers or due to old machinery and improper installation may cause fatal injury to the workers. Arrangement for urinals, latrine, washing facilities, place of sitting inside the factory, rest rooms, etc. are to be regularly inspected. But the ground reality is just opposite everywhere. The report says one thing but ground reality is just reverse. The managers cannot violate the specifications laid down in the Acts. He is now bound to follow strictly certain specified provisions, otherwise the licence is cancelled (Uday Kumar Varma, 2005).

Payment of Wages Act, 1936

This Act compels the management to make payment within specified period and there cannot be unauthorised deduction.

Plantation Labour Act (PLA), 1951

This Act is landmark in the history of labour legislation which has checked the tyrannical style of functioning of managers. The dictatorial role of garden managers was put under government control. The Act provides plethora of rights to plantation workers in the name of welfare measures. The management cannot terminate the services of any worker unless gross misconduct of worker is reported. The manager will have to serve show cause notice first, followed by charge sheet, proceedings, etc. Likewise various provisions regarding maternity benefits, creche facility, housing, drinking water, etc. have to be implemented. The management has to submit Annual Return to Tea Board and Labour Department of the respective State Government (Elizabeth Kaniampady, 2003). The Labour Department inspects the garden and keeps an eye on the various benefits given under statutory provision of Plantation Labour Act, 1951, Payment of Bonus Act, 1965. Inspection of the papers and documents (attendance register, wage rate, medical register, etc.) is important part through which the government checks the arbitrary style of the management of the garden. The manager cannot overlook or ignore the provisions of various Acts like Payment of Gratuity Act, 1972, Weekly Holiday Act, 1942 and Equal Remuneration Act, 1976 made for the welfare of workers.

Assam Tea Plantation Provident Fund Scheme, 1955 (ATPPF), Assam Plantation Labour Rules, 1956, Assam Tea Plantation PF and Pension Fund Scheme, 1968 and Assam Tea Plantation PF Deposit-linked Insurance Fund Scheme, 1984, put financial restrictions on the carefree style of functioning of the management. The Board of Trustees, controlling authority of the above funds, sends inspector to the gardens to inspect deposit of the PF amount to the Board office on time. Thus, the managers are bound to deduct the amount and deposit the same to the office. The State Government through land revenue at the rate of ₹ 9 per bigha realises huge money from the tea estates. The tea estates are bound to pay the enhanced revenue within the financial year.

The Government of India through Central Excise Duty on tea, income-tax return, corporate tax and the State Government through the agriculture tax, Assam taxation on specified land also control the tea estates (Piya Chatterjee, 2001).

Tea Board (Regional Office) also exercise control of all tea estates located in various states of our nation. The individual garden submits annual return to the Tea Board Office, Kolkata, West Bengal.

Railway Services

Railway lines in the Nilgiris' District, Tamil Nadu are not only cheap and quick means of transport but harbinger of cultural exchange and national understanding. The introduction of railways in the Nilgiris' District by the end of the 18th century is a boon in many respects for which the people of Green Valley would remain grateful to the colonial rulers. Though it is put forward for argument's sake that the entire communication system fabricated by the British for their own advantages and gains, yet an accountable impact on the overall development of the entire region in almost all respects of social, economic and industrial development along with the advancement of political awareness is a legacy of the communication network set up by the colonial power. It is true that British took interest to provide railway network in Tamil Nadu, particularly in the Nilgiris' District, Tamil Nadu with purely commercial motive. The extension of railway line in the the Nilgiris' District, Tamil Nadu in those days to connect this area with the States of Kerala and Karnataka was a gigantic task. However, it was planned by 1898 by the British administrators but could not be successfully completed by the Indian rulers after the independence. Udagamandalam (Ooty) was the last railway station in the Nilgris' Mountain Railway (NMR) line. It is a 46 kms stretch starting from Metupalaiyam passing through seven stations via Coonoor.

It is true that British exploited Tamil Nadu and extracted maximum benefit for themselves. But the fact remains that without infrastructure built by the early planters and the British administrators, Tamil Nadu would have been far behind the rest of the country that it is now (Rajani Kanta Das, 1931). It must be acknowledged today that tea is one of the major sources of Tamil Nadu economy. It contributes over hundreds of crores a year to the fund hungry Tamil Nadu Government through various taxes.

Postal Services

The postal services in the Nilgiris' District, Tamil Nadu were unknown till middle of the eighteenth century. The jurisdiction of the Wellington Post Office extended up to Udagamandalam (Ooty). Theoretically, the official packets and letters between Chennai and Ooty and places other than in Tamil Nadu were sent through messengers. However, later on, a Post Master for Ooty was appointed and regular post and telegraph services were introduced. Almost 30 post offices and 19 telecommunication centres were introduced in the Nilgiris' District. All these developments of postal services are rooted in the expansion of tea industry in Tamil Nadu (Deepak K. Mishra, 2012). The European tea planters had patronised the British administrators. Their relation at that time was cordial and depended on each other. The same relation is missing today to a great extent.

Welfare Measures by the Tea Planters and Tea Workers

Tea industry of the Nilgiris' District, Tamil Nadu from the very beginning has undertaken many benevolent schemes for which the people are obliged to the industry. The development of roads, paths, Coimbatore Aerodrome, civil hospital has been helped by the tea planters. Many tea garden labourers were deputed to work for the construction of the Nilgiris' Mountain Railway (NMR).

In the field of education, the European planters opened many vernacular schools in the gardens and provided teachers from the garden fund. Later on, these schools were taken over by the government in 1970. Further opening of middle schools and high schools has also been financed by the European planters. Further, it is needless to say that many charitable clubs like Lions Club, Rotary Club, and Red Cross have been funded by the tea planters for the greater interest of the people (Elizabeth Kaniampady, 2003).

Development-oriented Measures of the Employers of the Tea Gardens in Tamil Nadu

Tea industry is a boon for the State of Tamil Nadu. In its early period and even today, it is helpful to people in many ways.

Prior to the establishment of tea industry in Tamil Nadu the subsistence economy was the primary concern of the people. The tea industry brought radical change from subsistence economy to wage economy. There was perceptible change in the attitude of the people in respect of occupation and profession. The industry led them to open business centres, diversified business shops, technical workshops and job-oriented profession. The industry has brought indirect impact on the economy of the people of Tamil Nadu. The tea industry paved the way for urbanisation throughout the districts of Tamil Nadu and Ooty became a nodal town. It was a centre of attraction for the European planters and businessmen. Many other tourist places, small bazars/hats by the side of tea estates sprung up within short time. The industry gave employment to many educated indigenous people (Mahendra P. Lama, 1986). The scope of employment was extended to people of other districts of Tamil Nadu as well.

The communication networks, particularly the railway developed due to tea industry in the Nilgiris' District, Tamil Nadu which linked it with rest of India. Finally, the industry brought changes in the socio-economic and political perception of the people of the Nilgiris' District. Changes in population pattern and socio-economic and political activity of people of the Nilgiris' District—all these have great bearing on the development of tea industry of this district.

Measures Undertaken by the Trade Union Organisation

In order to maintain the integrity, independence, and continuity of service, a trade union organisation of workers is indispensable. It is the duty of trade union organisations to inculcate a sense of belonging in the tea workers. The prosperity of tea garden means the prosperity of the workers and this very attitude provides inspiration to the workers to maintain tea bushes like their own children. A remarkable feature about tea plantation is that while the employers in past were well organised, powerful economically as well as politically, the workers were unorganised, illiterate and ignorant with no one to represent their cases before the public or the government (Pranab Kumar Dasgupta, 1983). The European planters in past did not like any trade union organisation of the tea labourers. They neither encouraged nor sympathised with any attempt towards the organisation of labour in their estates. They viewed with disfavour the contacting of their workers by outsiders. Other than friends and relatives of the labourers, the outsiders had to take prior permission from the managers before entering into the garden. Planters did not like outsiders to organise the unions in the gardens, although the need to form labour union was also emphasised by the Assam Labour Enquiry Commission Report, 1921.

Trade union formation in tea plantation in Tamil Nadu was not an easy task during the British days. There were many difficulties in this task. The workers were mostly illiterate, spoke different languages and were timid and helpless. Again, isolated nature of the plantation area and the strenuous efforts made by the planters to prevent outsiders from contacting their labour had hindered the growth of trade unions in the Nilgiris' District, Tamil Nadu. The workers were afraid of the managers. They were made so due to the fear of victimisation. Tea garden workers' struggle did not however, crystallise into a unified and organised labour movement in Tamil Nadu until 1938.

The major constraints were the in-built systems operative in the garden such as restriction on mobility, enforced isolation, social and physical control of workers and the oppressive state machinery with the help of high caste businessmen from Chettiar community that prevented the emergence of a political leadership.

British managers realised that the country will go today or tomorrow out of the grip of the British rule and the labour would create problems in tea garden life. Hence, they began to change their colonial attitude and allowed the organisers from outside the valley to organise unions or panchayat in the gardens. They did not put any objection in making panchayat, or primary schools in the area. Thus, gradually many gardens came under the Panchayats of the areas concerned for the sole purpose of maintenance of schools located in the tea gardens.

Impact of Two Schools of Thought—Gandhian and Marxian

Trade unionism got inspiration from two schools of thought—Marxist and Gandhian. The philosophy of Marx emanated from his quest for liberation of toiling masses. His interpretation of human history as a product of class struggle and expected all changes to be crystallised in its crucible, but Gandhiji's action sprung from the inner recesses of his soul. He experimented with truth. Human lives were his laboratory, love his instrument and appeals of human heart his language. All India Trade Union Congress (AITUC) and Centre of Indian Trade Unions (CITU) followed the former whereas the Indian National Trade Union Congress (INTUC) and Hind Mazdoor Sabha (HSM) followed the latter as tenets of their organisation.

Trade Union and Workers' Participation in the Trade Union's Decision-making Process

Though tea garden workers are illiterate, ignorant, poor and politically quite unaware, they are moving forward due to their contact with Central Trade Unions such as INTUC, AITUC, CITU, communication devices like radio and media, both print and electronic. The newspapers and magazines are rarely used by the workers living in far flung gardens (Purnendu Kumar, 2006). However, the young generation of the same stock who is in the regular contact with other cross-sections of society, is quite familiar with day-to-day political development inside the country.

Tea garden workers in general are far behind in this respect. They live from hand to mouth; most of them are illiterate, socio-culturally less advanced, cut off from the mainstream of life due to heavily engaged in plantation environment. Consequently, the level of political participation, due to all these negative factors, is not admirable and up to the mark. They seldom apply their political wisdom and sagacity and they become victim of political indecision (Vandana Upadhyay, 2012). They are misled by their leaders and they fail to make correct assessment of the situation. Sometimes many other factors lead them to a state of utter confusion.

Labour vote is the solid vote bank in the hands of labour leaders belonging to their own caste and community. The leaders easily convince them in their own language, which generates emotional attachment. The per centage of poll in garden areas is higher than other general polling booths. This is because tea labourers are concentrated in labour lines and are very close to the polling centres. Further, all the voters remain present in the garden because they have limited employment or engagement outside the garden. Again, the division of votes is less in the garden. Either all will vote for this party or that candidate.

The tea garden labour, in fact, forms a real pressure group in the state politics as a whole (Iar Ali Khan, 1983). In Tamil Nadu too they are an important influencing factor. The entire constituencies of the Nilgiris' District, such as, Udagamandalam, Coonoor and Gudalur, tea plantation labour votes are the deciding factor.

Problems Encountered by the Tea Plantation Workers in India

The intellectual growth of the tea plantation workers is retarded due to poverty, socio-cultural backwardness, illiteracy and containerised plantation environment. Absence of leisure hours has dulled their thinking power. The workers never think of anything beyond arranging two square meals for themselves and their families. Excessive feudal dominance and tyrannical governance of the planters have kept them under perpetual slavery. Absence of freedom has made their mental faculty dormant. There is none to guide them to come out the pool of poverty, illiteracy and backwardness. They are virtually guardianless. Consequently, they are doomed intellectually. They lack political awareness. Higher income which brings in greater prosperity, more leisure, less anxiety and wider opportunity naturally—makes people more active in politics. Thus, the higher income groups are found to vote proportionally in larger numbers than those with lesser income group. The tea garden workers do not get opportunity to interact with neighbours.

Living in remote and isolated garden lines they fail to get exposure and remain deprived of the touches of modern civilisation. In fact, they are the victims of circumstances. Female workers are more politically unconscious. Their intellectual horizon is narrow and dwarf. This is due to their illiteracy, and having no contact with educated women organisations and consequent detachment from the mainstream of national life. No organisation (government or NGOs) have ever thought to ameliorate the condition of the women workers (Iar Ali Khan, 1983).

Industrial Relations

One of the most important labour questions is to relation between employers and employees. Since the beginning of the past century, there has been considerable improvement in labour conditions, but the relations between labour and capital has secretly improved in fact it has become much more strained (Purnendu Kumar, 2006). The fundamental reason of this growing antagonism is the rise of class consciousness and class solidarity among the workers which has been accompanied by an increasing demand for better working conditions higher wages and even the recognition of their status in business management. The capitalists guided by both self-interest and vested rights have scarcely shown any willingness to part with any of their rights and privileges The growth of organisation on both sides has often led them to open conflict leading to industrial and social disorganisation.

In India, these conflicts are no doubt more pronounced in factories, mines and transport than on plantations but even the latter industries have recently become subject to dispute. With increasing concerted action on the part of workers on plantation, industrial disputes are likely to increase. But the power of concerted action are still in the infant stage of development among the plantation workers. Planters have organised themselves for corporate activities from the very beginning. The most important of the Planters' Association, Indian Tea Association, and the United Planters' Association of Southern India (UPASI). The Bihar Planters' Association dates back to 1801, when the indigo planters formed themselves into an association for safeguarding their common interests. It was re-organised in 1905 under the present name (Rajani Kanta Das, 1931). The Indian Tea Association was founded in 1881 with the object of promoting the common interest of all persons concerned in the cultivation of tea in India. The membership consists of proprietors, managers and agents of tea estates. Since 1900 the association has maintained a scientific department for research in the interest of the industry and nominates one member to the Bengal Legislative Council.

The United Planters' Association of Southern India (incorporated) was organised in 1893 with the view to promoting the interest of various planting industries carried on in southern India. The association maintains a scientific department and four experimental stations and also publishes a weekly paper called *The Planters' Chronicle*. It elects an additional member to the Madras Legislative Council. The association has also a labour department with six divisional officers and agents throughout India. All these planters associations were organised for preserving their own business interests, namely research, cultivation, marketing and other facilities. On the question of labour they have a common policy. The Tea Planters' Association and The United Planters' Association of Southern India act together in demanding uniform law and regulations for recruitment of labour conditions of employment and terms of contract (Mahendra P. Lama, 1986). By their representatives on the Legislative Council and also in the various commission and committees appointed on the question of plantation labour they influence the policy of the government toward labour.

Industrial Disputes between Tea Plantation Employers and Workers

Nothing is definitely known about industrial disputes between employers and employees in the early years of the plantation industry except for the frictions in the form of assaults and riots already referred to. Considering the strength of the labour force, which, for instance, amounted to 323,000 in 1887, there was bound to be, to quote the official report, "a certain amount of harshness and oppression, at times possibly even of downright cruelty, on the one side, and of turbulence, conspiracies and maliciously concocted charges, on the other," which there were "criminal courts strong enough to deal with." "Speaking generally," continued the same report, "the relations between the employers and the labourers seem to be fairly good."

All these assaults and riots, especially the latter, which amounted to 106 in number in 1891, could not, however, be regarded as ordinary crimes. Organised opposition and "combination" among plantation labourers were noticeable as early as 1884, and some of these frictions were originally nothing but industrial disputes and became "riots" only for the lack of capable leadership among the illiterate and isolated groups of labourers working under the indenture system (Elizabeth Kaniampady, 2003). The very fact that labourers could be punished for "illegal assembly" shows that planters took ample precaution to prevent any concerted action on the part of labourers to redress their grievances, and that this provision of the law was effectively utilised by planters is indicated by the fact that in 1902-03, 82 labourers were imprisoned for illegal assembly including rioting.

Whatever might have been the case in the earlier years, there have grown up in recent years both consciousness of class interests and power of concerted action among plantation labourers.

The first sign of such consciousness and power was seen at a tea garden in Assam on September 6, 1920, when different sections of the labour force refused to turn out to work. It was soon followed by numerous strikes in various gardens in different parts of the province. The climax of these disputes was, however, reached in what is called the "Chargola exodus" early in May 1921, when following a dispute 750 labourers walked out of a garden and were soon joined by labourers in other gardens. In a few days, 8,799 labourers out of a total of 20,250 in different gardens of the district left work. Some of these disputes were accompanied by assaults, riots and lootings in which both plantations and government officials were attacked. Of 167 labourers imprisoned for illegal assembly and riots in 1920-21, the majority were the victims of these industrial disputes. The number of labourers imprisoned for similar offences declined to 96 in 1921-22 and to 24 in 1925-26 (Pranab Kumar Dasgupta, 1983). But these strikes and assaults are still in abundance. In 1929, a number of strikes involving from 100 to 672 workers took place both in the Surma and Assam Valleys and lasted from one to nine days.

The principal causes of these frictions and disputes were economic, especially in recent years. The rate of wages in the tea garden was low in the very beginning and had remained unchanged for a quarter of a century or more. It failed to respond to the great increase in the cost of living soon after the War. Moreover, owing to the depression in the tea industry, the first item of work to be reduced was the ticca or overtime earnings. The situation was still more aggravated by the fact that *pari passu* with decreased earnings, the prices of the so-called concession paddy went up. For example, previous to 1920, the price was fixed at ₹ 2.25 a mound and in July onwards of that year it was raised to ₹ 3.37. The result was the decrease in the real wages and in most cases, the labourers were worse off than they had been 20 years ago. Even in the case of the Chargola exodus, to which was generally ascribed a political cause, it was found that in many gardens the labourers were not earning a living wage before the exodus. In September 1929, a party of 85 Bombay labourers, including women and children, left the gardens in the Surma Valley on account of not receiving a living wage and flatly refused to return. Although the manager lodged a complaint of rioting against them, the Superintendent of Police on enquiry established the truth of the workers contention and found that they were insufficiently paid (Umananda Phukam, 1983).

Among the other economic causes of local character, the following might be mentioned to be the chief: First enforced work on Sundays, excessive work and inadequate leave, whenever there was a shortage of labour supply; second, fines for bad work, illegal deductions by the clerk from the wages and occasional withholding of wages by managers for keeping a hold on the workers. Third, short weights in measuring paddy, poor quality of paddy and high prices of food and clothing. Most of these allegations were found to be true by the Assam Labour Enquiry Committee of 1921-22.

There was a feeling among labourers that justice was not duly and impartially administrated by government in the controversies between the planters and themselves. "Europeans being administrators of justice in all disputes between European planters and labourers, it was impossible for them to be altogether uninfluenced by their natural feelings towards their fellow countrymen," as the official report put it in 1900 (Arul Sarma, 2012). "There is an undoubted tendency among magistrates in Assam," continues the report, "to inflict severe sentences in cases in which coolies are charged with committing offences against their employers and to impose light, and somewhat inadequate punishments, upon employers when they are convicted of offences against labourers." This feeling of injustice often loaded the labourers to take the law into their own hands in cases of grievances and to strike work.

Situation in Tamil Nadu Pertaining to Industrial Disputes

Personal insults in the form of kicks, blows or corporal punishment were still another cause of friction between planters and labourers, especially in the earlier years. The existence of such insults by planters to labourers was admitted by the government. "The Chief Commissioner is not so sanguine", says the Report on Plantation Labour Immigration into Tea Gardens of the Nilgiris, Tamil Nadu for 1899, "as to look forward to the day when Englishmen will altogether abandon the regrettable habit of giving a cuff or even a kick or a blow with a cane to natives of the labouring classes." That some of the riots were caused by such personal insults was also admitted by the Official Report the following year (Piya Chatterjee, 2001). "Blows given by managers," continued the report, "or more commonly assistant managers, to coolies, either for bad work or refusal to work, were the immediate causes of most of the rioting cases which occurred during the year. The striking and kicking of the labourers by managers exists even today in the private tea estates of the Nilgiris District, Tamil Nadu.

Of the contributory causes, especially in recent years, the most important was the success of a strike in 1950 on the tea gardens located along the Nilgiri Mountain Railway, which runs through the private tea estates where the first of the industrial disputes took place. Similarly important is the political condition of the State in 1920 and 1921. Although all of the disputes and disturbances did not result from the incitement from outside agitators, some of them, especially the exodus of labourers, were influenced by the non-co-operation movement, which swept all over the State during the period.

The fundamental cause of the industrial disputes and unrest in Tamil Nadu, especially in recent years, was the growing consciousness among the labourers themselves. A change in the attitude of the labourers not to pocket the insults at the hands of planters or other officials was noticeable even over a generation ago. "There was a growing tendency among the coolie class" observed the Report on Labour Immigration into Tea Gardens of the Nilgiris, Tamil Nadu in 1899, "to resent a blow by striking a blow in return, and this soon leads to serious results, as coolies act in combination among them and are armed with formidable weapons—the implements of their industries; but this very tendency exercises a healthy influence in restraining the hot-headed and impetuous European assistants from raising their hands against them (Piya Chatterjee, 2001). This spirit of self-assertion in the case of personal grievances has gradually developed into power of concerted action for the furtherance of class interests. In recent years, strikes, assaults and riots have their origin in the spirit of retaliation for the abuse and misuse of their power to which the workers have been subjected by managers and other high members of the staff.

The factors which have contributed most to the growth of class consciousness and concerted activities among labourers in Tamil Nadu might be classified under three headings: First, legislative measures, by which the government have gradually ameliorated labour conditions and abolished contract labour, especially since the inauguration of the International Labour Organisation in 1919. Second, the public attitude against contract labour, bad conditions and unjust treatment on plantations, as expressed especially by the vernacular Press in earlier years and both by the Press and Platform in recent years (Rajani Kanta Das, 1931). Although there were often "exaggerations and misrepresentations," "bitter hostility" towards the planters, and "indiscriminating opposition" towards emigration these agitations could not fail, yet to awaken a new consciousness among the labourers themselves. Third, the labour movement itself has been the most important factor in giving the labourers on plantations, though unorganised, a new viewpoint and in creating a new outlook.

Industrial peace on plantations as in other organised industries depends therefore upon full realisation by employers of this new situation and upon sympathetic appreciation by them of this new attitude.

WORKING CONDITIONS OF THE TEA PLANTATION LABOURERS IN INDIA

In the 1840s and early 1850s the wage rate in the plantations of Assam generally varied between ₹ 2.50 to ₹ 3.50 per month. It was only after the revolt of 1857, that it rose to ₹ 4.00. In this given context, these wages were not unjust, as indentured labour did not exist till then. This was mainly because of the strong bargaining power of the local labour force (Guha, 2006).

The situation changed their behaviour thereafter when indentured labour became the dominant mode of labour recruitment. The labour policy that was pursed by the planters and their governments did not encourage free movement of labour at competitive wages. The planters adopted coercion as the prime mechanism for ensuring labour supply. Their methods included extensive use of force to restrict free movement of labourers and it resulted in the creation of a type of serfdom, which was unheard of in any other public works departments at that time. A common free labourer earned ₹ 7 per month in 1864, while in the plantation sector they would earn between ₹ 4 to ₹ 5 during the same period (R.L. Sarkar, Mahendra P. Lama, 1986). The Transport of Native Labourers Act of 1863 did not stipulate the minimum wages (*ibid.*). Statutory wages were laid down by bringing amendments to existing legislation. Though the provisions were formally abolished in 1870 by the Act of 1882, and the same statutory wages continued in practice up to 1901. The minimum wages so set were ₹ 5 and ₹ 4 respectively for men and women and ₹ 3 for children per month under the mounting pressure of public opinion in India in support of increase of wages.

The demand-supply scenario in the tea labour market in India particularly in relation to the changes in employment growth and labour productivity, brings out the problems faced by the tea sector on the employment front. For the period 1980-2004, employment has grown at a higher rate at the all-India level than in Assam. Although at the all-India level growth of labour employed has been relatively robust during 1998-2000, mainly on account of the tremendous expansion of employment in Tamil Nadu. In Assam, the growth rate has decelerated to 0.87 per cent per annum. During 1998 and 2004, however, there has been some recovery of growth of labour per hectare at the all-India level, but the situation in Assam and West Bengal continues to be gloomy. As many as four out of seven districts in Assam under consideration, registered a negative growth in labour per hectare, while others experienced very low growth (Vandana Upadhyay, 2012). Although labour productivity had increased relatively and comfortably during the 1980s in Assam, during the 1990s labour productivity growth slumped in many districts in Assam. During the last six years, from 1998 to 2004, there has been substantial deterioration in labour productivity in almost all the major tea-producing states of India.

Perceptions on Working Conditions and Occupational Change

Workers' perception on their working conditions and the desire to change occupations provide important insights regarding the conditions of work inside and outside the gardens. However, an analysis of perceptions through a questionnaire method has some inherent limitations. Respondents may not be willing to share their real perceptions with the interviewer for a number of reasons.

Conditions of the Employment of the Plantation Labour

Terms of Labour Contract

It has already been noted that contract labour in India on plantations has been developed under two series of legislations, namely workmen's breach of Contract Act of 1859 and two sections of the Indian Penal Code and plantations legislation or Labour and Emigration Acts for Assam tea gardens since 1963 the former leading to the contract system under penal sanction and latter to the indenture system (Rajani Kanta Das, 1931). The object of the breach of Contract Act of 1859 was to safeguard employers against "the fraudulent breach of contract on the part of artificers, workmen and labourers who received money in advance on account of work which they had contracted to perform." It began to be taken as advantage of by tea planters in India in sixties as noted before and the terms of contract under it were often mixed with those under plantations Acts. The most important terms in favour of the employer were as follows first, verbal contracts were legal, whether they could be verified or redeemed. On most of the plantations, a record of verbal contracts was however invariably kept either in the garden cash book or advance registers, or the register for the advancement of money and the labourer's thumb impression was generally added to the entry. Second although the contract was generally limited to a period of 313 days, it was often extended to 939 days. Third a labourer could be prosecuted and imprisoned for breaking his agreement, though it contained no compensating provision for his protection. Among the features more or less favourable to the labourer might be mentioned the following. First under the original Act, the employer had no power of arrest without warrant. Second the magistrate was granted a wide discretion as to the reasonableness for the non-performance of the contract and the amount of punishment to be inflicted. Third when a labourer was once sentenced to imprisonment, he was no longer liable to prosecution in respect to the contract under this Act.

Beside the contract under the other two system of legislation which could be executed either in recruiting districts or at Dhubri in Assam there was also the system of local contracts which had already existed in the districts of Sylhet and Cachar and which was sanctioned by the Act of 1882 (Umananda Phukam, 1983). The objects of the local contract system were as follows: (i) Providing the planter with system of penal contract instead of civil contract so that he might have better control over his labour force. (ii) Securing to the planter a uniform system of contract and to the labourers a uniform system of protection. (iii) Encouragement to free emigration into Assam. Local contracts as a method for the establishment of free immigration failed to get materialised. The Assam Labour Enquiry Committee of 1906 recommended its withdrawal on the following grounds: first, free emigration was impossible unless there was also free labour. Second, if an emigrant was to be put under an agreement it was better done in his own village where he was still a free agent and among his own people and could appear before a magistrate who knew his language. Moreover there is no necessity for a local contract as Act XIII of 1859 was sufficient to take its place.

Hours of Work

Unlike other agricultural industries, the question of hours of work is an important one on plantations. This is due to the fact that it is an organized and large-scale industry and capitalistic enterprises. The very fact that labourers live on or near the plantations with their wives and children suggests that there is a possibility of overwork on the part of both adults and children, unless there is a specific provision against it (Purnendu Kumar, 2006).

1. *Legal Hours*

The hours of labour on plantations, especially on tea gardens in Assam, were in fact regulated from the very beginning. The Plantation Act of 1870, which amended the terms of the indenture system for Assam tea gardens, fixed also the hours of labour at nine a day. Subsequent amendments and re-enactments of this Act made scarcely any alteration in the hours of labour (Elizabeth Kaniampady, 2003). The indenture system has been abolished, but the standard of the hours of work once established still remains.

The legal hours of work fixed for Assam tea gardens applied to men and women alike. Children or persons under the age of sixteen could not become indentured or contract labourers, but they often worked the same number of hours as adults.

2. *Overtime Work*

The actual hours of work are, however, quite different from those limited by the law. There are two important factors which influence the actual length of work on plantations.

- First, the basis of remuneration on plantations is piece work or task, and in order to earn the full wages, the task must be completed irrespective of the time. The fact that many labourers cannot earn the regular wages, as to be noted later on, indicates that the task is by no means an easy one. In fact, Section 5 of The Plantation Act of 1870 specifically laid down that during the first six months labourers shall be entitled to full pay on the completion of half the daily task, unless the inspector testified that the labourer was physically fit to perform the whole task. That the task is still heavy is also proved by the fact that on the 5th September 1927, 80 Munda workers of a garden left work and returned to it only on the assurance that it would be reduced, which was ultimately done by the manager.
- Second, as in other agricultural industries, the work on plantations undergoes variation according to season. The possibility of engaging labourers for overtime work was stipulated by the terms of contract from the very beginning and a good part of the labourers' income depended upon overtime work. During the cold weather, however, there is a great depression in plantation industries and many labourers have to depend in part on subsidiary industries.

The main purpose of weekly holidays is, however, rest, which means not only cessation from work for recuperation, but also enjoyment of sociability and other amenities of life. Nothing is more important to labourers on plantations, who are mostly immigrants and live in isolated communities on hillsides, than the companionship of their friends and relatives on the same or neighbouring plantations (Uday Kumar Varma, 2005). It was perhaps the realisation of this fact that led Captain Mackie, President of the Darjeeling Planters' Association, to suggest that, in addition to the weekly holiday, there should be half holiday on Saturday, especially during the non-manufacturing season. "In all countries," said Captain Mackie, "the working man has a half holiday on Saturday, and there seems no reason to deprive the tea garden coolies of this privilege." This suggestion has not received any serious consideration by the plantation industries. In fact, the labourers are compelled to work even on Sundays, as noted before. It would be much better for them to have a full holiday once every week.

It is needless to say that long hours do not necessarily lead to a larger income. The task or overtime work, as once stipulated by the contract, and as is still in vigour on most plantations, does not in reality help the workers to earn higher wages, although it appears to do so. Had it not been for this stipulation, the rate of wages for regular work would have been much higher from the very beginning. What is true of the shorter hours is also true of Sunday or holiday work. The workers, including one or two members of the family willing to work overtime to meet their expenses, and if they do not work overtime or on holidays, they have to earn the same amount during the regular hours of the day, and the fixed days of the week. Both overtime work and holiday work are disadvantageous to the workers.

Industrial Efficiency

1. *Absenteeism and Turnover*

Regularity of attendance is one of the essentials of industrial efficiency. A great defect of the Indian labourer is his constant absence from the place of work. This is true in the case of labourers on plantations as in any other organized industry in India (Rajani Kanta Das, 1931).

The study of average daily working strength on the tea gardens of the tea-producing States as compared with the total number of workers on the books for several years shows that the regularity of attendance varies from 75 to 77 per cent. In the case of men, from 71 to 74 per cent in the case of women, from 68 to 73 per cent. In the case of children, and from 72 of 74.5 per cent. In the case of all the workers taken together, as shown in Table 1.6. It is thus seen that from 25.5 to 28 per cent of the workers, that is, over one-quarter of the total, are generally absent from work.

Table 1.6: Absenteeism on the Tea Gardens of the Tea Producing States (At Specific Years)

Year	Per centage of Average Daily Working Strength to total Number on the Books			Percentage of Absenteeism	
	Men	Women	Children	Total	Percentage absenteeism
1906	76.5	71	68	72	28
1914	75	72	73	73	27
1922	77	74	72.5	74.5	25.5
1928-29	76	73	69	74	26

Next to absenteeism, labour turnover, or the number of labourers who are discharged every year in comparison with the annual labour strength, is an important obstacle to the achievement of efficiency. The number of labourers annually discharged, including transfers and deaths, amounted as high as 192,541 in 1920-21, as compared with the total labour force of 1,060,948, giving the labour turnover of 18 per cent, as shown in Table 1.7. The labour turnover in 1928-29 amounted only to 11 per cent, as compared with 14 per cent in 1902-03 (Purnendu Kumar, 2006).

Table 1.7: Labour Turnover on the Tea Gardens of the Tea Producing States (At specified periods)

Year	Annual Strength	Annual Discharge (Including Transfer and Deaths)	Per Cent of Turnover
1902-03	547,870	76,934	14
1910-11	736,955	86,817	12
1920-21	1,060,948	192,541	18
1928-29	1,046,441	116,632	11

In comparison with other industries, the labour turnover on plantations cannot be said to be very high. The reason for this low rate of turnover is the fact that these labourers are generally appointed permanently and live on plantations or in the vicinity (R.L. Sarkar, 1986). But even a very small rate of turnover involves a high cost for the plantations, and interferes with the rate of wages, on the one hand, and with the achievement of skill on the other.

2. *Vigour and Skill*

While attendance and steadiness are preliminary conditions, the efficiency of labour depends mostly upon vigour and skill. Regarding vigour, it has already been pointed out that the efficiency of the labourers on plantation is greatly diminished by the frequent outbreak of epidemics and the presence of other diseases, especially anaemia. The average labourer without sufficient vigour cannot be expected to do a day's work, and the cultivation of gardens must suffer or additional labour force must be imported (Purnendu Kumar, 2006).

Still greater is the problem of skill. Practically, all the workers on plantations, as in fact in all other industries in India, are illiterate and untrained. Plantation workers, as noted before, are generally drawn from agricultural labourers, casual workers and peasants and artisans who are, as a rule, not only illiterate but also untrained in any industrial career.

Plantations scarcely give them any chance of achieving any general or technical education, the labourers as a class, therefore, remaining unskilled on plantations. It has been estimated that not more than 2 per cent on tea, coffee and rubber plantations are skilled, even in the very broad sense of the word.

3. *Supervision and Management*

The most important condition of industrial success is, however, business administration, which consists, among other things, of supervision and management. There are not, however, sufficient data on the supervision and management of plantations for drawing any conclusion.

The two most important features of plantation industries in India are that they are mostly the property of joint stock companies, and that most of them are financed by Europeans, as noted before. Out of 795 tea plantations in Assam in 1921, for instance, 632, or 70 per cent, belonged to joint stock companies (Iar Ali Khan, 1983). The coffee plantations in South India are, however, smaller concerns and are owned by private individuals. Out of 127 and 242 plantations in Madras and Mysore respectively, 104 and 232 were owned by private individuals.

4. *Comparative Productivity*

One of the best indications of industrial efficiency is increasing productivity. Productivity is, however, the result of several factors, namely land, labour and capital; and a comprehensive study of efficiency must take into consideration the part played by each of them. Other factors being equal, the increasing productivity per acre in one country as compared with that in other countries, cannot fail to give some idea of industrial efficiency.

Industrial Remunerations: A Special Reference to Tamil Nadu

Plantation industries are scattered all over the country, where both business conditions and standards of living differ from one another. The system of remuneration, including rate of wages, bonus and concession and earnings and incomes, therefore, varies from place to place.

1. *Basis of Rate-making*

The rate of wages on plantations, especially on the tea gardens of Tamil Nadu, is mostly based upon piecework and is determined by both the quality and quantity of the work. Whether expressed in terms of daily or monthly wages, the rate is contingent upon the execution of a certain daily task (Piya Chatterjee, 2001).

The unit of rate-making on tea gardens varies according to the season, location, and type of work. As the most important types of the work on plantations are those of hoeing and plucking, some idea of rate-making may be had from their detailed accounts. Hoeing is of two different kinds, namely light or surface hoeing and deep or medium hoeing. The former is done from five to seven times a year and the latter only once a year. The unit of measuring hoeing is a *nal* which is equivalent to twelve or thirteen feet. The day's work consists of from 25 to 30 square *nals* in the case of light hoeing and from twelve to sixteen square *nals* in the case of deep hoeing.

In plucking, the day's work varies from 20 to 24 lbs. of leaves, depending upon the quality, season of the year, methods of plucking and species of tea-bushes. In weighing the leaf deductions are made for the weight of the basket, wet leaf and wastage of manufacture, called "factory charges." The calculation is generally made on the supposition that four pounds of green leaf make one pound of manufactured tea. The usual rate of payment for fine plucking is based on certain kgs of leaf collected (Piya Chatterjee, 2001). Any quantity plucked over and above this fixed quantity is paid for proportionately and sometimes at an increased rate.

2. *Mode and Time of Payment*

Since the wages of workers on plantations, especially on the tea gardens of Tamil Nadu, consist of both money rates and concessions, the payment is also made both in cash and kind. Formerly, when rice was sold to contract labourers at a fixed rate, payment in kind was more common than in cash. On many gardens the daily payment was often made in brass tokens which were cashed weekly on the gardens or commissioned to a shop. But with the gradual disappearance of the rice concession, except in the time of high prices, payment in kind has also begun to disappear (Pranab Kumar Dasgupta). In cases where the rate of wages was fixed by the month and paid by the day or week, sometimes the worker did not get the full share of his earnings.

Similarly from 1905-06 to 1920-21 the monthly rate of wages increased from ₹ 7.11 to ₹ 8.97 or 23 per cent. For men, from ₹ 5.54 to ₹ 7.46 or 36 per cent for women and from ₹ 3.48 to ₹ 4.67 or 31 per cent for children among non-Act labourers in the course of 16 years.

Table 1.8: Variation in Wage-Rate in Tea-Gardens.
1905-06 To 1920-21 (Monthly Rates in ₹)

Class of Workers	1905-06	1920-21	Percentage Increase
Men	7.11	8.97	23
Women	5.54	7.46	36
Children	3.48	4.67	31

3. *Bonus and Concession*

Besides regular wages, bonus and concession are also common in almost all plantation industries. These terms are used to mean any payment over and above the stipulated rate of wages. But while the former usually implies consideration of some special service or condition, the latter means payment without such consideration. Moreover, unlike bonus, concession has some element of gratuities and is often called so. There exist various kinds of bonuses on tea gardens, but the bonus on profits, though granted to the managers and other members of the staff, is never granted to the labourers (Arul Sarma, 2012). In the opinion of planters, such bonus is difficult to operate on plantations, as the withdrawal or reduction of it in bad years is liable to be misunderstood by labourers.

Besides wages and bonus, the most common form of industrial remuneration in India is the payment of gratuities or concessions. It has been in existence since the beginning of organised industries and is the most widespread practice all over the country today. There are different forms in which concessions are made such as free or cheap housing, wholesale or cheap rate of grain and other necessities, and free fuel and medicine.

Concessions form, however, one of the most important sources of income to the labourers in the tea-gardens of the Nilgiris' District, Tamil Nadu. Formerly, they were made under contract and formed a part of the wages. Under the sections pertaining to the health and welfare of the plantation workers under The Plantation Labour Act, 1951 and Tamil Nadu Plantation Rules, 1952, for instance, provisions were made for housing accommodation, water supply, sanitary arrangement, hospital service and medical attendance free of charge for all workers. With the abolition of the indenture system, some of the anti-labour practices were withdrawn, while others were retained by the employers of the tea gardens out of colonial self-interest, so that a solid block of labour force might always be available on the gardens. The very nature of plantation work requires the granting of some of these concessions.

The leave of absence to pregnant women with allowances is also a kind of concession to women workers. Before the Second World War many gardens used to give blankets free of cost or at reduced rates to the new workers or to the sick. When the prices of clothing rose during and after the war, the concession was extended, but at present free or cheap clothing is not given to any large extent. Of other similar concessions, the most important are free firewood and advance of money without any interest.

Standard of Living of the Tea Plantation Labour in Tamil Nadu

The most important phase of the labour question is, however, the standard of living. The object of all production is consumption, and material welfare as indicated by the standard of living is a preliminary condition to intellectual and moral progress (Elizabeth Kaniampady, 2003). While an industry may not concern itself with anything outside the material aspects of life, it must share, in order to justify its existence, a part of its profit with the workers, who contribute to its success and who are thus entitled to a decent standard of living.

The standard of living is, however, a vague term. It varies in time and place. It contains, nevertheless. several elements which need to be taken into consideration. In the first place, any kind of standard must provide the *necessities* of life, without which life is impossible. Moreover, with the progress of society there also arise new desires and aspirations, the satisfaction of which leads to new necessaries of life. In the second place, a standard of living must also provide for those *decencies*, which are needed for the increasing craving for finer things in conformity with both the increasing personal taste and social ideals. In the third place, the instinct of self-display also leads to *luxuries.* While there is no limit to "conspicuous consumption," a certain amount of it is still essential for the gratification of human nature.

It must be remembered that there is no sharp line of demarcation between necessaries, decencies and luxuries, and what are luxuries today become decencies or even necessaries tomorrow (Rajani Kanta Das, 1931). Finally, to save for the future is also a natural impulse in man, and one must also have chances for savings after meeting the annual expenditure. In judging the standard of living, all these factors must be taken into consideration.

1. *Housing Conditions*

The first question in connection with the standard of living is that of housing. The housing of labour population is, however, a part of the organisation of plantation industries. This is due to the fact that most of the plantations are located in isolated localities and are worked by imported labour (Piya Chatterjee, 2001). To supply housing accommodation to workers and their dependents has, therefore, become a general policy of the plantations.

By far the largest number of plantation labourers, in fact, live on or near the plantations. It has been noted before that out of 1,053,944 workers on tea, coffee and rubber plantations in 1928-29, 834,588 workers, or about four-fifths, were living on the plantations themselves. Including their dependents, the number of labour population on plantations must be much larger. On the tea gardens of Tamil Nadu alone, for instance, the number of dependents amounted to 45 per cent of the total labour population. On that basis the total number of plantation workers living on all plantations would be about 1,517,432.

The labour population on plantations are housed in "lines" or colonies. The greatest defect of these "lines" is the fact that they are overcrowded. The houses are built very close to one another, without a proper outlet for conservancy and ventilation, thus subjecting them to insanitation and epidemics. This is one of the main reasons for the high rate of mortality on plantations until very recently (Deepak K. Mishra, 2012). Regarding water supply, sanitary arrangements, and other aspects of the labour "lines" much has been already said in the earlier discussions.

Besides overcrowding, insufficiency of accommodation for all the members of the family is a great defect. In most cases, several members of the family sleep in the same room. Very few, if any houses have separate accommodation for children and adult people. Decency, convenience and comfort are thus lacking in most of the houses on the plantations.

The labour population living outside the plantations would amount to about one-fifth. It has been the policy of the plantations to grant or secure land for the workers so that when settled, they might become a source of labour supply.

The dwelling of the labour population living outside the plantations resemble more or less those in the villages. Besides overcrowding, convenience, comfort and decency are as much lacking in these settlements as in the lines. As regards sanitation and water supply, there is scarcely any improvement in the former as compared with those in the latter (Mahendra P. Lama, 1986).

2. *Food and Clothing*

A still more important question is that of food and clothing. Besides sanitary, convenient and comfortable dwellings, what the workers need is wholesome and sufficient diet. Insufficient nourishment is a national calamity in India, and the workers on the plantations are no exception to this rule.

In the study of diet as an element of the standard of living, three things must be taken into consideration, namely quantity, quality and the proportionate value in the whole family budget. While the first two items contribute to the health and vigour of the workers, the last one indicates the relative value of other elements in the standard of living. What is the exact amount of food necessary for the normal growth and the power maintenance of the body is a question which it is difficult to determine. It depends not only upon the quantity but also on the quality of the food.

3. *Alcohol and Narcotics*

One of the worst features of the labourers' conditions on plantations is the consumption of liquors and narcotics. The habit of consuming the country-made liquors, opium and *ganja* (an intoxicating preparation of Indian hemp) prevails extensively among different classes of the population, although varying in extent and kind according to the races and castes. Drinking is a common practice among the aboriginal races, but it is interdicted among the Mahommedans. The consumption of opium is more common among the Assamese that among the inhabitants of any other province in general and Tamil Nadu in particular. The smoking of *ganja* is, however, a widely spread practice among a large class of the people.

That the use of liquors and narcotics is injurious to health and interferes with the efficiency and welfare of the workers needs scarcely any discussion. The problem is how to discourage the growth of this habit (Umananda Phukam,1983). There is an appeal frequently noticed from the trade unions to bring in restriction of the consumption of opium to the medical and scientific needs and the creation of public opinion against its use by education and by agitation in the press, platform and educational system.

4. *Loans and Savings*

Indebtedness is another hardship from which the majority of the workers suffer on plantations. The high rent of land and exorbitant rate of interest are two of the evils from which all the Indian masses suffer more or less. Even before going to the tea gardens of Tamil Nadu, a large number of emigrants are in debt and one of the most difficult tasks of recruitment is to settle the debt before embarkation. Even after arrival at the gardens, most of the labourers remain in debt.

One of the reasons of heavy indebtedness on the part of the labourers, as in fact, of all classes of people in India, is extravagant expenditure on the occasion of births, marriages and deaths. The money on such occasions is generally advanced by the moneylender at an exorbitant rate of interest (Rajani Kanta Das, 1931). Though it is difficult to estimate the extent of such advances on plantations, the existence of them cannot be denied.

Another sign of a decent standard of living is that after balancing the income and expenditure there is left some savings. In this world of constant economic struggles, nothing cheers a man so much as the fact that he has been able to save something from his income for his old age or unforeseen events.

5. *Education and Recreation*

One of the most important questions of plantation labour is that of education. The very fact that most of the children on plantations live with their parents means that their education must be provided on the plantations themselves if they are to be educated at all. But up to the present there is scarcely any provision for their education on the plantations, although the employers have been under the obligation to provide for the same as per The Plantation Labour Act, 1951. Neither do the workers spend anything on their children's education on the plantations, nor do the employers spend anything for the education of their workers' children, None of the family budgets on the plantations have any item for education.

6. *Welfare Work*

One of the most important methods of ameliorating the conditions of labour is welfare work. The importance of welfare work becomes all the greater in India, where social legislation still lags behind, and workers specially on plantations, are still unable to ameliorate their own conditions (Uday Kumar Varma, 2005). The most important phases of welfare work on plantations, specially in Tamil Nadu, are sick payments, pensions, housing and maternity benefits.

According to the UPASI, some of the gardens give adequate assistance to men and women who are not able to work owing to sickness. Earlier under the contract system, the total number of the days due to absence through sickness was added to the contract under Act XIII of 1859, when they were employed in terms of working days. Under Section 130 of Act VI of 1901, this was permissible only when the total number of days absent exceeded thirty days in any one year, and the inspector in charge had given his sanction to that effect. But with the abolition of the contract system, these conditions do not exist any more. The present system is to give the sick half pay or hospital diet. In the case of the labourers employed on a weekly basis, it is usual in many gardens to give them light work on full pay until they recover full strength.

Another important question is the provision for old age is the case of labourers who have spent all their life on plantations. Some of the gardens give small pensions in cash to the deserving workers who have earned them by long and faithful service, but such practices are rare. As a rule, old workers are given light work, and sometimes allotments of garden land for cultivation.

While this system of pensions is very much appreciated, its scope is very much limited. The provision of superannuation on a large scale can only be undertaken by the State and the Central Government alone which will be in a position to undertake this system of old age pensions on a nationwide basis.

Maternity benefit is still another system of welfare work on plantations. The question is becoming important not only because of its international significance since the inauguration of the International Labour Organisation, but also because of its practical and economic value (M.M. Rehman, 2005). The difficulty and expense of recruiting labourers for plantations have led the planters to become more generous and liberal in the treatment of women during and after confinement. Secondly, maternity allowance is granted only when absolutely necessary, that is, when there is no working member in the family, third, some of the gardens give leave of absence for three months before and after confinement with full pay for the whole period while others give a similar period of leave of absence and ten pounds of rice a week free of cost apart from applicable wages. But this generous treatment is not common. There is, however, a tendency towards increased liberality in granting leave of absence to women before and after childbirth and also some kind of remuneration during the period. However, majority of the workers did not acknowledge such a privilege in the tea gardens.

The question of maternity benefits can scarcely be solved by philanthropy or welfare work. The importance of adequate legislation has been realised by almost all advanced countries and such legislation has been passed even by the Government of India in the case of the women employed in factories (Rajani Kanta Das,

1931). It is not only sufficient that the Legislations are enacted by the government of India and the respective State Governments of the top tea-producing States for maternity benefits to women in plantations, where are employed the largest number of women labourers in India, but it should be strictly implemented and monitored on an on-going basis. The present Maternity Benefit Act, 1961 is not effectively implemented as well as administered by the Government of Tamil Nadu. Adding to their crisis, the excellent scheme of insurance under the Employees' State Insurance Act, 1948 does not cover the plantation workers at all. The government, tea planters' associations or workers' trade unions do not pay attention to covering the plantation workers under the said act. As everybody is aware of the fact that under the ESI Act, 1948 the insured person and his/her family members are entitled to receive the following benefits: (a) Medical, (b) Sickness, (c) Maternity, (d) Dependents, (e) Disablement and (f) Payment of funeral expenses.

The scope of welfare work is much wider than that which can be covered by payments to the sick and to the old, or the maternity benefits. The provision for medical help and medicine is an important item in welfare work, but since the labourers work and live on plantations, this is a part of plantation organisation. As noted before, education and recreation offer special opportunities for welfare work, which can be easily undertaken by plantations for the benefit of the workers as well as for themselves.

Health Problems Faced by the Tea Plantation Labour in India

Sanitation and Health—An Overview

Another important question in connection with sanitary arrangements was that of the latrine system, attention to which was drawn as early as 1884. In spite of the fact that the plantation industry has been in existence for over half a century, the installation of a conservancy system has scarcely advanced beyond the experimental stage (Piya Chatterjee, 2001). Most of the tea gardens in Assam, for instance, lack an adequate system of conservancy and it is due to this fact that there prevail several diseases such as hookworm. In the opinion of several authorities, hookworm is contracted on the gardens and the anaemia and inefficiency arising out of it cause a good deal of loss to the gardens. Contrary to the prevailing notion, the Assam Labour Enquiry Committee of 1921-22 have found the worker willing to take advantage of latrine accommodation and have noted that wherever the latrines have been provided the result has been accompanied by appreciable fall in the incidence of anaemia.

Scenario in Tamil Nadu

The existing system of latrine accommodation might be classified under four heading: first, the bucket system, which is liable to become insanitary and for which there is always a necessity for keeping a class of sweepers; second, the trench system, which often runs the risk of infection by flies; third, the aqua-privy system, which although very convenient and sanitary, is very much limited in scope, being dependent upon the availability of streams and rivers; fourth, the septic tank system, which is the ideal system of conservancy. There are two difficulties in the installation of this system: In the first place, lack of sufficient water supply, since it requires about four or five gallons of water per person using it.

In the second place, the high initial expenses. But according to some medical authorities the septic tank system is the cheapest in the long run, as it secures the sanitary condition, which is essential for the exertion of human energy. Only a very few of the tea gardens in the Nilgiris' District, Tamil Nadu have, however, installed the latrine system, especially the septic tank (Pranab Kumar Dasgupta,1983).

Births and Deaths

Since the health of a people is best indicated by vital statistics, the birth and death rates on plantations as compared with those outside will give a clearer idea of the conditions of health of plantation labourers. It must, however, be mentioned that the system of calculating statistics is much more accurate on plantations than that outside and any comparative study based on such data is liable to involve a certain amount of error.

Complete statistics on birth and death rates in the tea gardens of Tamil Nadu are available since 1878. Owing to the fact that the number of women in the earlier years was very small as compared with that of men, the birth rates have been shown both per thousand women and per thousand total population. On the basis of women population, the birth-rate fell down from 101.3 per mille in 1878 to 70.1 per mille in 1920; and on the basis of total population, the birth-rate fell from 31.9 per mille in 1878 to 19.3 per mille in 1920 and was 31.5 per mille in 1928-29, as shown in Table 1.9.

Table 1.9: Birth-Rates on Tea Gardens in the Nilgris District,Tamil Nadu (Shown only at specified period)

Year	Birth-rate Per 1000 Women	Per 1000 of Total Population
1878	101.3	31.9
1900	80.2	27.6
1919-20	70.1	19.3
1928-29	–	31.5

An important feature of the birth-rate on the tea gardens of Tamil Nadu is its variation.

There are several causes of this variation:

- First, periodical unhealthy seasons induced by excessive rain and prolonged drought, or by the outbreak of epidemics, reduce productive power on the one hand and induce miscarriage on the other.
- Second, variation in the number of immigrants has some influence on the birth-rate. It is a known fact that acclimatised women are healthier than the new arrivals and are, therefore, more prolific.
- Third, the composition of the immigrants as to the local sources of supply has also an effect upon the birth-rate. In 1897, for instance, while the general birth-rate per thousand women for all Tamil Nadu tea garden workers was 77.4, the birth-rate varied from 94.6 in the case of the immigrants from Assam to 48.5 in case of those from the Central Provinces.

- Fourth, the distribution of the immigrants over different parts of the Madras Province is still another cause. In 1895, for instance, the birth-rate per thousand varied from 56.8 in the district of coimbatore to 105.6 in the Nilgiris' District. It must be mentioned that in addition to the differences in the climatic conditions of these two districts the sanitary arrangements in different gardens has also been an important effect upon the birth-rate.

Another important feature of the birth-rate in the tea gardens of Tamil Nadu is that there has been almost a steady decline except in very recent years. Negligence in registration of births and declining vitality among plantation labourers, as suggested by some, can scarcely be accepted as valid reasons for such a phenomenon. As suggested by the district authorities, the changes in the character and the composition of the immigrants, which are partly the results of the changes in the recruiting system, might possibly account for this gradual decline of the birth-rate.

Until very recently, however, a low birth-rate was the outstanding feature among the labourers of Tamil Nadu tea gardens. In the earlier years, the number of women was much smaller than that of men and the birth-rate was consequently very low, but even in 1901, when the number of women exceeded that of men (for instance, there were 204,150 women as compared with 200,088 men), the birth-rate on the gardens was 29.1 per thousand total population and 93.2 per thousand adult women, as compared with 33.9 and 101.6, respectively in the then Province of Madras (Purnendu Kumar, 2006). This lower rate continued to be the case until 1923-24 when the birth-rate on the tea gardens reached the same level, or was even a little higher than that in the whole province, that is, 31.11 in the case of the former as compared with 31.04 in the case of the latter.

There has been a good deal of speculation as to the causes of this lower birth-rate on tea gardens of the Nilgiris' District, Tamil Nadu:

- First, the women lack adaptability to the changes of conditions of food and climate on arrival from a different country and their whole strength seems to be required to resist the insidious effect of the climate of the hilly area, so that there is left scarcely "sufficient vital force to allow them to reproduce their species with success."

- Second, hard work, on which women were often employed, was not calculated to raise the birth-rate.
- Third, the character and composition of the immigrants had also great influence upon the birth-rate. The recruitment of starving and diseased people from famine and pestilence-prevailing regions was liable to bring to Tamil Nadu such women as were most probably unable to retain their normal fecundity.
- Fourth, the age as well as the capacity and willingness for motherhood were among the factors of the low birth-rate. A large number of immigrant women recruited by contractors were infertile. This was due to the fact that the interest of contractors was to get any class of women for their recruits as they were paid per head, whereas the immigrants recruited by the Head Kanganis mostly came with their families and were more prolific.
- Fifth, miscarriage and still births were also among the causes leading to a low birth-rate. Miscarriage was often the result of syphilis and anaemia, and of the lack of sufficient care bestowed on women while pregnant.
- Sixth, abortion was still another cause of the low birth-rate. It was a well-known fact that abortion was performed by professional women permanently living on the gardens, the main objection to child-bearing by tea garden women being the trouble caused by having to work and look after children as well. The loss of wages during the period following child-birth and often before was an additional reason.

Finally, irregularity in the marriage or union of men and women was still another cause. In the contractor's depot single men and women were sometimes paired off, regardless of caste and inclination, and sent off as "family coolies." These "depot marriages," as they were generally called, were rarely fruitful. The system of herding men and women of different castes in the lines also led to irregular and fruitless unions. Moreover, single women frequently refrained from settling down finally with one man till they had been for some time on the gardens. It is an ascertained fact that there was scarcely any offspring from temporary and irregular unions.

Death Rate in the Tea Plantation Sector in India

There are several reasons for the heavy mortality on the several tea-gardens (Purnendu Kumar, 2006) in the pre-independence India:

- First, the general unhealthiness of the Province, especially in the earlier years, when the gardens were first opened and the sanitary arrangements were inadequate.
- Secondly, the change from one to another climate. It is a recognised fact that mortality varied among immigrants of various Provinces. The death-rates for several years tend to show that the native Assamese were healthier than the imported labourers, and immigrants from Bengal were healthier than those from more distant Provinces. In short, the greater the change in climate between the recruiting and the labouring districts, the greater is likely to be the death-rate among the immigrants.
- Thirdly, change in diet.
- Fourthly, composition of immigrants. The immigrants of poor physique and coming from poverty-stricken districts.
- Fifthly, "the want of proper houses, overcrowding, unhealthy sites, insufficient and unsuitable food, impure water and want of proper medical attendance."

Finally, despair and melancholy, to which the majority of the immigrants fell victim. The disillusion often falling upon immigrants.

The variation in the death-rate is another noticeable feature on the tea-gardens of the top tea producing states. This is due to several factors, namely:

- The exceptional unhealthiness of the plantation workers for some years resulting from heavy floods or a long period of drought naturally affects the death rate.
- An outbreak of epidemics which every now and then visit the tea gardens is also responsible for a variation in the death rate.
- The proportion of the newly arrived as compared with the older section among the total labour force is also an important cause. It is a well-known fact that the death rate is higher among the newly arrived immigrants and falls greatly as the length of residence increases.

This decline in the rate of mortality in recent years has been brought about by several factors of which the most important are the following: (1) The gradual clearance of jungles; (2) a closer supervision and better provision of sanitary arrangements; (3) the gradual adaptation of workers to the physical and social conditions, a large number of whom have gradually settled down in the tea districts of the tea producing states; and (4) the comparatively small number of new immigrants. The increasing facilities in travel and the abolition of contract labour have also led to their indirect effect upon mortality.

Prevalent Diseases among the Tea Plantation Labourers in India

The immediate causes of death are usually various diseases of which the most prevalent on the tea gardens of the tea-producing states in India are-cholera, diarrhoea, dysentery, malaria, hookworm and various respiratory complications, causing for instance, 13,044 deaths out of a total of 22,581 deaths in 1928-29, as shown in Table 1.10. The table also shows the variation in the number of deaths caused by different diseases.

Table 1.10: Causes of Death on the Tea-Gardens of the Tea-producing States in India

(Shown at Specific Periods)

Causes	1893	1900	1918-19	1928-29
Cholera	2,301	1,754	5,288	375
Diarrhoea	1,155	1,994	2,647	1,373
Dysentery	3,217	3,760	4,145	2,512
Malaria	2,122	2,825	3,380	3,038
Hookworm	1,399	1,854	2,361	1,448
Respiratory Diseases	572	2,398	6,310	4,398
Other Causes	5,276	5,015	38,045	9,437
TOTAL	15,982	19,603	62,176	22,581

Table 1.11: Variation in Death-Rate in the Tea Gardens of the Nilgiris' District, Tamil Nadu

(At Specified Years)

Death Rates Per Mill				
Years	**Act-Workers**	**Non-Act Workers**	**Children**	**All Persons**
1878	106.2	38.9	63.1	66.1
1900	43.5	26.2	25.4	29.4
1920-21	–	31.9	21.1	27.3
1928-29	–	22.5	20.2	21.5

Diarrhoea and dysentery are common diseases in India, especially in the provinces of Bengal, Assam and Madras, and a large number of deaths are attributed to them every year. They have long been known to be among the chief causes of deaths in the tea gardens, causing respectively 2,447 and 4,145 deaths in 1918 and 1919 when influenza was also most prevalent. The number of deaths caused by these diseases are generally higher on the tea gardens than in the whole province of Assam (Umananda Phukam, 1983).

The most common disease is, however, malaria and it is also prevalent on the tea gardens. In fact, there are few labourers on the gardens who at one time or other do not suffer from it. In 1928-29, 3038 deaths, over 13 per cent of the total, were caused by malaria alone, but the sufferings and devitalising effect of malaria are more common than the actual deaths. Attention has been drawn to the high spleen index on certain gardens especially among children. Prophylactic dozes of quinine, especially during the rainy season, are often administered to check its growth.

About a generation ago kala-azar was one of the causes of the high mortality among the workers on the tea gardens. Even now it is liable to become an epidemic and to play havoc on plantations. Between 1916 and 1929, for instance, 270 workers out of about 550 attacked died of it in one single garden, causing a loss of between ₹ 40,000 and ₹ 50,000 to the garden. Hundreds of infected houses had to be burnt and new lines erected and a hospital established.

Among the epidemics cholera is the most important as it appears about every year, though in different degrees of severity (Piya Chatterjee, 2001). Formerly, it was often introduced into the Assam tea gardens by the new immigrants, who contracted it in insanitary detention depots in Bengal. On some gardens unrestricted communication between new arrivals and old workers was followed by severe outbreaks.

With regard to deaths from Cholera, it must be remembered that when once it appears in the neighbourhood it causes, in spite of sanitary precaution, great mortality in the lines of tea gardens where people are more closely congregated together than in an ordinary village. The highest number of deaths was caused by Cholera in 1918-19, the year of the influenza epidemic, the number of deaths amounting to 5,288.

In recent years, influenza has become one of the most vital epidemics in India as all over the world. The number of deaths caused by influenza on plantations was 28,552 in 1918-19. Accompanied by Cholera, dysentery and respiratory diseases, it raised the total number of deaths from 23.5 per mill in 1917-18 to 61.4 per mill in 1918-19.

Anaemia is another common disease on the tea gardens of Assam and Tamil Nadu. In 1888, beri-beri, another common disease in Bengal, was found to be identical with anaemia. It is caused, however, by several diseases such as malaria, dysentery, and hookworm. The most severe type of anaemia is, however, that caused by hookworm, as it is very difficult to get rid of the initial infection.

The majority of the cases returned as dropsy, and anaemia is really due to hookworm infection. It has been estimated that about 71.3 per cent of the population in Bengal has been infected with hookworm. The number of cases amounted to 3,001 in the Duars tea garden in Bengal in 1918 and 4,028 on the Assam tea gardens in 1919-20 (Purnendu Kumar, 2006).

The most important method of controlling diseases consists of prevention of infection and direct treatment. Prevention means simply the regulation of the latrine system so that the ova of the worms cannot spread and contaminate drinking water. The treatment consists of the administration of thymol in 30 grain dozes by which dead parasites are discharged by hundreds and the patients are found to be rapidly restored to health.

Other diseases taking a heavy toll of life are the various respiratory complications, which caused 4,398 deaths or about one-fifth of the total in 1928-29. The death of 9,437 persons or about 44 per cent of the total were caused by various other diseases, a number of which remain unidentified (Elizabeth Kaniampady, 2003).

Provisions have been made, under plantation legislation for adequate treatment of labourers suffering from the above diseases on the tea gardens and some of the gardens have qualified physicians and adequate hospital supplies, as noted before. It has often been said that workers do not take advantage of hospital service even when such is provided free of cost, and that hospital treatment is the last resort to be taken advantage of by them. But when a hospital is attractive and where good and careful treatment is provided, there seems to be no reason why in-door treatment should not be more popular.

In spite of provision for medical attendance to the workers, there is a need for further extension of the service, especially for those who are living in the lines. It is revealed by the fact that a large number of time-expired labourers resorted to government dispensaries for treatment. In a number of cases, workers whose contract did not expire were also sent to these dispensaries for treatment. In such cases, the expenses of food were borne by the gardens on which the contract workers were employed.

An unfortunate aspect of labour conditions on the tea gardens is borne out by the fact that a considerable number of workers became infirm and destitute even after long service (Purnendu Kumar, 2006). "It is impossible to visit an estate," says the Report on Labour Immigration to Assam for 1897, "without noticing the number of infirm persons who are supported practically by the charity of their employees."

Although consideration and sympathy were displayed by the great majority of planters towards labourers who had worn themselves out in the service of tea gardens, some planters were short sighted and unkind enough to turn such persons out of their gardens.

2

Studies Conducted in India

Study I: Conducted by the Labour Bureau, Ministry of Labour and Employment, Government of India

To solve the problems faced by the women tea plantation workers engaged in various industries, a sound planning based on accurate and reliable data bank is needed. Accordingly, the present scheme titled "Socio-economic Conditions of Women Workers in Industry" was taken up by the Bureau, during the year 1975—"The International Women's Year". Initially, the scheme was confined to the organised sector only. However, keeping in view the utility of the data so generated, it was considered to extend the scope of scheme to the unorganised sector as well. The present report relates to the plantation sector. To assess the socio-economic condition of women labour in Plantation Industry the survey is conducted in six states where plantations are grown, i.e. Assam, West Bengal, Tamil Nadu, Kerala, Karnataka and Tripura. Field work was undertaken during the period September-October 2008. The survey has been conducted in four plantations, viz. tea, coffee, rubber and cardamom. The findings of the study were as follows:

(a) A total of 132 unit level and 827 worker level schedules were canvassed during the survey.

(b) More than 50 per cent of the total workers employed in the plantations were women workers.

(c) In non-manual jobs majority of the workers were male.

(d) Majority of the workers were unskilled and employed as plantation labourers.

(e) Most of the units surveyed were found paying annual bonus to their workers.

(f) Majority of the units were allowing weekly off without wages to the workers.

(g) A few cases of sexual harassment 3.0 per cent were reported during the last two years.

(h) About 60 per cent of units have put in place the mechanism to redress the grievances of workers.

(i) Around 63 per cent of the units surveyed were member of employers' association.

(j) Among manual workers plantation labourers constitute majority. Their average per day earnings work out to be ₹ 67.6 at aggregate level.

(k) Only 48.5 per cent of the units were providing medical facilities to workers and their family members.

(l) In Karnataka state very few units were found providing medical facilities to workers.

(m) Crèche facility has been provided by only 37.1 per cent of the total units surveyed. In tea, coffee, rubber and cardamom plantations very few units were providing crèche facility.

(n) In tea plantations, 5.3 per cent of the women workers were provided with education facility to their children. In coffee and cardamom, no unit was found providing education facility to the children of its workers.

(o) Housing facility has been provided by 77.3 per cent of the total units surveyed. Housing facility to workers has been provided by maximum units (97.9 per cent) in tea plantations and minimum units (50.0 per cent) in cardamom units.

(p) Maternity benefits were provided by 73.5 per cent of the total units surveyed. Among the cardamom plantation units, only 38.9 per cent were providing maternity benefit to their women workers.

(q) Only 17.4 per cent of the total units surveyed have appointed welfare officers. In coffee and cardamom units no welfare officers was found appointed. Concessional items were found to be provided only in the tea plantation units. At aggregate level, 23.5 per cent of the units are providing various types of concession to the workers.

(r) Canteen facility has been provided by only 12.9 per cent of the units surveyed. In Assam state, from which maximum number of sample units were drawn, and which employed majority of the tea plantation workers, only 16.7 per cent units were providing canteen facility.

(s) The basic welfare amenities like urinals and latrines were provided by only 9.8 per cent of the units surveyed. Rest shelter was provided by 25.0 per cent of the units surveyed.

(t) Separate welfare facilities for women tea plantation workers like washing facility, separate urinals, rest shelter were provided by 6.1 per cent, 7.6 per cent and 6.8 per cent and unit respectively. More than five per cent of the plantation workers were migrated from other states.

(u) Average family size of the sampled women workers was 4.2 members at overall level.

(v) Majority of the sampled women workers (54.4 per cent) were found to be illiterate. Average number of earners per women worker house hold was found to be two members.

(w) Very meager i.e. 1.1 per cent, women tea plantation workers were found to be working beyond the normal daily hours of work.

(x) Around 59 per cent of the women workers had membership of a trade union.

(y) Only 34.7 per cent, 18.5 per cent and 43.5 per cent women workers were aware of Minimum Wage Act,

1948, Equal Remuneration Act, 1976 and Maternity Benefits Act, 1961.

(z) About 42 per cent of the women workers were saving money.

Study II: Economic Organization of the Labour Force, M.M. Rehman (2005)

About nine-tenth of the workforce in a tea industry is attached to the gardens. Their work concern preparation of the nursery bed, transplanting, pruning, cleaning and clearing, drainage, loosening of the soil, etc., and the most important work of plucking of tea leaves. All the works which require spade-work is done by men. Pruning is done both by men and women. Cutting away of dead woods and unnecessary twigs is done by women mainly with the help of small knives. Weeding is also women's job, during transplantation. Plucking is done mainly by women but men also works as pluckers. Plucking continues almost throughout the year. Plucking is done for about eight hours a day. It starts at 8.00 a.m. and continues up to 12.00 noon. Then there is lunch break for one and half hours. Work is resumed at 1.30 p.m. and lasts up to 5.30 p.m. The leaves are deposited in front of the factory gate twice a day, once after the first session of plucking and then labourers carry the leaf load in gunny cloth on their heads while some carry the same on their back with the help of a carrying strap passing over the forehead.

If there is no extra hand in the family, a women labourer gets up at 4.00 a.m. in the morning, attends nature's call, plasters the courtyard with cow dung and earth solution and then sits in her kitchen. She cooks, rice and vegetables. She takes and serves the breakfast to her family members which consists of rice, a little vegetable and tea. Then with sound of the factory siren, she proceeds to the garden for plucking. She returns home at about 12.30 noon, takes bath and then eats rice and vegetable already prepared in the morning. Then again she goes for plucking and returns in the evening. She cooks again rice and vegetables for dinner. She goes to bed about 8.00 p.m. after finishing dinner. Women goes through more physical strain compared to men as they work in the garden as well as look after domestic work and cooking. Lactating mothers carry their babies to the garden and keep them under the shed of the tree. While mother is busy in plucking, the babies are looked after by the old ladies called patti-ma or baby nurse. The mothers feed the babies at intervals. Drinking water is carried to the gardens where plucking is in progress in tractor vehicle and is supplied to the labourers by the water mans or water suppliers.

Study III: Work Operations and Wages of the Tea Plantation Workers, Umananda Phukam (1983)

There is a fixed quota of leaves which a labourer should pluck in a day. It is 25 kgs. for a male and the quota for a female labourer is equally the same. And the remuneration is also the same. For every additional kg. of leaves plucked, an incentive of one rupee and fifty paise above the normal rate is given. The income of a labourer fluctuates according to the leaf position in a garden. A labourer does not get any wage on the weekly holidays and monthly income of a male worker ranges from ₹ 150 to ₹ 180. The income of a female labourer is little less. But the overall family income is not very low as a number of members from each family work in the garden.

During peak plucking season which runs between may and September, temporary hands are employed to complete the plucking in appropriate time. Leaves are to be plucked at certain stage of its growth. Plucking from a plant is done at an interval of seven or eight days which allows new shoots to grow and the operation should be completed in time, otherwise the quality of tea will deteriorate. The women pluckers sing, chat and cut jokes while plucking, and no sign of boredom is noticed during work. It is known to all that the women have unbound love for flowers.

Other economic benefits which a worker derives from the company are gratuity and contributory provident fund. Each worker and his/her two dependants get weekly ration in rice and wheat/flour at subsidized rates. The company also supplies fuel free of cost to the labourers and provides free quarters and offers medical aid though the medical part is denied by the labour force.

Study IV: Work, Wages and Staff Distribution: Elizabeth Kaniampady (2003)

Charagpur Tea Estate maintains 39 monthly-paid staff in various categories in the sector, i.e., the garden and the factory. All of them are men expect only one woman who worked as dai or midwife attached to the dispensary. There are only 11 members in the monthly-paid staff who belonged to scheduled tribes and six of them are munda. All the top positions are held by Bengalee Hindus.

Total member of permanent weekly-paid staff is 195 which include 85 women. There are nine jogali sirdars (all men) in this permanent staff. A jogali sirdar is the head of a group of workers who maintains attendance, etc. Of the workers and receives a lump sum remuneration of ₹ 100 per year besides his regular wage. Majority of the permanent weekly-paid staff are tribes and six of them are jogali sirdars. Expecting the monthly-paid staff all the workers including the permanent weekly-paid staff get for six days a week (on Monday no work and no pay).

The chawalas of the factory are daily-rated workers (i.e. the wage is ₹ 3.77 per day0 but they get pay for full month and paid once a month. The sirdars of the garden and the factory enjoy a scale of pay like that of monthly-paid staff. Sirdars of both garden and factory and the chowkidars enjoy the scale of ₹ 100-150 with ₹ 2.50 as annual increment. Besides they get D.A. @ 14.5 per cent and variable D.A. @25.5 per cent.

The difference of benefits provided to the permanent and temporary labourers is in the ratio, fuel, gratuity and provident fund. The provident fund is contributory and is 12 per cent of the total wage and is deducted at source from all monthly-paid workers and they are entitled to all the statutory welfare measures according to the provisions of The Tamil Nadu Plantation Labour Rules, 1955 and subsequent amendments made to the Act.

All permanent workers including their dependants get ration which is much lower than the market price. Temporary workers also get ration at a subsidized rate but they have to pay more and no ration is provided for their dependants.

Managerial and supervisory staff gets free fuel for their kitchen. Other monthly-paid and permanent workers are paid some fuel allowance which varies according to the category of workers. Monthly-paid and permanent workers get gratuity to the tune of 15 day's wages for every year of service with the maximum of twenty month's gratuity. The amount of gratuity is calculated taking into account the wages (excluding servant allowance, bonus, leave wage, overtime or any other special grant) as payable on the date of retirement. Workers of all categories are entitled to have maximum bonus of 20 per cent of annual wages.

3

The Socio-Economic and Working Conditions of the Tea Plantation Workers of the Tamil Nadu Tea Plantation Corporation Limited [TANTEA] in Tamil Nadu

Research Objectives

General

To know the socio-economic and working conditions of the Tea Plantation workers of the Tamil Nadu Tea Plantation Corporation Limited [TANTEA].

Specific

- To find out the socio-economic conditions of the plantation workers of the TANTEA.
- To know about their occupational profile and working conditions and job satisfaction.
- To know about the occupational risks and health problems of the tea plantation workers.
- To find out the health, welfare and social security measures made available to the tea plantation workers.
- To know about the perception of the plantation workers about the functioning of the management.
- To highlight the role of trade union in protecting the interests of the labour force as viewed.

Operational Definitions

- **Socio-economic status** refers to socio-economic standard of people which is conventionally expressed in terms of various social classes as specified in the Kuppuswamy's socio-economic status scale. This scale is based on three variables—education, occupation and income. This term refers to the socio-economic status of the tea plantation workers employed by the Tamil Nadu Tea Plantation Corporation Limited (TANTEA).
- **Education** refers to the level of literacy of the tea plantation workers of the TANTEA.
- **Occupation** refers to the nature of work of the tea plantation workers, such as, plucking, weeding, pruning and other related work on the tea gardens of the TANTEA.
- **Income** specifies the earning capacity of the tea plantation workers of the TANTEA which also influences their socio-economic status.
- **Economic status** refers to the standard of living, income and lifestyle of the tea plantation workers of the TANTEA. These tea plantation workers, based on their income, are classified into following classes—upper, upper middle, lower middle, upper lower and lower as defined by the Kuppuswamy's scale.
- **Social security** means protection through public programmes designed to protect the tea plantation workers engaged by the TANTEA and their families from income losses due to unemployment, old age, sickness or death and to improve their welfare through public services, e.g. medical care, E.S.I., Provident Fund and other health and welfare services.
- **Job satisfaction** refers to the perception of the tea plantation workers of the TANTEA to remain in the state of satisfaction over their job.
- **Plantation:** According to Section 2(f) of the Plantations Labour Act, 1951, "Plantation means any plantation to

which this Act applies and includes offices, hospitals, dispensaries, schools and any other premises used for any purpose connected with such plantation, but does not include any factory covered under the Factories Act, 1948:-

The Act extends to the whole of India except the state of Jammu and Kashmir. It applies to the following plantations:

(a) Any land used or intended to be used for growing tea, coffee, rubber, cinchona or cardamom which admeasures five hectares or more and in which fifteen or more persons are employed or were employed on any day of the preceding twelve months.

(b) Any land used or intended to be used for growing any other plant, which admeasures five hectares or more and in which fifteen or more persons are employed or were employed on any day of the preceding twelve months, and so notified by the State Government.

The State Government may apply the provisions of the Act to any land used or intended to be used for growing tea, coffee, rubber, cinchona, cardamom or any other plant, even if it admeasures less than five hectares or employs less than 15 persons."

- **Worker:** According to Section 2(k) of the Plantations Labour Act, 1951, "worker means a person employed in a plantation for hire or reward, whether directly or through any agency, to do any work, skilled, unskilled, manual or clerical but does not include (a) medical officer employed in plantation, (b) any person employed in plantation including any member of medical staff whose monthly wages exceed ₹ 750, (c) any person employed in the plantation primarily in a managerial capacity, not withstanding that his monthly wages do not exceed ₹ 750 and (d) any person temporarily employed in the plantation in any work relating to the construction, development or maintenance of buildings, roads, bridges, drains, or canals."

- **Employer [Section 2(e)]:** Employer when used in relation to a plantation, means the person who has the ultimate control over the affairs of the plantation, and where the affairs of any plantation are entrusted to any other person (whether called a managing agent, manager, superintendent or by any other name) such other person shall be deemed to be the employer in relation to that plantation.
- **Adult [Section 2(b)]:** Adult means a person who has completed his eighteenth year.
- **Child [Section 2(c)]:** Child means a person who has not completed his fourteenth year.
- **Day [Section 2(d)]:** Day means a period of twenty-four hours beginning at midnight.
- **Week [Section 2(j)]:** Week means a period of seven days beginning at midnight on Saturday night or such other night as may be fixed by the State Government in relation to plantations in any area after such consultation as may be prescribed with reference to the plantations concerned in that area.
- **Wages [Section 2(i)]:** Wages has the meaning assigned to it in clause (h) of Section 2 of the Minimum Wages Act, 1948 (11 of 1948).

As per Section 2(h) of the Minimum Wages Act, 1948 "Wages" means all remuneration, capable of being expressed in terms of money, which would, if the terms of the contract of employment, express or implied, were fulfilled, be payable to a person employed in respect of his employment or of work done in such employment and includes house rent allowance, but does not include—

(i) The value of (a) any house accommodation, supply of light, water, medical attendance, or [b] any other amenity or any service excluded by general or special order of the appropriate government;

(ii) Any contribution paid by the employer to any pension fund or provident fund or under any scheme of social insurance;

(iii) Any travelling allowance or the value of any travelling concession;

(iv) Any sum paid to the person employed to defray special expenses entailed on him by the nature of his employment; or

(v) Any gratuity payable on discharge.

Welfare Measures

The following welfare measures are to be provided to the plantation workers as per the Plantations Labour Act, 1951.

(a) Canteens in plantations employing 150 or more workers [Section 11].

(b) Crèches in plantations employing 50 or more women workers [Section 12].

(c) Recreational facilities for the workers and their children [Section 13].

(d) Educational facilities in the estate for the children of workers, where there are 25 workers' children between the age of 6 and 12 [Section 14].

(e) Housing facilities for every worker and his family residing in the plantation. The standard and specification of the accommodation, procedure for the allotment and rent chargeable from workers, are to be prescribed in the rules by the State Governments [Sections 15 and 16].

(f) The State Government may make rules requiring every plantation employer to provide the workers with such number and type of umbrellas, blankets, rain coats or other like amenities for the protection of workers from rain or cold as may be prescribed [Section 17].

(g) Appointment of a welfare officer in plantations employing 300 or more workers [Section 18]. The exact standards of these facilities have been prescribed under the rules framed by the State Government.

Health Measures to be Provided to the Workers [The Plantation Labor Act, 1951]

(a) Supply of wholesome drinking water to the workers at convenient places. [Section 8]

(b) Sufficient number of Latrines and Urinals separately for male and female workers and conveniently accessible to them by the employer and maintained in a clean and sanitary condition. [Section 9]

(c) Medical Facilities: The employers required to provide and maintain the prescribed medical facilities for the plantation workers and their families.

Variables Used in the Study

(a) General Information: Gender, income, class, caste/community, educational qualification and marital status.

(b) Occupational Profile: Category of work, nature of work and designation.

(c) Socio-economic Conditions: Religion, political and caste, nature of housing, salary, expense, savings, assets and borrowing.

(d) Working Conditions: Leave facilities, weekly rest, work load, daily working hours, over time, rest and lunch interval and compensation for sickness.

(e) Health Provisions: Access to drinking water, ambulance facility and health care system.

(f) Welfare Provisions: Canteen facility, crèche facility, recreational facility, educational facility and housing facility.

(g) Social Security: Employee State Insurance Scheme, Workmen Compensation Act, Bonus, Employee Provident Fund, Gratuity, Workers Benefit Fund and Insurance Scheme.

(h) Role of Trade Union in safeguarding the interests of plantation workers.

(i) Perception of the plantation workers about the functioning of TANTEA Management.

(j) Occupational Risks: Work place injury, cause of injury and pain, exposure to attacks by the wild animals, insects, spraying of pesticides and absence of first aid kit.

(k) Health problems of the plantation workers and their level of health education.

Research Setting—Divisions of the TANTEA

TANTEA—Tea divisions: 1. Coonoor, 2. Naduvattam, 3. Kotagiri, 4. Cherambady, 5. Cherangode, 6. Nelliyalam, 7. Kolapally, 8. Devala, 9. Pandiar, 10. Lawson and 11. Ryan.

Research Design

This study has adopted the framework of descriptive design. The major goal of a descriptive research is to describe events, phenomena and situations. The researcher has engaged descriptive design since descriptions are made on the basis of scientific observations to be more accurate and precise than casual.

Source of Data and Unit of Analysis

The primary source of data was respondents from the TANTEA who were the tea plantation workers permanently employed in the Coonoor and Naduvattam divisions of the TANTEA. The respondents were drawn from the permanent workers. Out of eleven divisions of the TANTEA, data were collected only from the tea plantation workers of these two divisions, who were selected by applying the method of multi-stage sampling along with simple random sampling (Lottery Method). The list of the workers has been collected by the researcher from the personnel department functioning in the headquarters office of the TANTEA at Coonoor. The other primary source of data was the management representatives of the TANTEA who were interviewed personally by the researcher. Apart from the primary source, secondary sources of information were also tapped for this study in the form of published papers in journals and books. The secondary sources of information were mainly used to pull together available literature in the research topic and to generate the variables for the study.

Sampling Design and Sample Size

This study has adopted multi-stage sampling along with simple random sampling (lottery method). While selecting each cluster, simple random sampling (lottery method) has been simultaneously applied to go into the next level. The size of the sample for the research study has been 300.

The following were the eleven divisions of the Tamil Nadu Tea Plantation Corporation Limited [TANTEA]: 1. Coonoor, 2. Kothagiri, 3. Cherambady, 4. Cherangode, 5. Nelliyalam, 6. Kollapally, 7. Devala, 8. Pandiar, 9. Naduvattam, 10. Lawson and 11. Ryan. In the first stage, two divisions were selected by lottery method out of the eleven divisions of the TANTEA. The second stage involved the selection of centres through lottery method from the selected Coonoor and Naduvattam divisions. From each division, five centres were selected through lottery. In the third stage, five working fields were selected, by applying lottery method, from each of the five centres falling under the divisions of Coonoor and Naduvattam. The fourth and final stage involved the selection of workers through lottery method from the selected working fields of the selected centres representing the divisions of Coonoor and Naduvattam respectively. From each field, six workers were selected as the respondents for the research study. Multi-stage sampling was used because of the larger population and geographical location. Simple random sampling (lottery method) has been used to select the particular divisions, centres, working fields and the tea plantation workers.

The researcher had collected data from the tea plantation workers permanently employed in the Naduvattam and Coonoor Divisions. Out of the 469 workers employed in the Coonoor Division, the researcher interviewed 150 tea plantation workers. Similarly, he collected data from 150 tea plantation workers out of the 483 workers in the Naduvattam Division. The sample size fixed for this research study has been 300. The sample size was five per cent of the total working population (sampling frame). The sample size was fixed by the researcher after consulting the members of the Doctoral Committee, statisticians and subject experts; besides keeping in mind the time and economic considerations.

While selecting the respondents for the research study, following criteria has been fixed: (a) A worker must have completed his/her eighteenth year of age, (b) A worker must have been made permanent in his/her job and designated as plantation worker, (c) He/she must have completed at least one year of service with the TANTEA, and (d) He/she must have been working in one of the working fields of the respective divisions, i.e., Coonoor and Naduvattam.

Fieldwork, Pilot Study and Pre-testing of Tools of Data Collection

The first phase of the field work was conducted from 28 April to 13 June 2010 as the lists of tea plantation workers from the respective divisions of the TANTEA were available with the researcher. The researcher interviewed thirty tea plantation workers each from the Coonoor and Naduvattam divisions to assess the feasibility of the study. This pilot study has been undertaken by the researcher with plantation workers to find out the extent of the problem in the tea industry. The second phase of fieldwork continued from 3 to 10 May 2011. The tool was pretested with respondents representing the Coonoor and Naduvattam divisions of the TANTEA.

Tools of Data Collection

Interview Schedule

The primary tool of data collection used was a detailed interview schedule consisting of questions on personal and family details of the respondents, their socio-economic conditions, occupational profile, working conditions including occupational risks and health problems of the tea plantation workers.

The researcher preferred to choose a detailed interview schedule as the main tool of data collection for two major reasons:

(1) The interview schedule could be used for the tea plantations workers who were either illiterate or hardly completed their primary education.

(2) The researcher got an opportunity to contact the prospective respondents in person and also to explain to them difficult terms. Clarifications were made possible which saved the researcher a lot of time, money and duplication of data.

Apart from several researcher generated questions and statements, the interview schedule contained two standardized tools: 1. Kuppuswamy's scale on the socio-economic status (conversion factor modified in the year 2008) and 2. Job satisfaction scale developed by D. Murali and M.S. Kulkarni (1991).

Job Satisfaction Scale

To measure the level of job satisfaction of working women, the scale developed by D. Murali and M.S. Kulkarni (1991) is adopted.

The scale consists of 40 statements out of which 20 statements are positive and other 20 statements are negative. The total job satisfaction score range from 40 to 200. The increasing score was indicative of the higher degree of job satisfaction. The higher degree of job satisfaction is defined, i.e., above the third tertile of the total score obtained from the respondents.

Kuppuswamy's Scale

The socio-economic status scale (urban) developed by Kuppuswamy's attempts to measure the socio-economic class of family in urban community. It is based on three variables—education, occupation, and income. A weight age is assigned to each variable according to seven point predefined scale. The total of three weight ages gives the socio-economic status score which is graded to indicate the five classes, as per details in Table 3.1. To get current income group, a conversion factor based on current All India Consumer Price Index (AICPI) is used, which is given later.

For income, the conversion factor can be obtained by dividing AICPI by 60.04. The income group in the Kuppuswamy's scale are multiplied with the conversions factor to get the appropriate income group (*Indian Journal of Pediatrics*, Volume 70, March

2003). Now, since AICPI in June 2008 was approximately 650, hence 650 divided by 60.04 = 10.83. Thus all the income groups in the Kuppuswamy's scale in the above table are multiplied with the conversion factor to get the appropriated income group. Thus, the conversion factor 10.83 is multiplied by ₹ 2000 which comes to ₹ 21,660 and rest income groups would be as given in Table 3.2.

The total score in Kuppuswamy's classification is calculated as the sum total of the three scores, i.e., Education (A) + Occupation (B) + Income (C).

Questionnaire for the Management Staff (TANTEA)

A questionnaire was administered with all the management staff of the Tamil Nadu Tea Plantation Corporation Limited (TANTEA). This was to find out the perception of the management staff in the cadres of Managing Director, Joint Managing Director, General Manager, Assistant Manager, Divisional Managers of the two divisions, Chief Personnel Officer, Administrative Officer, Senior Manager (Industrial Relation) and Senior Manager (Sales and Marketing). This tool is to find out their perception about the plight of the tea plantation workers of the TANTEA keeping in view their working conditions, occupational risks, health problems and socio-economic status.

Period of Data Collection

Data collection for the study was carried out from 2 December 2011-22nd January 2012. The researcher had collected data from the tea plantation workers permanently employed in the Naduvattam and Coonoor divisions.

Analysis of Data

The analysis of data was based on the specific objectives framed for the study. Analysis of data has been concerned with planning the most optimal manner in which the voluminous data collected were summarized and analyzed to arrive at the answers to the questions that have been raised by the study.

Statistical Tools

Statistical analysis of data has been carried out with the help of statistical package for social sciences—SPSS ver.12 (Leech,

Barrett and Morgan, 2005). The data has been described using frequency tables and figures wherever applicable. Variables pertaining to the following dimensions have been described through uni-variate and bi-variate tables: Demographic profile; occupational profile; socio-economic status; working conditions; health, welfare and social security measures; occupational risks and health problems; role of trade union in protecting the interests of the labour force; and perception of the tea plantation workers about the functioning of the management. Association between demographic profile, socio-economic status variables and job satisfaction has been tested using chi-square test.

Limitations of the Study

- The findings of this research study entirely confined to the Tamil Nadu Tea Plantation Corporation Limited [TANTEA] which has been run and controlled by the Government of Tamil Nadu. The findings could not be generalized to the tea plantation workers of the private tea companies in Tamil Nadu who appear to have been enjoying better privileges and occupying higher status in the society.
- The researcher faced threats from the trade unions of the tea plantation workers. They thought that the researcher has been spoiling the minds of the workers by trying to know about the working conditions of the tea plantation workers. Questions relating to the socio-economic conditions, wages, leave, social security measures, welfare and health problems had really disturbed the functionaries of the trade unions.
- Though the entire management of the TANTEA has been supportive for the research study, questions relating to occupational risks and health of the workers have caused embarrassment to a few of the TANTEA officials.

Prevalent Diseases among the Tea Plantation Labourers in India

The immediate causes of death are usually various diseases of which the most prevalent on the tea-gardens of the tea producing states in India are cholera, diarrhoea, dysentery, malaria, hookworm and various respiratory complications, causing for instance, 13,044 deaths out of a total of 22,581 deaths in 1928-29, as shown in the table below. The table also shows the variation in the number of deaths caused by different diseases.

Table 3.1: Causes of Death on the Tea-Gardens of Top Tea Producing States in India

(Shown at Specific Periods)

Causes	1893	1900	1918-19	1928-29
Cholera	2,301	1,754	5,288	375
Diarrhoea	1,155	1,994	2,647	1,373
Dysentery	3,217	3,760	4,145	2,512
Malaria	2,122	2,825	3,380	3,038
Hookworm	1,399	1,854	2,361	1,448
Respiratory Diseases	572	2,398	6,310	4,398
Other causes	5,276	5,015	38,045	9,437
TOTAL	15,982	19,603	62,176	22,581

Source: Tea Board, Kolkata, West Bengal

Table 3.2: Variation in Death-Rate in the Tea-Gardens of Top Tea Producing States in India (At Specified Years) Death Rates per mille

Years	Act-workers	Non-Act workers	Children	All Persons
1878	106.2	38.9	63.14	66.1
1900	43.5	26.2	25.4	29.4
1920-21	-	31.9	21.1	27.3
1928-29	-	22.5	20.2	21.5

Source: Tea Board, Kolkata, West Bengal

Diarrhoea and dysentery are common diseases in India, especially in the provinces of Bengal, Assam and Madras, and a large number of deaths are attributed to them every year. They have long been known to be among the chief causes of deaths in the tea-gardens, causing respectively 2,647 and 4,145 deaths in 1918 and 1919 when influenza was also most prevalent. The number of deaths caused by these diseases is generally higher on the tea-gardens than in the whole province of Assam (Umananda Phukam, 1983).

The most common disease is however, malaria, and it is also prevalent on the tea-gardens. In fact, there are few labourers on the gardens who at one time or other do not suffer from it. In 1928-29, 3,038 deaths, over 13 per cent of the total, were caused by malaria alone, but the sufferings and devitalising effect of malaria are more common than the actual deaths. Attention has been drawn to the high spleen index on certain gardens especially among children. Prophylactic dozes of quinine, especially during the rainy season, are often administered to check its growth.

About a generation ago kalazar was one of the causes of the high mortality among the workers on the tea-gardens. Even now it is liable to become an epidemic and to play havoc on plantations. Between 1916 and 1929, for instance, 270 workers out of about 550 attacked died of it in one single garden, causing a loss of between ₹ 40,000 and ₹ 50,000 to the garden. Hundreds of infected houses had to be burnt and new lines erected and a hospital established (Tea Board, Kolkata, West Bengal). Among the epidemics cholera is the most important as it appears about every year, though in different degrees of severity (Piya Chatterjee, 2001). Formerly, it was often introduced into the Assam tea-gardens by the new immigrants, who contracted it in insanitary detention depots in Bengal. On some gardens unrestricted communication between new arrivals and old workers was followed by severe outbreaks.

With regard to deaths from cholera, it must be remembered that when once it appears in the neighbourhood it causes, in spite of sanitary precaution, great mortality in the lines of tea-gardens where people are more closely congregated together than in an ordinary village. The highest number of deaths was caused by cholera in 1918-19, the year of the influenza epidemic, the number of deaths amounting to 5,288.

In recent years influenza has become one of the most vital epidemics in India as all over the world. The number of deaths caused by influenza on plantations was 28,552 in 1918-19. Accompanied by cholera, dysentery and respiratory diseases, it raised the total number of deaths from 23.5 per mille in 1917-18 to 61.4 per mille in 1918-19 (Tea Board, Kolkata, West Bengal).

Anaemia is another common disease on the tea gardens of Assam and Tamil Nadu. In 1888, beri-beri, another common disease in Bengal, was found to be identical with anaemia. It is caused, however, by several diseases, such as malaria, dysentery, and hookworm. The most severe type of anaemia is, however, that caused by hookworm, as it is very difficult to get rid of the initial infection.

Health Measures to be Provided to the Tea Plantation Workers Under The Plantation Labour Act, 1951

It is a fact that the labourers were starved, illiterate, innocent and exploited people in their place of origin. They were allured by the agents touring them to this inhospitable and inaccessible tea plantation area. Bribery, coercion, deceit, false promises were the tactics applied by the agents to bring them here. In course of their journey, they suffered immensely and many men, women and children died due to various diseases (cholera, dysentery), hunger and congestion (Purnendu Kumar, 2006).

Though the climate was favourable of tea plantation, it was not favourable for the workers. The extreme humid climate, high temperature, diseases like malaria, cholera, kalazar, small pox, dysentery, and typhoid were wide spread (Umananda Phukam, 1983). While on journey for more than a month indentured labourers were given limited quantity of dry ration and were forced to embark the country boat beyond its capacity. They were virtually packed up in the boat like animals and no human consideration was even thought of regarding the privacy of woman. Due to long journey and bad climate many labourers and their children who were poor and ill-nourished, died on route because they were unable to withstand the hostile climate of the tea plantations.

The general health of the workers in the tea-gardens of Tamil Nadu is very poor. The tropical climate with heavy rainfall, high temperature and observers. But the underfed and malnutrition of the tea-garden labourers are the main problems even today which is responsible for their poor health. They are under nourished, hence, they lack vitality and they live in most unhygienic condition. Consequently they have weak physique having no glamour on their faces.

In this section, the researcher presents a detailed note as to whether the TANTEA management adhered to the following statutory health measures: potable drinking water, latrines and urinals, ambulance facility, hospital facility and provision for appointment of medical practitioner to attend to the health needs of the tea plantation workers.

Table 3.3: Statutory Health Measures made available to the tea plantation workers by the TANTEA management

Sl. No.	Health measures for Tea Plantation Workers	Divisions								Total	
		Coonoor				Naduvattam				Provided [n (%)]	Not Provided [n (%)]
		Provided				Not Provided					
		Frequency	Percentage	Frequency	Percentage	Frequency	Percentage	Frequency	Percentage		
1.	Potable drinking water	0	0	150	100	0	0	150	100	0 (0%)	300 (100%)
2.	Latrines and urinals	0	0	150	100	0	0	150	100	0 (0%)	300 (100%)
3.	Ambulance	0	0	150	100	0	0	150	100	0 (0%)	300 (100%)
4.	Hospital facility (group or garden hospital)	0	0	150	100	0	0	150	100	0 (0%)	300 (100%)
5.	Availability of medical practitioner to attend the health problems of tea plantation workers.	0	0	150	100	0	0	150	100	0 (0%)	300 (100%)

All the respondents were denied the above-mentioned health provisions though they have been guaranteed under The Plantations Labour Act, 1951. All those tea plantation workers who were interviewed by the researcher rejected the claims of the TANTEA management that all these statutory measures have been adhered to.

Though every employer of a plantation has been obligated to provide the following statutory welfare measures: (a) Potable drinking water, (b) Latrines and urinals separately provided for male and female workers, (c) Medical facility including a hospital to treat the ill workers, (d) Ambulance facility and (e) Appointment of a medical practitioner either permanently or on temporary basis to attend to the health problems of the tea plantation workers and should also visit the plantation fields during the normal working hours of the tea plantation workers.

Occupational Risks of the Workers

Occupational Risks of the Tea Plantation Workers

Occupational Dermatitis is also a common form of injury caused to workers on the plantations. Amputations as a result of an injury were also common on the estates. Amputations result in a neglected injury of a serious fracture or cut. Burns are caused due negligent handling of chemicals and in some cases due to inadequate safety precautions when igniting fires. Occupational injuries due to contact with chemical substances were prevalent in the estates. Injuries occurring to internal organs due to occupational hazards were also common in the estates. Injuries to the respiratory system could be also possible and directly linked to hazardous exposures where workers suffer from temporary or permanent lung disorders. The nasal cavity and mouth are the major routes through which toxic substances enter the respiratory system of the body, and, are easily affected by gases, dust or fumes. The nervous system is highly sensitive to the hazardous effects of organic solvents. Organophosphate insecticides such as malathion and parathion that are used interfere severely with the functions of the nervous system leading to weakness and paralysis and sometimes death.

Table 3.4: Sustained Injury at the Workplace in the Last One Year due to Attacks of Wild Animals and Insects Bites

Sl. No.	Sustained Injury at the Workplace	Division				Total	
		Coonoor		Naduvattam			
		Frequency	Percentage	Frequency	Percentage	Injured n (%)	Not Injured n (%)
1.	Injured	129	86	141	94	270 (90%)	0 (0%)
2.	Not Injured	21	14	9	6	0 (0%)	30 (10%)
	Total	150	100	150	100	270 (90%)	30 (10%)

Most of the respondents (90 per cent) had injury at the workplace last one year. These injuries were caused by attacks of wild animals and insect bites in the divisions of Coonoor (43 per cent) and Naduvattam (47 per cent). A one tenth (10 per cent) of the respondents were not injured due to such

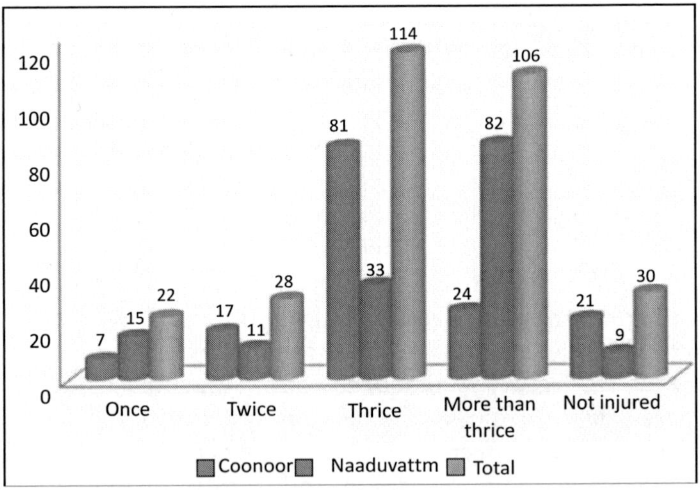

(Coonoor: N = 150 and Naduvattam: N = 150 & Total: N = 300)

Fig. 3.1: Number of times the injury was caused to the respondents in the last one year.

incidents. Hence it could be inferred that the possibility of attacks by wild animals and insects was more on the plantation workers due to their nature of work and work environment.

More than one third, i.e., 114 (38 per cent) of the respondents had been injured thrice, while comparably an equal number 106 (35 per cent) of the respondents sustained injury more than thrice in the last one year. It could be inferred that many occupational risks were associated with the work of the tea plantation workers.

Table 3.5: Nature of Injury Sustained by the Respondents and Reporting the Same

Sl. No.	Nature of Injury	Division				Total Frequency	Total Per centage
		Coonoor		Naduvattam			
		Frequency	Per centage	Frequency	Per centage		
1.	Minor	125	83	134	89	259	86
2.	Major	4	3	7	5	11	4
3.	Did not sustain injury	21	14	9	6	30	10
Total		150	100	150	50	300	100

A majority (86 per cent) of the respondents had minor injury while four per cent of the respondents had major injury. The respondents from both the divisions were almost equally attacked by the wild animals and insect bites. This reflected the occupational risks involved in the tea plantations sector.

It could be inferred that tea plantation workers were more prone to leech-bite as many, i.e., 183 (61 per cent) respondents had leech-bite. Each four per cent of the respondents had snake bite and attacked by the elephants. A less number, i.e., 25 (8 per cent) of the respondents were bitten by wasps while only two per cent, i.e., 7 of the respondents were attacked by bison, the incidents of which were noticed more in Coonoor compared to the Naduvattam division. A negligible number, i.e., 3 (1 per cent) of the respondents were allegedly attacked by wild animals, such as, leopard, jackals, etc., while ten per cent of the respondents were bitten by wild insects, such as, scorpion, etc.

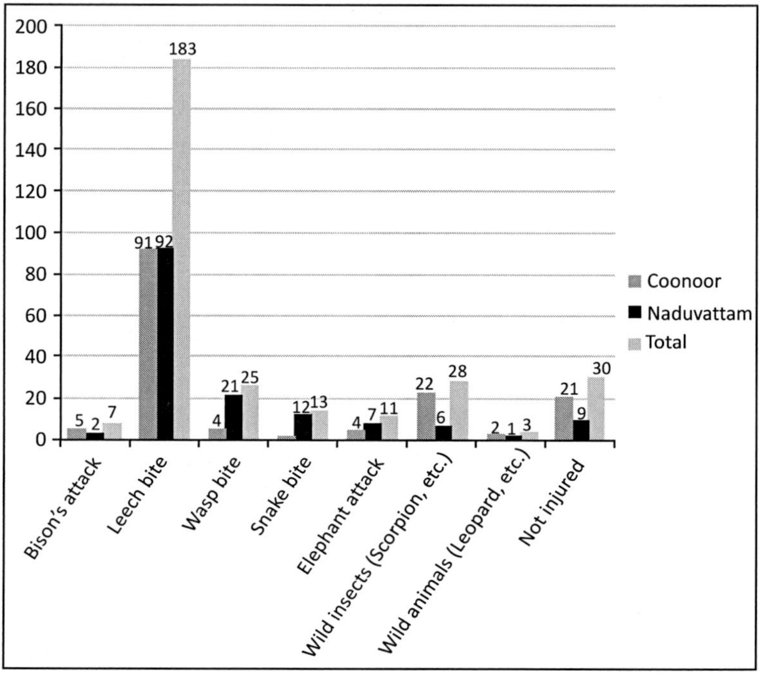

(Coonoor: N = 150 and Naduvattam: N = 150 and Total: N = 300)

Fig. 3.2: Causes of injury meted out to the respondents

The researcher noticed that more than half, i.e., 163 (54 per cent) of the respondents had injury on their lower limbs, while nearly one sixth, i.e., 48 (16 per cent) of them had injury on their upper limbs. Very small number, i.e., 15 (5 per cent) of the respondents were injured on the trunk/abdomen of their body. This was so because they were obligated to work on standing position and their lower part of the body was always in touch with the ground filled with bushes. Fourteen per cent of the respondents had injury on their head and neck. The researcher was informed by the respondents that when they had a fall from high positioned slopes there was more possibility of getting their lower limbs injured, and sometimes it led to fractures as well.

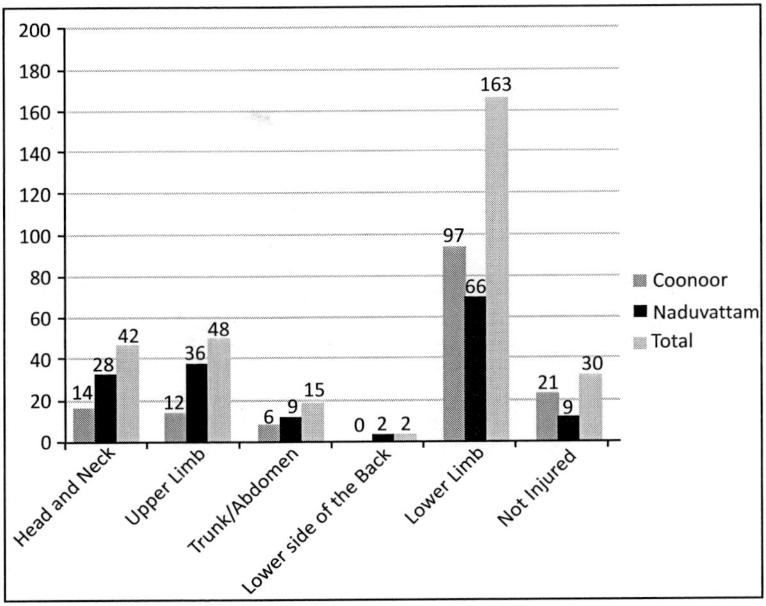

(Coonoor: N = 150 and Naduvattam: N = 150 and Total: N = 300)

Fig. 3.3: Site of Injury caused to the respondents

A one third, i.e., 98 (33 per cent) of the respondents had reported the injury caused to them to their colleagues, while more than one third, i.e., 103 (34 per cent) of the respondents did not report it to anybody. More than one tenth, i.e., 35 (12 per cent) of the respondents had reported the injury to their supervisors, while an equal figure, i.e., 34 (11 per cent) of the respondents had intimated about their injury to others, such as, Field Conductor (F.C.) and Assistant Field Conductor (A.F.C.). It could be inferred that none of the respondents reported their injury to the medical officer since most of the time the medical practitioner was either not available or inaccessible in the plantation fields for the tea plantation workers to treat injury, if any and other health ailments. There were very few respondents who had noticed the medical officer visiting the concerned division offices of Coonoor and Naduvattam that too only to receive their monthly honorarium.

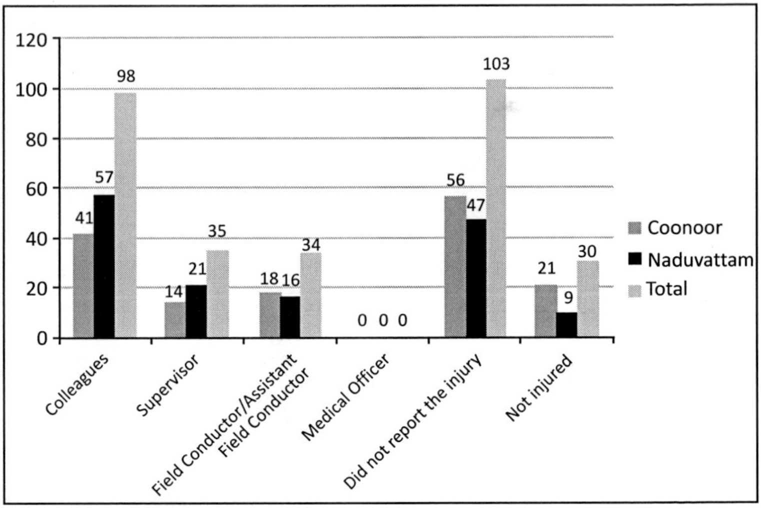

(Coonoor: N = 150 and Naduvattam: N = 150 and Total: N = 300)

Fig. 3.4: Reporting the Injury to others

Nearly half of the respondents, i.e., 137 (46 per cent) who had been injured were administered first aid, while a small number, i.e., 22 (7 per cent) of the respondents had to undergo minor

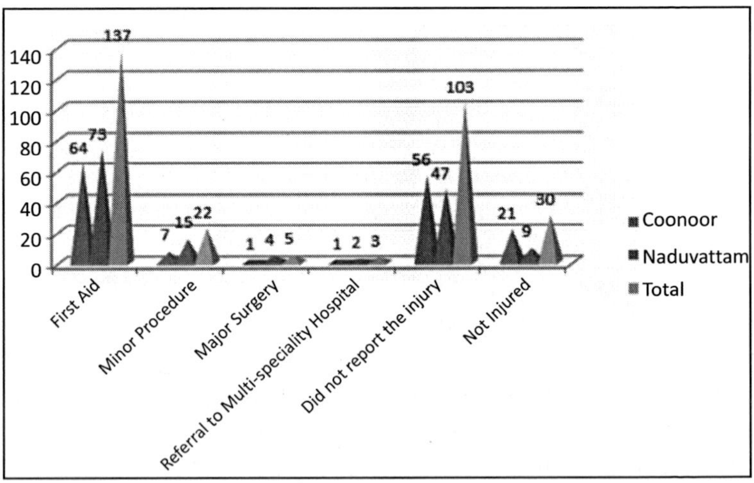

(Coonoor: N = 150 and Naduvattam: N = 150 and Total: N = 300)

Fig. 3.5: Nature of Treatment Provided to the Respondents when they were Injured

procedures to treat their injury. It could be inferred that though only two per cent, i.e., five of the respondents underwent major surgery to treat their injury, this was quite alarming that required immediate attention of the employer, i.e. TANTEA to take suitable measures to prevent injury caused to the workers. Usually it took considerable amount of time to rush the injured to the nearest clinic or hospital for medical help. A negligible number, i.e., 3 (1 per cent) of the respondents were referred to multi-speciality hospitals located in the Coimbatore District, Tamil Nadu. More than one third, i.e., 103 (34 per cent) of the respondents did not report their injury, while ten per cent of the respondents were not injured at all.

More than three fourth, i.e., 258 (86 per cent) of the respondents experienced pain due to work-related activity in the last one month, while more than one tenth, i.e., 42 (14 per cent) of

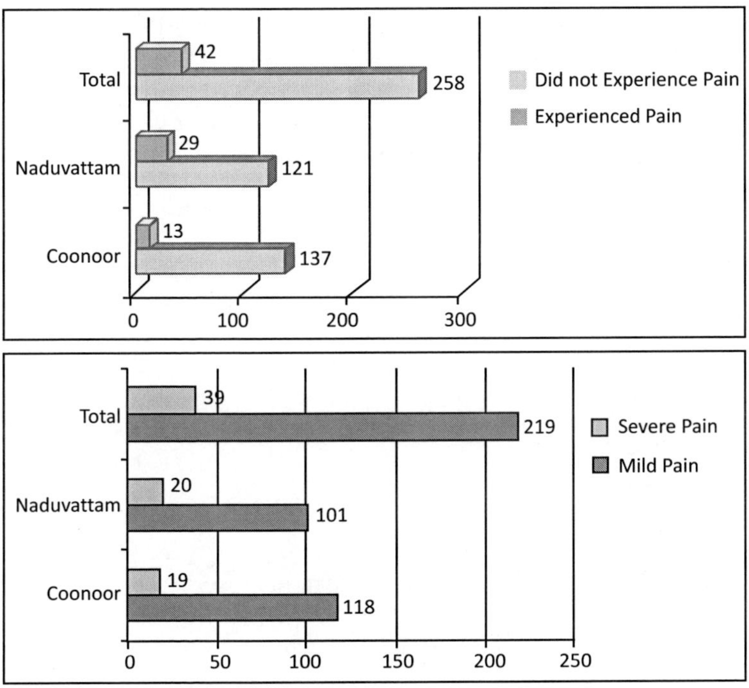

(Coonoor: N = 150 and Naduvattam: N = 150 and Total: N = 300)

Fig. 3.6: Work-related pain experienced by the respondents in the last one month

the respondents did not experience it. Out of those respondents, who experienced pain due to work-related activity, nearly three fourth, i.e., 219 (73 per cent) of the respondents experienced pain which was mild in nature, while more than one tenth, i.e., 39 (13 per cent) of the respondents experienced severe pain. It could be inferred that body postures maintained by the workers was the major reason for experiencing pain at their workplace. The researcher came to now that the tasks of pruning and plucking caused pain to the tea plantation workers.

More than three fourth (86 per cent) of the respondents experienced pain due to work related activity in the last month from the time the researcher collected data from them. Among them, nearly half, i.e., 146 (49 per cent) of the respondents had work-related pain less than three times, while more than one tenth, i.e., 42 (14 per cent) of the respondents experienced pain between three to less than five times. More than one tenth, i.e., 37 (12 per cent) of the respondents experienced pain in their body between five times to less than eight times, while eleven per cent of the respondents had experienced pain more than eight times.

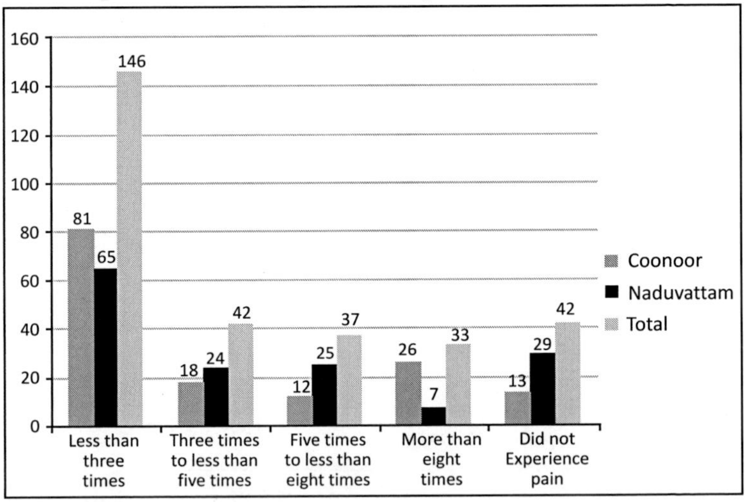

(Coonoor: N = 150 and Naduvattam: N = 150 and Total: N = 300)

Fig. 3.7: Number of times the pain was experienced in the last one month due to work related activity

More than three fourth, i.e., 231 (77 per cent) of the respondents attributed the activity of plucking to be the main cause of pain, while a very less number, i.e., 15 and 9 (5 and 3 per cent) of the respondents associated developing pain with carrying out the tasks of pruning and chopping respectively. A negligible number, i.e., 3 (1 per cent) of the respondents who did the work of tipping and weeding experienced pain out of it.

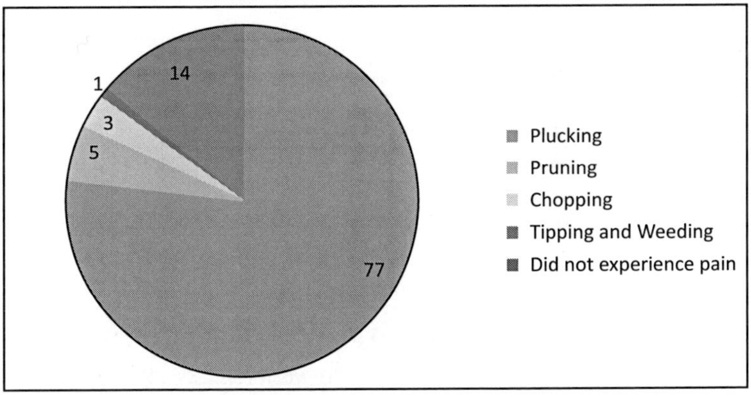

(Coonoor: N = 150 and Naduvattam: N = 150 and Total: N = 300)

Fig. 3.8: Causes of pain experienced by the respondents

It could be inferred that tea plantation workers were prone to get pain on their back and shoulder as nearly one third, i.e., 96 (32 per cent) and one fourth, i.e., 78 (26 per cent) of the respondents suffered from work-related pain on the above-mentioned site of their body, respectively. Each five per cent, i.e., 15 of the respondents experienced headache and pain in their neck and upper limbs. Nearly one fifth, i.e., 54 (18 per cent) of the respondents experienced pain at lower limbs. The researcher while interviewing the respondents came to know that long standing hours of work and nature of work led to the muscular-skeletal pain experienced by the respondents in their body.

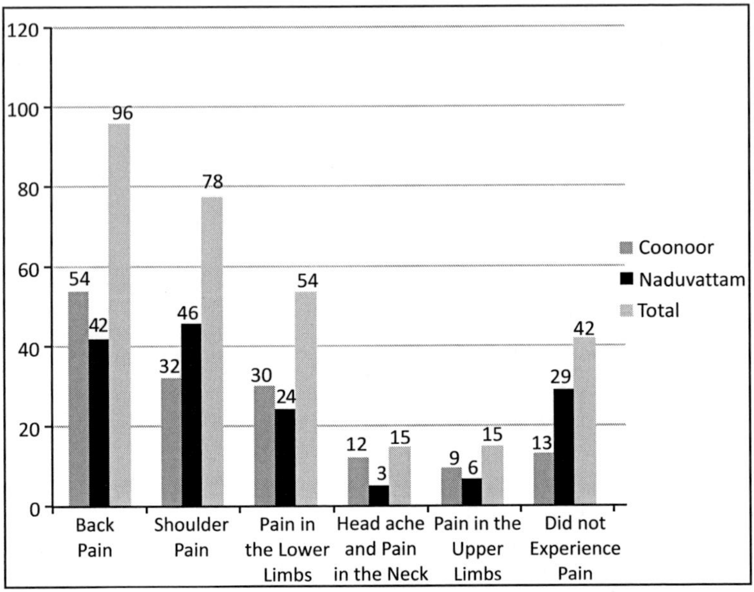

(Coonoor: N = 150 and Naduvattam: N = 150 and Total: N = 300)

Fig. 3.9: Site of the pain due to work related activity on the body of the respondents

Table 3.6: Nature of Treatment Provided to the Respondents Who Experienced Pain Due to Work Related Activity

Sl. No.	Nature of treatment provided for the pain experienced	Division				Total Frequency	Total Per centage
		Coonoor		Naduvattam			
		Frequency	Percentage	Frequency	Percentage		
1.	First aid	23	15	47	31	70	23
2.	Minor surgery/ procedure at dispensary or hospital (e.g. dressing, suturing, application of plaster cast	4	3	1	1	5	2

Sl. No.	Nature of treatment provided for the pain experienced	Division				Total Frequency	Total Per centage
		Coonoor		Naduvattam			
		Frequency	Percentage	Frequency	Percentage		
3.	Major surgery / procedure at hospital	2	1	1	1	3	1
4.	Did not receive medical treatment	108	72	72	48	180	60
5.	Did not experience pain	13	7	29	19	42	14
Total		150	100	150	100	300	100

Many (60 per cent) of the respondents did not receive medical care and treatment even though they experienced pain and wanted to treat the same. Nearly one fourth (23 per cent) of the respondents received first aid after having experienced pain and reported the same either to their colleagues or to their superiors, such as, Supervisor, Field Conductor, Assistant Field Conductor, etc. A negligible number (2 and 1 per cent) of the respondents underwent minor and major surgery for their pain caused due to the work-related activities.

It could be inferred that the workers were denied by the employer the basic health care and allied service even in case of emergency and immediate need. This has caused the respondents to develop an attitude whereby they did not even want to share with others including their colleagues that they experienced pain due to work-related activity.

Health Problems of the Tea Plantation Workers

Table 3.7: Personal Practices Affecting the Health of the Respondents.

Sl. No.	Practices affecting the health of the respondents	Division								Total	
		Coonoor				Naduvattam					
		Practiced		Not Practiced		Practiced		Not Practiced			
		Frequency	Per centage	Frequency	Percentage	Frequency	Percentage	Frequency	Per centage	Practiced [n (%)]	Not Practiced [n (%)]
1.	Consumption of Alcohol	107	71	43	29	132	88	18	12	239 (80%)	61 (20%)
2.	Smoking	34	23	116	77	13	9	137	91	47 (16%)	253 (84%)
3.	Use of Betel Leaf and Nuts	119	79	31	21	141	94	9	6	260 (87%)	40 (13%)
4.	Use of Substance	13	9	137	91	24	16	126	84	37 (12%)	263 (88%)
5.	Consumption of Illicit Liquor	13	9	137	91	24	16	126	84	37 (12%)	263 (88%)
6.	Gambling	5	3	145	97	12	8	138	92	17 (6%)	283 (94%)

It was noticed by the researcher that the tea plantation workers resorted to various practices that affected their health. It could be inferred that more than three fourth (80 per cent) of the respondents had alcoholic dependence. The researcher was informed by the respondents during data collection that they preferred to take rum and brandy and stated further that it helped them to adapt to their climatic conditions. The researcher noticed that compared to Coonoor division, number of workers was more in the Naduvattam division in terms of consumption of alcoholic drinks. It was a common practice among the women tea plantation workers to consume alcoholic drinks as it gave them relief from body pain and other health ailments, such as, cough, cold, headache, etc.

With regard to smoking, nearly one sixth (16 per cent) of the respondents resorted to such a practice, while more than three fourth (84 per cent) of the respondents preferred using betel leaf and nuts. Though, smoking was practiced among the male workers, the usage of betel leaf and a nut was practiced by women workers. Though more than one tenth (12 per cent) of the respondents resorted to both substance usage and consumption of illicit liquor, it could be assumed that all male workers preferred taking both.

It could be inferred that tea plantation workers preferred taking alcohol since many, i.e., 204 (68 per cent) respondents consumed it on daily basis, while only five per cent, i.e., 15 of the respondents took alcoholic drinks every week. A very small number, i.e., 12 (4 per cent) of the respondents consumed alcohol during the festive seasons, while a similar figure, i.e., 9 (3 per cent) of the respondents consumed the same occassionally. Twenty per cent of the respondents did not consume alcohol.

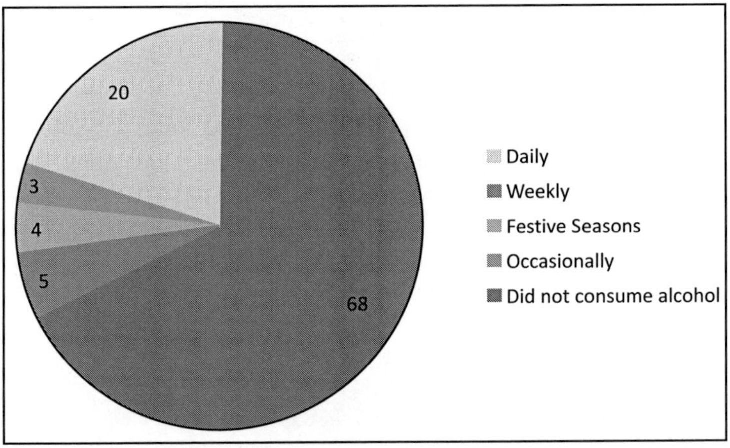

(Coonoor: N = 150 and Naduvattam: N = 150 and Total: N = 300)

Fig. 3.10: Frequency of consumption of Alcohol among the respondents

Each five per cent, i.e., 14 of the respondents were either chain smokers or smoked cigarettes two to four times a day, while each two per cent, i.e., five of the respondents either resorted to smoking once in a week or did it occassionally. More than three fourth (83 per cent) of the respondents did not smoke since women workers dominated the tea plantations as far as the strength of the labour force was concerned. It was interesting to note that only three per cent, i.e., nine of the respondents did smoke once a day.

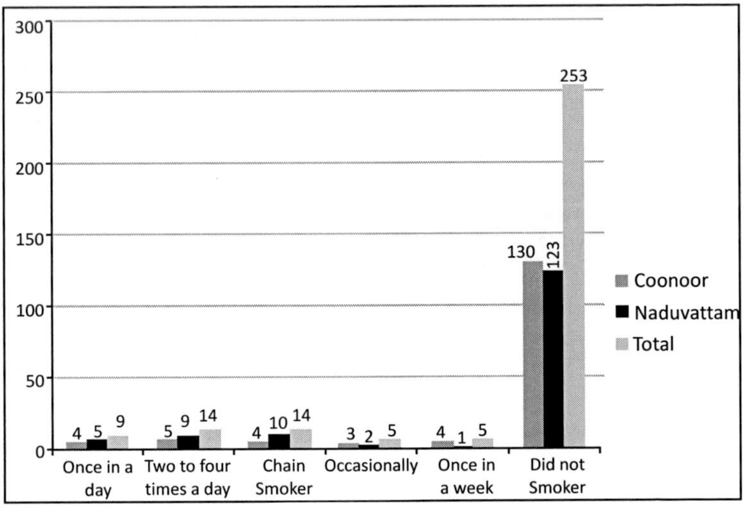

(Coonoor: N = 150 and Naduvattam: N = 150 and Total: N = 300)

Fig. 3.11: Frequency of smoking among the respondents

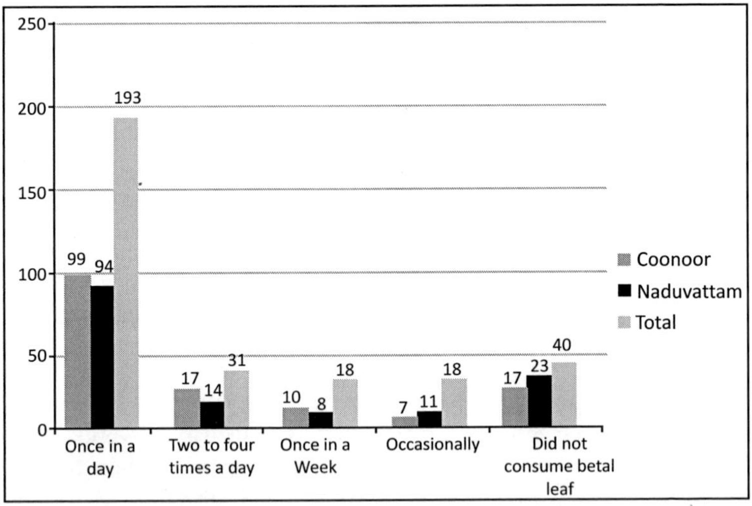

(Coonoor: N = 150 and Naduvattam: N = 150 and Total: N = 300)

Fig. 3.12: Frequency of usage of betel leaf and a nut among the respondents

Many, i.e., 193 (64 per cent) respondents all of whom were women have consumed betel leaf and a nut once in a day, while each six per cent, i.e., 18 of the respondents either consumed it once in a week or occasionally. One tenth, i.e., 31 (10 per cent) of the respondents consumed it two to four times in day, while fourteen per cent, i.e., 40 of the respondents refrained from using it.

Table 3.8: Exposure to Chemicals and Health Problems Caused the Respondents

Sl. No.	Exposure to chemicals and Health problems caused	Divisions								Total	
		Coonoor				Naduvattam				Yes [n (%)]	No [n (%)]
		Yes		No		Yes		No			
		F	P	F	P	F	P	F	P		
1	Direct or indirect exposure to chemicals	108	72	42	28	121	81	29	19	229 (76%)	71 (24%)
2	Explained about the dangers of the chemicals before it was sprayed	19	13	131	87	36	24	114	76	55 (18%)	245 (82%)
3	Washing hands after spraying the chemicals and before eating after the work was done	113	75	37	25	91	61	59	39	204 (68%)	96 (32%)
4	Exposure to dermatology /skin problems	21	14	129	86	13	9	137	91	34 (11%)	266 (89%)
5	Whether skin problems caused due to spraying of pesticides to the leaves	57	38	93	62	41	27	109	73	98 (33%)	202 (67%)

Sl. No.	Exposure to chemicals and Health problems caused	Divisions								Total	
		Coonoor				Naduvattam				Yes [n (%)]	No [n (%)]
		Yes		No		Yes		No			
		F	P	F	P	F	P	F	P		
6	Whether noticed women workers who were unable to conceive	26	17	124	83	11	7	139	93	37 (12%)	263 (88%)
7	Associating inability to conceive with inhalation of pesticides and fertilizers	21	14	129	86	9	6	141	94	27 (9%)	273 (91%)

A majority (89 per cent) of the respondents felt that the chances of developing skin problems were bright for the tea plantation workers, while seventy-seven per cent of the respondents had associated such as health problem due to spraying of pesticides to the tea leaves. A majority (87 per cent) of the respondents accepted the existence of labour infertility rate among women workers, while eighty-nine per cent of the respondents had associated it with the inhalation of pesticides and fertilizers.

Table 3.9: Other Health Problems Faced by the Workers

Sl. No.	Other health problems faced by the workers	Divisions								Total	
		Coonoor				Naduvattam					
		Yes		No		Yes		No		Yes [n (%)]	No [n (%)]
		F	P	F	P	F	P	F	P		
1	Fever and cough	71	47	79	53	43	29	107	71	114 (38%)	186 (62%)
2	Body pain	89	59	61	41	76	51	74	49	165 (55%)	135 (45%)

A considerable number (38 per cent) of the respondents had fever with cough, while a majority (55 per cent) of the respondents experienced body pain due to carrying out work-related activities.

The researcher has been informed by the respondents that they mostly had pain in their spinal cord which they associated with the necessity of frequently bending to collect tea leaves.

Table 3.10: Sexual Practices Noticed Among the Tea Plantation Workers in the Opinion of the Respondents

Sl. No	Sexual practices	Divisions								Total	
		Coonoor				Naduvattam				Yes [n (%)]	No [n (%)]
		Yes		No		Yes		No			
		F	P	F	P	F	P	F	P		
1	Practice of extra-marital affairs noticed by the respondents among the workers	26	17	124	83	11	7	139	93	37 (12%)	263 (88%)
2	Practice of pre-marital sex noticed by the respondents among the workers	4	3	146	97	7	5	143	95	11 (4%)	289 (96%)
3	Incidents of sexual harassment of women workers by male workers as noticed by the respondents	17	11	133	89	9	6	141	94	26 (9%)	274 (91%)

Only a less number (13 per cent) of the respondents accepted the existence of extra-marital affairs among the workers, while only three per cent of the workers admitted the existence of pre-marital sex among the workers. A little number (9 per cent) of the respondents acknowledged that these women workers were subjected to sexual harassment by the male workers.

Main Findings of the Study

The findings of the study have clearly indicated the socio-economic and working conditions of the tea plantation workers in Tamil Nadu. The researcher has presented the main findings based on the objectives of the study. References to other relevant studies have been made in order to understand the similarities and differences in the findings.

Demographic Details of the Respondents

Sex: More than three fourth (88 per cent) of the respondents were females, while more than one-tenth (12 per cent) of them were males. Similar findings were observed in the research study carried out in the four plantations, i.e. tea, coffee, rubber and cardamom from the States of Assam, West Bengal, Tamil Nadu, Kerala, Karnataka and Tripura (Labour Bureau, Ministry of Labour and Employment, Government of India, 1975).

More than two-fifth (41 per cent) of the respondents were aged between 41 to 50 years, while one third (33 per cent) of them belonged to the age group of 31-40 years, sixteen per cent of them were between the age group of 51 to 60 years. Similar findings were noticed in the tea and coffee plantations from the States of Assam, West Bengal, Tamil Nadu and Kerala (Labour Bureau, Ministry of Labour and Employment, Government of India, 1975). Differences in the findings were also noticed in the study conducted in the Sri Lankan tea plantations of the Uva, Sabaragamuva, Southern, Central and Western provinces, where nearly two per cent (1.8%) of the labourers were children, who did not even complete fourteen years (Employers' Federation of Ceylon in collaboration with the ILO, 1997). Similarly, a study carried out on the Bolivian Sugar Cane Plantations found out that children and youths account for half of the eight million people living in Bolivia. The ILO and UNICEF estimated that the sugar cane harvest mobilizes almost 10,000 children and adolescents (National Institute of Statistics, 2006). 2,540 children worked in the sugar cane harvest (Zafra) in Santa Cruz and 2,619 youths participated in the Zafra of Tarija (Laura Baas, G.K. Lieten, 2011). In Bermejo, in 2004, there were 2,349 children and adolescents of whom 1,315 were of school-going age (Guevara, 2004).

Marital Status: Most (94 per cent) of the respondents were married, while a very small number (6 per cent) of them were unmarried. Differences in the findings were observed in the study carried out among the tea plantation workers of the State of Assam, where many (62) respondents were unmarried and a very small number (3 per cent) of the respondents were divorcees (Gadapani Sarma, 2007).

Educational Qualification: Nearly one third (31 per cent) of the respondents had studied up to Vth Std., while two-fifth (20 per cent) of them had never attended formal schooling. Similar findings were observed in the study carried out in state of Assam (Elizabeth Kaniambady, 2003). Majority of the sampled women workers (54.4 per cent) were found to be illiterate (Labour Bureau, Ministry of Labour and Employment, Government of India, 1975). A research study conducted in the coffee plantations in Brazil revealed similar findings that the literacy rates in the Municipio were the lowest in Minas Gerais, where children attended school in one-room classes with mixed age groups (Watson, Kelly; Achinelli, Moira Laura, 2008). Differences in the findings were observed over the outcome of the research study conducted in the Bolivian sugar cane plantations, which stated that school going children of 11 and 12 years old participated in the same activities as older permanent helpers like cutting, de-topping and stacking sugar cane, after classes or on non-school days (Laura Baas, G.K. Lieten, 2011).

Number of Family Members: Nearly two-third (65 per cent) of the respondents had a family consisting of four adults and two children which included their dependents, while more than one third (35 per cent) of them had three adults and one child, living in the extended type of family. Similar findings were observed in the study of the tea plantations from the state of West Bengal (Umananda Phukam, 1983). The average family size of the sampled women workers was 4.2 members at overall level. The average number of earners per women worker house hold was found to be two members (Labour Bureau, Ministry of Labour and Employment, Government of India, 1975).

Ethnicity and Migratory Character: Most (94 per cent) of the respondents were Sri Lankan repatriates (Estate Tamils), while only five per cent of them were Tamils of Indian origin. Similar findings were observed from the tea plantations in the states of Assam, West Bengal, Tamil Nadu and Tripura (Labour

Bureau, Ministry of Labour and Employment, Government of India, 1975). About 60 per cent of the sugar cane harvesters in Bolivia were temporary migrants (Laura Baas, G.K. Lieten, 2011).

Occupational Profile

Designation of Workers: All of the respondents were permanent workers, while none of them was a casual worker. Similar findings were noticed in the tea gardens of the state of Assam (Gadapani Sarma, 2007). Another study conducted in the Bolivian sugar cane plantations brought out similar finding, where the year-round maintenance and work operations were undertaken only by the permanent workers (Laura Baas, G.K. Lieten, 2011).

Nature of Work and Years of Experience: Most (91 per cent) of the respondents' nature of work was plucking, while a very small number (5 per cent) of them had to do pruning, three per cent of them weeding and chopping. More than two fifth (41 per cent) of the respondents had less than ten years of working experience with TANTEA, while an equal figure (41 per cent) of them were serving the organization for 20 to 30 years. Similar findings were noticed in the tea gardens of the state of Assam, which stated that about nine-tenth of the work force in a tea industry were attached to the gardens. Their work involved preparation of nursery bed, transplanting, pruning, cleaning and clearing, drainage, loosening of the soil, etc., and the most important work of plucking of tea leaves (M.M. Rehman, 2005).

Socio-economic Status

(a) *Social Status*

Religion: Most (92 per cent) of the respondents were Hindus, while a small number (8 per cent) of the respondents were Christians. Similar findings were observed in the tea plantations of the state of Assam (Gadapani Sarma, 2007) and Sri Lanka tea plantations (Employers' Federation of Ceylon in collaboration with the ILO, 1997).

Community: Nearly three-fourth (73 per cent) of the respondents were Scheduled Castes, while nearly one-fourth (24 per cent) of them belonged to backward class community.

Differences in the findings were observed in the study carried out in the State of Assam, where majority of the workers belonged to the Scheduled Tribes (Elizabeth Kaniambady, 2003).

Toilet facility: Nearly three-fourth (73 per cent) of the respondents did not have toilet facility at their home, while more than one-fourth (27 per cent) of them had toilet facility which they themselves established it.

Other Indicators of Social Status: The socio-economic status scale developed by Kuppuswamy (2008) was used by the researcher to measure the socio-economic class of the families of the respondents. It was done based on three variables such as education, occupation and income.

Two-fifth (40 per cent) of the respondents' family head had never been to schools and not studied, while, nearly half (46 per cent) of the respondents' head of the family had studied up to primary level of education. Only eight per cent of the respondents' family head had completed high schooling.

All of the tea plantation workers were unskilled as the job did not require specialized training to handle operations carried out in the fields.

Nearly half of the respondents (46 per cent) belonged to the upper middle class, while two-fifth (40 per cent) of the respondents were grouped under lower middle class. Nearly one-sixth (14 per cent) of the respondents were categorized under the upper lower class. None of the respondents' socio-economic class status fell either under the upper or lower class the two extreme classes.

Most (91 per cent) of the respondents' family income per month was greater than rupees two thousand while around six per cent of the respondents earned a family income of between rupees one thousand and less than rupees two thousand. A negligible number (3 per cent) of the respondents' family income was between rupees five hundred and less than rupees seven hundred and fifty.

Similar findings were recorded in the study carried out in the tea gardens of the Jorhat District, Assam (Gadapani Sarma, 2007) and Hailakandy, Assam (Raman Vasantili, 2008). A study carried out in the Brazilian coffee plantations revealed similar findings which stated that coffee was often grown in rural, isolated and poverty-stricken areas. Plantation workers in these areas were most vulnerable to instability on the world coffee market, as their incomes were precariously tied to world coffee prices (Vakis et al., 2004). Largely unpredictable, price fluctuations left workers laden with risk. Many workers were financially dependent solely upon coffee dedicating their labour to its production. The roads were unpaved. Most of the workers lived in simple homes without privacy, which they often built themselves and they had very few possessions. Most homes lacked electricity and running water (FAEMG, 1996). Most families did not have their own means of transportation. Some families shared a horse and cart to meet their transportation needs (Watson, Kelly; Achinelli, Moira Laura, 2008). Similarly, in Santa Cruz as well as in Bermejo, the living conditions of the workers and their families were precarious. For 4-6 months, they slept in a well-constructed building that separated the families from the solteros (single men). Each family was allocated about 2 × 2 meter by the contractor. The worker, his wife and his children all slept together in one bed. Families tried creating some privacy by hanging sheets between their own bed and their neighbours' (Laura Baas, G.K. Lieten, 2011).

The researcher noticed prevalence of similar type of bonded labour in the plantation in general, and tea plantations in particular. In Assam and West Bengal, Arkati system of labour supply was practiced. Arkatis were agents of supplying labour to the tea gardens and exploited the workers. They earned direct commission from the British employers and the local elites, and they paid very meager wages to the workers (Umananda Phukam, 1983). Similar form of practice, known as Kangani system and Indentured system of labour supply was noticed in Tamil Nadu (India), Sri Lanka and a few of the Middle East countries (as far as indentured labour system is concerned (Oddvar Hollup, 1994). In the same way, a system involving advanced payments through intermediaries, known as *enganche* (debt bondage) was prevalent in the Bolivian sugar cane plantations (Laura Baas, G.K. Lieten, 2011).

(b) *Economic Status*

Ownership of House: Most (90 per cent) of the respondents did not own a house, while one-tenth (10 per cent) of them did own a house. Similar findings were observed among the workers serving the tea plantations of the state of Assam (Elizabeth Kaniambady, 2003).

Type of Accommodation: More than three-fourth (82 per cent) of the respondents lived in workers' quarters provided by the TANTEA. Though similar findings were observed in intra-national studies such as (Elizabeth Kaniambady, 2003) and (M.M. Rehman, 2005) differences in the findings were noticed in international studies carried out in Brazilian coffee plantations (Watson, Kelly; Achinelli, Moira Laura, 2008) and Bolivian sugar cane plantations (Laura Baas, G.K. Lieten, 2011), which revealed that the workers were not offered housing facility by their employers and workers themselves built it with simple materials that they had and most of the time put up in the camps. The living conditions of the workers and their families were precarious in both the countries, i.e. Brazil and Bolivia.

Wages: More than three-fourth (85 per cent) of the respondents received wages between three thousand rupees to four thousand rupees. This could be associated with their level of socio-economic status. Similar findings were observed among the workers in the tea plantations of Assam and West Bengal (M.M. Rehman, 2005). The tea plantation workers in India were governed by The Minimum Wages Act, 1948 and paid accordingly. The minimum daily wage of a tea plantation worker has been ₹ 136 in Tamil Nadu (2011). Though the plantation workers in the coffee sector in Brazil were governed by the Brazilian Minimum Wage FAEMG, 1996 (Watson, Kelly; Achinelli, Moira Laura, 2008), sugar cane plantation workers in Bolivia earned wages depending on the volume they manage to cut (Laura Baas, G.K. Lieten, 2011). They earned a wage between 1,000 and 4,000 Boliviano (100-400 Euros) a month.

Saving Habit: Ninety-eight per cent of the respondents did not possess saving habit. It could be interpreted that due to their low wages, the workers had to incur expenses on basic amenities and other requirements which led to non-possession of saving habit. Differences in the findings were observed from the tea plantations in the States of Assam, West Bengal, Tamil Nadu and Tripura, which stated that 42 per cent of the women workers were saving money (Labour Bureau, Ministry of Labour and Employment, Government of India, 1975).

Owning Assets: None of the respondents had either movable or immovable assets. All the respondents had borrowed money from others, mostly (97 per cent) from moneylenders. Similar findings were observed in intra-national studies such as (Elizabeth Kaniambady, 2003) and (M.M. Rehman, 2005) and study carried out in the Sri Lankan tea plantations (Oddvar Hollup, 1994).

Working Conditions

Leave Eligibility: All of the respondents were entitled to the following types of leave: casual leave (12 days), earned leave (14 days), medical or sick leave (15 days) and leave on loss of pay (LLP) up to any number of days. But all the respondents denied payment of wages during casual leave and many rejected the claim made by the TANTEA that 50 per cent of wages were paid to the workers as and when they availed sick or medical leave. Similar findings were noticed in the tea plantations of prime tea producing states in India (Labour Bureau, Ministry of Labour and Employment, Government of India, 1975). Differences in findings were noticed in coffee and sugar cane plantation sectors in Brazil and Bolivia, where workers seemed to be in a disadvantageous position due to absence of labour legislations and other labor protective mechanism to protect the rights of the labour (Watson, Kelly; Achinelli, Moira Laura, 2008), and (Laura Baas, G.K. Lieten, 2011).

Weekly rest: All the respondents were entitled to avail weekly rest which was acknowledged by the workers in both the divisions. But workers availing weekly rest had to forego the wages during such days. This practice was confirmed by other studies as well (Elizabeth Kaniambady, 2003) and (M.M. Rehman, 2005). This practice has been followed in other countries such as Sri Lanka, Cambodia, Fiji islands, Maldives, Philippines and a few Latin American countries where plantations are grown.

Maternity Leave: All of the respondents acknowledged that women workers who were pregnant were sanctioned twelve weeks of maternity leave with wages. Differences in the findings were observed in the tea plantations of Karnataka and Tripura, where the pregnant women tea plantation workers in the private companies were denied maternity leave with wages. (Labour Bureau, Ministry of Labour and Employment, Government of India, 1975).

Obligatory Workload: Every respondent has been expected to collect at least twenty-five kilograms of green leaf everyday failing which they were paid only fifty per cent of the daily wages. Similar findings were observed in the study of the tea plantations from the State of West Bengal (Umananda Phukam, 1983). Differences in findings were observed in coffee plantations of Brazil (60 kgs. of coffee beans) and sugar cane plantations of Bolivia (40-50 kgs. of sugar cane stalks) (Watson, Kelly; Achinelli, Moira Laura, 2008) and (Laura Baas, G.K. Lieten, 2011).

Daily and Weekly Hours of Work: More than two-third (67 per cent) of the respondents had worked six days per week and obviously availed their weekly rest, and others did not avail it. Every one undertook eight hours of work in a day and forty-eight hours a week. None of the respondents was paid wages as and when they availed weekly rest. Similar findings were observed in other studies as well (Elizabeth Kaniambady, 2003) and (M.M. Rehman, 2005). Differences in findings were observed in coffee plantations of Brazil and sugar cane plantations of Bolivia, where the workers and adolescents worked all morning without any real breaks; they only stopped every once in a while to drink some water, smoke a cigarette, chew coca leaves and sharpen their machetes. From morning 04:30 to 06:00 in the evening, workers were expected to be engaged in work, apart from lunch break which usually went on from an hour to an hour and a half (Watson, Kelly; Achinelli, Moira Laura, 2008) and (Laura Baas, G.K. Lieten, 2011).

Over-time Wages: Sixty-six per cent of the respondents worked over time and received only ordinary rate of wages (single wages), while workers in the tea factories received double the wages for their overtime work, as they were covered under The Factories Act, 1948. Similar findings were observed in the study of the tea plantations from the State of West Bengal (Umananda Phukam, 1983). Differences in findings were observed in the Bolivian sugar cane plantations, whereby, 'extra work' has been compensated in terms of volume of work undertaken by the workers. There was no concept of over-time and payment of double the wages for the same (Laura Baas, G.K. Lieten, 2011).

Daily rest interval and prohibition of engaging the workers between 07:00 p.m. and 06:00 a.m.: All the respondents were allowed to take fifteen minutes of rest interval every day during which refreshments were supplied by the TANTEA. None of the respondents was engaged to work on the tea plantations from 07:00 p.m. to 06:00 a.m. Similar findings were observed in the study of the tea plantations from the State of West Bengal (Umananda Phukam, 1983). Differences in findings were observed in coffee plantations of Brazil and sugar cane plantations of Bolivia, where the workers did not have rest interval at all, apart from lunch break which usually went on from an hour to an hour and a half. Sometimes, since the loading machine was available only in the middle of the night, workers were expected to get up to use it (Watson, Kelly; Achinelli, Moira Laura, 2008) and (Laura Baas, G.K. Lieten, 2011).

Health Measures (Statutory)

All of the respondents were denied the following health provisions: (a) potable drinking water, (b) latrines and urinals, (c) ambulance facility, (d) hospital facility (group or garden hospital), and (e) appointment of medical practitioner to visit the tea plantations to attend to the health issues of the workers, though they have been guaranteed by The Plantations Labour Act, 1951. All those tea plantation workers who were interviewed by the researcher rejected the claims of the TANTEA management that all these statutory measures have been adhered to.

Differences in findings were observed in the research study carried out in the four plantations, i.e. tea, coffee, rubber and cardamom from the States of Assam, West Bengal, Tamil Nadu, Kerala, Karnataka and Tripura, which stated that some (48.5 per cent) of the units in Karnataka were providing medical facilities to workers and their family members, while around ten per cent of the units surveyed in Assam complied with the provision of urinals and latrines separately for male and female workers (Labour Bureau, Ministry of Labour and Employment, Government of India, 1975). Another study undertaken on the tea plantation workers of Assam showed that drinking water has been carried to the tea gardens where plucking was in progress in tractor vehicle and supplied to the labourers (M.M. Rehman).

Similar findings were observed in the coffee plantations of Brazil and sugar cane plantations of Bolivia, where the workers did not have health centre close to their dwellings. The little children contracted diseases related to the unhygienic conditions in the camp, like diarrhoea, and were often malnourished, which caused them anaemia. Similarly, medicines were not available for the sick and those injured at workplace lacked medical attention (Watson, Kelly; Achinelli, Moira Laura, 2008) and (Laura Baas, G.K. Lieten, 2011).

Welfare Measures (Statutory)

Canteen Facility: None of the respondents was provided with canteen facility by the management. Differences in findings were observed in the research study carried out in the four plantations, i.e. tea, coffee, rubber and cardamom from the States of Assam, West Bengal, Tamil Nadu, Kerala, Karnataka and Tripura, which showed that canteen facility has been provided in 12.9 per cent of the units surveyed in tea plantations of Assam (Labour Bureau, Ministry of Labour and Employment, Government of India, 1975).

Creche and Recreation: Half of the respondents (50 per cent) all from Coonoor division were provided with crèche and recreation facility, though not well maintained and did not serve the purpose for which they were provided. Similar findings were observed in the research study carried out in the four plantations, i.e. tea, coffee, rubber and cardamom from the States of Assam, West Bengal, Tamil Nadu, Kerala, Karnataka and Tripura, which claimed that crèche facility (37.1 per cent) and recreational (25.0 per cent) facilities were provided in the tea and coffee plantations (Labour Bureau, Ministry of Labour and Employment, Government of India, 1975).

Education Facility: Half of the respondents (50 per cent) all from Naduvattam division were provided with education facility for their children between the age group of six and twelve years. Similar findings were observed in the research study carried out in the four plantations, i.e. tea, coffee, rubber and cardamom from the States of Assam, West Bengal, Tamil Nadu, Kerala, Karnataka and Tripura, which claimed that education facility was provided to the workers' children in the tea plantations (5.3 per cent), while it was not provided in the coffee and cardamom plantations (Labour Bureau, Ministry of Labour and Employment, Government of India, 1975).

Housing Facility: More than three-fourth (82 per cent) of the respondents were provided housing facility and subsequently had occupied the workers' quarters. Similar findings were observed in the research study carried out in the four plantations, i.e. tea, coffee, rubber and cardamom from the States of Assam, West Bengal, Tamil Nadu, Kerala, Karnataka and Tripura, which claimed that housing facility has been provided in the tea (77.3 per cent) and cardamom (50.0 per cent) plantations (Labour Bureau, Ministry of Labour and Employment, Government of India, 1975).

Other Welfare Measures: None of the respondents admitted receiving umbrella, blanket and raincoat, which were supposed to be provided under The Plantations Labour Act, 1951.

Appointment of Labour Welfare Officer: The statutory provision of the appointment of a labour welfare officer has also been not adhered by the TANTEA management as none of the respondents acknowledged it and the researcher also verified it.

Social Security Measures and Other Benefits (Statutory and Voluntary)

Statutory Welfare Measures: All of the respondents were entitled to the following statutory social security measures: (a) Provident Fund scheme under The Provident Fund and Miscellaneous Provisions Act, 1952, (b) Employees' State Insurance under The Employees' State Insurance Act, 1948, (c) Payment of Gratuity under The Payment of Gratuity Act, 1972, (d) Maternity Benefit scheme under The Maternity Benefit Act, 1961, (e) Bonus scheme under The Payment of Bonus Act, 1965, and (f) Payment of compensation for death, disablement—either permanent or temporary under the Workmen's' Compensation Act, 1923. Similar findings were observed in the research study carried out in the four plantations, i.e. tea, coffee, rubber and cardamom from the States of Assam, West Bengal, Tamil Nadu, Kerala, Karnataka and Tripura, which claimed that all of the above-mentioned statutory welfare measures such as maternity benefit (38.9 per cent), appointment of welfare officer (17.4 per cent), payment of bonus (88 per cent), etc. were provided in the tea and coffee plantations (Labour Bureau, Ministry of Labour and Employment, Government of India, 1975).

Voluntary Welfare Measures: Following voluntary welfare measures were provided to all of the respondents: (a) Employees' Benefit Fund, (b) Insurance Scheme provided by the United Planters' Association of South India (UPASI), and (c) Credit, Cooperative and Thrift Society. Library and reading room facility was not available for none of the respondents.

Trade Union Membership of the Respondents

Most (94 per cent) of the respondents had membership of any one of the registered trade unions, consisting of forty-five and forty-nine per cent from the divisions of Coonoor and Naduvattam, respectively. Similar findings were observed in the research study carried out in the four plantations, i.e. tea, coffee, rubber and cardamom from the States of Assam, West Bengal, Tamil Nadu, Kerala, Karnataka and Tripura, which claimed that 59 per cent of women workers in the tea plantations had membership of a trade union (Labour Bureau, Ministry of Labour and Employment, Government of India, 1975).

Occupational Risks of the Tea Plantation Workers

Injury at Workplace: Most of the respondents (90 per cent) had injury at the workplace last one year. The injuries were caused by attacks of the wild animals and insect bites in the divisions of Coonoor (43 per cent) and Naduvattam (47 per cent). Only one-tenth (10 per cent) of the respondents were not injured due to such incidents. Similar findings were observed in the Sri Lankan tea plantations (Employers' Federation of Ceylon in collaboration with the ILO, 1997).

Nature of Injury: More than three-fourth (86 per cent) of the respondents had minor injury, while a very small number (4 per cent) of the respondents had major injury. The respondents, from both the divisions, were almost equally attacked by the wild animals and insect bites.

Number of Times the Injury was Caused: More than one third (38 per cent) of the respondents had been injured thrice, while comparably an equal figure (35 per cent) of the respondents sustained injury more than thrice in the last one year.

Causes of injury: It could be inferred that tea plantation workers were more prone to leech-bite as many (61 per cent) of the respondents had leech-bite. Each four per cent of the respondents had snake bite and attacked by the wild elephants. A less number (8 per cent) of the respondents were bitten by wasps, while two per cent of the respondents were attacked by bison, the incidents of which were more noticed in Coonoor compared to the Naduvattam division. Only one per cent of the respondents were allegedly attacked by wild animals, such as leopard, jackal, etc. Ten per cent of the respondents were bitten by wild insects such as scorpion, etc. Similar findings were observed in the Sri Lankan tea plantations (Employers' Federation of Ceylon in collaboration with the ILO, 1997).

Site of Injury Caused to the Respondents: The researcher could notice that more than half of the respondents (54 per cent) had injury on their lower limbs, while one-sixth (16 per cent) of them had injury on their upper limbs. A very small number

(5 per cent) of the respondents were injured on the trunk/abdomen of their body. Similar findings were observed in the Sri Lankan tea plantations (Employers' Federation of Ceylon in collaboration with the ILO, 1997).

Reporting of Injury to Others: Nearly one-third (33 per cent) of the respondents had reported the injury to their colleagues, while one-third (34 per cent) of the respondents did not report it to anybody. More than one-tenth (12 per cent) of the respondents had reported the injury to their superiors, while an equal figure (11 per cent) of the respondents had intimated about their injury to others such as field conductor (AFC).

Nature of Treatment Provided to the Respondents: Nearly half of the respondents (46 per cent) who had been injured were administered first aid, while a small number (7 per cent) of the respondents had to undergo minor procedures to treat their injury.

Work-related Pain Experienced by the Respondents: More than three-fourth (86 per cent) of the respondents experienced pain due to work-related activity in the last one month, while nearly one-sixth (14 per cent) of the respondents did not feel it. Out of those respondents, who experienced pain due to work-related activity, nearly three-fourth (73 per cent) of the respondents experienced pain which was minor in nature, while more than one-tenth (13 per cent) of the respondents experienced severe pain. Similar findings were observed in the Sri Lankan tea plantations (Employers' Federation of Ceylon in collaboration with the ILO, 1997).

Number of Times the Pain was Experienced in the Last One Month Due to Work-related Activity: Nearly half of the respondents (49 per cent) had work-related pain less than three times, while nearly one-sixth (14 per cent) of the respondents experienced pain between three to less than five times. More than one-tenth (12 per cent) of the respondents felt pain in their body between five times to less than eight times.

Causes of Pain Experienced by the Respondents: More than three-fourth (77 per cent) of the respondents associated their pain with the task of plucking, while five and three per cent of the respondents linked it to the task of pruning and tipping, respectively. A negligible number (1 per cent) of the respondents felt that the pain was caused due to the work of chopping and weeding in the plantation fields. Similar findings were observed in the Sri Lankan tea plantations (Employers' Federation of Ceylon in collaboration with the ILO, 1997).

Site of the Pain Due to Work-related Activity on the Body of the Respondents: Nearly one-third (32 per cent) and one-fourth (26 per cent) of the respondents suffered from work-related pain on their back and shoulder, respectively. Each a very small number (5 per cent) of the respondents experienced head ache and pain in their neck, and upper limbs. Nearly two-fifth (18 per cent) of the respondents experienced pain at their lower limbs. Similar findings were observed in the Sri Lankan tea plantations (Employers' Federation of Ceylon in collaboration with the ILO, 1997).

Nature of Treatment Provided to the respondents who experienced pain due to work-related activity: Many (60 per cent) of the respondents did not receive medical care and treatment even though they experienced pain and wanted to treat the same. Nearly one-fourth (23 per cent) of the respondents received first aid after having experienced pain and reported the same either to their colleagues or to their superiors, field conductor, assistant field conductor, etc. A negligible number (2 and 1 per cent) of the respondents underwent minor and major surgery for their pain caused due to their work-related activities.

Health Problems of the Tea Plantation Workers

Practices Affecting the Health of the Respondents: It was noticed by the researcher that the tea plantation workers resorted to various practices that affected their health. More than three-fourth (88 per cent) of the respondents consumed alcoholic drinks which they felt that it helped them to adopt to their climatic conditions. Compared to Coonoor division, number of workers was more in the Naduvattam division in terms of usage of alcoholic drinks.

With regard to smoking, nearly one-sixth (16 per cent) of the respondents resorted to such a practice, while more than three-fourth (84 per cent) of the respondents preferred using betel leaf and nuts. Though smoking was practiced among the male workers, the usage of betel leaf and a nut was practiced by women workers.

It could be inferred that male workers preferred consuming illicit liquor, though available in limited quantity and preferred using substances such as mava, pan and other similar items inducing kick. Though more than one-tenth (12 per cent) of the respondents resorted to both substance usage and consumption of illicit liquor, it could be assumed that all male workers preferred taking both. A very small number (6 per cent) of the respondents, all of them being male workers, played gambling in both the divisions of Coonoor and Naduvattam.

Similar findings were observed in coffee plantations of Brazil and sugar cane plantations of Bolivia (Watson, Kelly; Achinelli, Moira Laura, 2008) and (Laura Baas, G.K. Lieten, 2011)

Exposure to Chemicals and Health Problems Caused the Respondents: More than three-fourth (89 per cent) of the respondents felt that the chances of developing skin problems were bright for the tea plantation workers, while more than three-fourth (77 per cent) of the respondents had associated such as health problem due to spraying of pesticides to the tea leaves. More than three-fourth (87 per cent) of the respondents accepted the existence of labour infertility rate among women workers, while an equal figure (89 per cent) of the respondents had associated it with the inhalation of pesticides and fertilizers. Similar findings were observed in the Sri Lankan tea plantations (Employers' Federation of Ceylon in collaboration with the ILO, 1997).

Other Health Problems Faced by the Workers: More than one-third (38 per cent) of the respondents had fever with cough, while more than half (55 per cent) of the respondents experienced body pain due to carrying out work-related activities. Nearly one-third (32 per cent) of the respondents had pain in their spinal cord which they associated with the necessity of frequently bending to collect tea leaves. Similar findings were observed in the Sri Lankan tea plantations (Employers' Federation of Ceylon in collaboration with the ILO, 1997).

Sexual Practices Noticed among the Tea Plantation Workers in the Opinion of the Respondents: More than one-tenth (13 per cent) of the respondents accepted the existence of extra-marital affairs among the workers, while only three per cent of the workers admitted the existence of pre-marital sex among the workers. Nearly one-tenth (9 per cent) of the respondents acknowledged that these women workers were subjected to sexual harassment by the male workers. Similar findings were observed in the research study carried out in the four plantations, i.e. tea, coffee, rubber and cardamom from the states of Assam, West Bengal, Tamil Nadu, Kerala, Karnataka and Tripura, which showed that (3.0 per cent) of the cases of sexual harassment were reported (Labour Bureau, Ministry of Labour and Employment, Government of India, 1975).

Perception of the Plantation Workers about the Overall Functioning of the TANTEA Management: More than three-fourth (79 per cent) of the respondents acknowledged that the trade unions were insensitive in handling the grievances of the workers, while more than three-fourth (87 per cent) of the respondents were of the opinion that the unions did not facilitate the workers to ventilate their grievances arising out of working conditions. An equal figure (85 per cent) of the respondents felt that the trade union functionaries did not take efforts for securing the statutory welfare measures meant for them. Ninety-one per cent of the respondents felt that the trade unions were not concerned about problems faced by the workers, while eighty seven per cent of the respondents said that the trade unions were not interested in their welfare.

Most (96 per cent) of the respondent felt that the trade unions did not undertake negotiations with the TANTEA management in good faith. Many (65 per cent) of the respondents denied the claims made by the trade unions that they get jobs to the family members of the deceased workers. Most (95 per cent) of the respondents felt that the trade unions were more interested in the collection of the subscription fee from the workers than anything else.

More than three-fourth (83 per cent) of the respondents felt that the management has not been concerned about the general welfare of the plantation workers. A similar figure (83 per cent) of the respondents felt that the divisional manager was not available as well as accessible for the workers to know about their problems. All of the respondents were of the opinion that the senior manager-industrial relations were not available and inaccessible for them to address their grievances.

None of the respondents felt that the concerned senior level superiors encouraged the workers to discuss with him any issues that affected their working conditions. More than three-fourth (89 per cent) of the respondents felt that the top level superiors did not have effective control over the entire divisions of the TANTEA. Most (95 per cent) of the respondents did not agree that the joint managing director has been holding frequent meetings with the respective workers, while an equal figure (94 per cent) of the respondents felt that the management could handle the general administration and labour problems in a better way. None of the respondents acknowledged that the top most superior has been encouraging the workers to ventilate their grievances.

Job Satisfaction of the Tea Plantation Workers

Gender and Job Satisfaction: The proportion of job satisfaction observed among the female and male tea plantation workers has been 33 per cent and 25 per cent, respectively. Though the proportion of job satisfaction was found to be higher among female workers compared to the male workers, the difference was not statistically significant.

Age and Job Satisfaction: It has been found that the proportion of job satisfaction across the various age groups ranged from 25 per cent to 39 per cent. It has been noted that as the age group increased, the proportion of job satisfaction also increased.

Educational Qualification and Job Satisfaction: It has been observed that the proportion of job satisfaction across the various educational statuses was not significantly different.

Experience and Job Satisfaction: The working experience of the tea plantation workers was classified as one to less than ten years, ten years to twenty years, and more than twenty years. The association between working experience and job satisfaction has been examined.

Ethnicity and Job Satisfaction: As regards to association between ethnicity of the tea plantation workers and the job satisfaction, the proportion of the job satisfaction observed among the Sri Lankan refugees/estate Tamils and local Tamils was 32.3 per cent and 33.3 per cent, respectively.

Type of Residence and Job Satisfaction: The proportion of job satisfaction was significantly different with respect to the type of residence possessed. It implied that there was an association between type of residence of the workers and job satisfaction. It has been noted that majority of the respondents who owned their house had job satisfaction compared to those staying either in the company quarters or in the rented/leased house.

Recommendations and Suggestions

For the Government of Tamil Nadu

Optimal Utilization of Resources and Effective Management of Cost Cutting Measures

Effective Management of the Guest Houses: The guest houses of the TANTEA in the Nilgiris' District being located in the prime locations could have been leased out to either Tamil Nadu Tourism Development Corporation Limited or private corporate hotels. This would amount to greater profit generation and could support the loss driven TANTEA, since most of the time, these guest houses were vacant. During the occupancy of these guest houses under the control of the TANTEA, many plantation workers (numbering from six to ten) have been deployed in the guest houses to attend to the needs of the VIPs who stayed over there. This has caused havoc to the farm operations of the tea industry. The deputed tea plantation workers are also skilled in carrying out electrical repair works, plumbing, civil, inner decorations and household work and to be specific cooking as well. Hence, the resources of these tea plantation workers are placed at the disposal of these VIPs who take possession of the guest houses. The guest houses are usually occupied by the Ministers of Tamil Nadu State Government and Central Government and their relatives, Governor of the respective states, their relatives, politicians, executives in the rank of IAS, IPS and second-line officers. Sometimes, it is allotted to the higher authorities and officials of the TANTEA to entertain their family members and guests. This could have been avoided by taking suitable action in this regard.

There should be a fair and transparent system in allotting these guest houses as there is always an allegation that there is no official recording of allotting the guest houses in many occasions.

Colonial mindset of the top most officials of the TANTEA, who used to avail maximum benefits and welfare measures apart from highest pay packets and other privileges pose real threat to the development of the tea industry. They enjoy all luxurious lifestyles, privileges and welfare amenities at the cost of interests of the labour in the form of absence of statutory and voluntary welfare measures, otherwise made available to the workers with the huge sum allocated for the top brass of the TANTEA.

Effective Management of Human Resources: Excessive and undue middle and top level management staff could be absorbed in other government departments or Public Sector Undertakings (PSUs) of the State Government of Tamil Nadu, since there is no much work load for these middle and top level management staff.

Infrastructure: These infrastructural bottlenecks faced by this hill tea industry are not a new problem. The topographical variation in the region has made the accessibility poor. There is tremendous lack of transport and communication, energy and irrigation which have profoundly hampered the productivity in these tea estates. Transport systems are still at nascent stage that some terrains are still inaccessible. This make the task of reaching (in some areas) adequate bush care varying from manuring to managerial supervision almost a formidable venture. The underdeveloped nature of roads and communication has made the cost of production extra ordinarily high in these areas. Besides, this has a negative impact on the health, psychology and socio-economic welfare of the poor labour class. Though this sector attracted immense importance in the past, neither the management nor the government machineries endeavored to development these facilities. Since these are the arteries of development, a strong plea should be made by the trade unions to construct and complete this essential field of development.

The international upheaval in the prices of crude have an adverse impact on these languishing tea gardens. The expensive fuel (petroleum and coal) along with the record power crisis in Tamil Nadu, in the last ten years have virtually made some of the systems and operations redundant. Now, no tea garden can rely on this ever-fluctuating supply. It is high to explore the possibility of harnessing the perennial rivers of the hills like Upper Bavani and the Pycara for multipurpose projects. They can be a major source of energy. The State Government should expedite the construction and the completion of projects already on the card.

Besides, tea garden situated by the side of streams and waterfalls can always test the feasibility of exploiting them for power from water driven turbines.

Further, it is essential on the part of the management to find out the possibility of developing water reservoirs by taping the nearby seasonal streams and rivulets which could help in irrigating the gardens during the dry season. This way, they can intensify the cropping pattern.

However, while undertaking all these costly ventures the question about financial resources would naturally acquire eminence. Who would finance these schemes? So the best alternative is to adequately exploit the Central Government's present rehabilitation scheme.

Common Fund: Another alternative would be to make a Hill Tea Gardens Common Fund for the TANTEA on the basis of size and production of the estates. This can be made by pulling together all the estates somewhat in the framework of International Monetary Fund (IMF) which in times of extreme necessity or any major financial misbalance can lend money to the deserving gardens. This is more realistic in the backdrop of the present costly borrowings from the banking and the non-banking financial intermediaries.

For the TANTEA

Betterment of Working Conditions: Management has to reorient their strategy if they want a quick rejuvenation of their tea gardens. This includes not only the fulfillment of labourers' genuine demands but a new socio-economic orientation. They should open up more and more training institutions in all phase of tea production. By organizing training camps and other technical demonstrations they can give a scientific and more advanced orientation to the labour productivity. The concept of industrial democracy should be introduced so as to provide labourers with the sense of belonging and ample scope for their participation. The reduction of the excise duty in 1984 from a heavy amount of ₹ 1.33 per kg to a meager 20 paise per kg., till December 1986 by the Centre and State Governments' relief in the rural employment cess, would certainly encourage the management as it would reduce the overall cost of production and at the same time fetch a higher profit margin. Taking advantage of this relief, the management must consider equitably dividing this dividend and ensuring that it trickles down to each labour household. The government should extend this relief at least as long as the financial crisis is overcome.

Payment of better wages, provision of better health, welfare and social security measures to the tea plantation workers.

Recognition of Trade Unions and Bargaining with them in Good Faith: The management with the help of governmental machinery should open up more and more schools and health amenities in the garden. Special programme for female education right up to high school level and other adult education facilities should be introduced. The labourers should be increasingly made aware of importance and incentives of family welfare measures floated by the government. As the labourers become more educated the probability of their resorting in violence and getting misguided would be drastically reduced. Because, if we analyze the present scenario, the misunderstanding between the management and labourers are mainly on petty issues generally misguided and instigated by some vested interests. Incidents of strikes and demonstrations are sheer waste of human capital.

This exacerbates the whole society creating a permanent disunity and feeling of animosity. The weak and minority labourers get frightened, the majorities get overwhelmed and in both the cases, they will lack their interest and effective participation in tea production further affecting the productivity.

Harmony between the Workers and the Management: So, the productivity in the labour front can be increased only if there is adequate promotion of harmonious labour-management relations, adequate economic incentives, avoidance of multiplicity of trade unions, encouraging participative process, eliminating fear of retrenchment and exploitation of the labour class and by setting up of the more and more technical, health and educational institutions for the toiling class and of course the motivation to adopt newer technologies.

Replantation and Extension: TANTEA extra-ordinarily lags behind in the replantation, extension and in fillings of the vacancies schemes. The management appears to be looking for a quick and short-period profit, did not dare and like to face the loss of crop emerging out of the period between uprooting of the old bushes and commencement of harvest from the new plants. The management of the TANTEA has been discouraged by the prevailing acute sickness of the tea industry, fiscal structure, internationally low prices for the final products, high cost of production, increasing labour unrest and other technological drawback. But there is no escape from the present situation. The issue of replantation should be given utmost priority and importance at any cost. Any delay in doing so would only place the whole economy into doldrums which may take any critical dimension making the TANTEA vulnerable to any sort of political and social mismanagement and chaos.

Bush Care and Plucking: The planting of first quality of clones and the mere use of fertilizer would not yield any fruitful results until and unless the gardens go for proper bush care, efficient plucking and strict managerial supervision. The labour attitudes and performance of labour cannot be overlooked. From the very inception, the tea nurseries play a prominent role. It has been found that nurseries were sometimes neglected and built at inapproachable location. An appropriate location of nurseries and a constant and expert supervision would enhance a probability of getting maximum number of healthy bushes. Systematic and scientific pruning must be done to avoid bush sickness like creation of knots (due to continuous pruning at the same height) on the hamperage causing constriction of the flow of the sap. This further result into disproportionate return of the crop in comparison to the inputs applied.

Bush Sanitation: Bush sanitation is another major aspect generally not taken care of in the tea gardens. Tea bushes can be healthy and high yielding only if they get rid of knotting frames, congested top hamper mosses and lichens and other obnoxious grasses. Plantation protection can be ensured through cleanliness of the tea sections, proper drainage, effective soil culture and proper shading of the area and required spraying based on seasonal needs with appropriate chemical application and correct dose.

Soil Erosion: Soil erosion has been caused due to excessive rain fall which saturates the upper mantle of the soil. This, however, could be prevented to a large extent by a scientific pruning method. The bushes should be slope pruned and made to touch each other so that all beating action of rain directly falling upon the exposed soil surface can be checked. A substantial quantity of crops is lost because of the estates' inability to pluck. This low plucking occurs mainly because of ineffective management and lacking devotion of the labourers. There are examples that some of the tea gardens in Darjeeling have improved their productivity simply by more careful and concentrated plucking. Plucking are done of maximum quantity of leaf of the desired quality and secondly, it does not adversely affect the health and vigor of the bush.

Labour and Management

For the Workers: There is nothing like human capital in this universe. Labourers are not only the vital instruments of tea production but are also the moving force in the tea economy. Whatever technological progress, improvement in seed varieties may be made, they will bear the least fruit in the absence of effective participation by the labourers. Labourers play a significant role in enhancing overall productivity in the tea industry as they are involved at every stage of production starting from nursery development to the final preparation of tea packets.

Strictly speaking, the labour force is not a homogeneous entity. It is made up of range of skills and specialties that embody varying amount of education and training. So it is reasonable to suppose that their contribution to the productive process vary accordingly. This has been mainly attributed to the factors like inadequate training to the workers, socio-economic backwardness of the workers, lack of technological and technical aid to the workers, existence of a huge surplus labour force in the form of disguised unemployment, the increasing bandhs and violence by the labourers resulting into diminution in working desire and quality, effort and psychological depression.

For the Employer: Management are usually of the view that the labourers have been increasingly displaying negligence on the part of their duties. The available sample of a study revealed that the time that should have been spent on plucking by the labour in peak period is spent on something else. The result was that in a day of eight to nine hours in some garden 3.6 to 3.7 hours was spent on actual plucking. The rest was wasted. This is generally accepted by the workers also. They attribute this slackness mainly to the unattractive incentive in the form of money and other facilities from the management side. The monetary incentive on the extra leave plucked over and above the allotted task is generally found to be much lower in the tea gardens owned by the TANTEA than in the gardens controlled by the private tea companies. Further, this is made more difficult by the increasing politicization of the labourers and their upward participation in the local politics.

For the Trade Unions: Awareness of responsibilities and effectively managing the problems faced by them: Trade unionism is a prerogative in a democratic nation like ours. The duties of a trade union are not simply limited to pressurize management to fall in the lines of fulfilling workers' demand. Trade unions have to be more dynamic. In other words, they have to make labour class aware of not only their socio-political and economic rights but also of their duties, discipline and devotion to their professions. They should be given the chance to understand the charm of non-violent and democratic politics based on humanitarian goals and aspirations. Trade unions should educate the labour class on the line that they are as vital as management in any tea gardens and about their role in increasing the productivity in the gardens. The trade unions through its affiliated federations must effectively manage the following problems facing them: multiplicity of trade unions, intra-union rivalry, lack of internal leadership in the tea plantations and lack of coordination and support among the external trade union leadership.

Source of supply of labour must be regulated by the trade unions: One of the most critical problems faced by this hill tea industry is the onslaught of labour supply. This has not only upset the whole economic structure but has also led to huge health and unemployment problem. The alarming growth of labour population in numbers outstripping available or anticipated resources essential for sustaining such growth is a threat to the whole tea industry. The qualitative dimension of this growth has caused even greater concern. This is the steady deterioration of the physical and mental calibrate of labourers through persistent ill health and under-nutrition afflicting large proportions of successive generation of their children, during the crucial years of their growth and development. This frightening scenario is not an isolated case. It is an impact of the general deterioration in the national health and nutrition scene, only difference being the magnitude of its impact.

It is unexpected from a labourer having impaired physical stamina and poor mental abilities to provide a high productivity in his performance.

The number of women labourer is quite high in the hill tea gardens of the nilgiris district. Most of them are educationally backward and superstitious. It is an established fact that higher the literacy rates among the women folk, the lower the birth rate. This is amply proved by the experience of Kerala. Their backwardness along with many socio-cultural reasons, these women labourers preferred to ignore the governmental family welfare measures thereby putting spurt in the population pressure. This further leads to all sorts of economic and social tension making them vulnerable to any mischief's prompted by the vested interest to have petty political gains.

For the Government of India

Marketing: Marketing is one of the most menacing and critical problems for the hill tea garden of the Nilgiris' District. About 12 million kg of the total production of the Nilgiris' District is exported. Cochin and Pollachi auction is by far the most important disposal centre of Nilgiris tea.

Auction System: Before analyzing the marketing trend, a short overview of the auction system is worth noting. Auctions are held fortnightly or monthly. Quantities coming up for sale are catalogued beforehand and catalogues are closed a few days before the auction. Quantities are generally regulated in an attempt to maintain an even supply over the year mainly to minimize price fluctuation. Samples of the teas catalogued for each auction are circulated to buyers. The selling of the tea at the auction is entrusted to the brokers who work on a commission from both seller and buyer. Prior to the sale, selling brokers make their valuations of the teas catalogued, based on the market at the previous week's auction.

Before the auction, selling brokers visit buyers, obtain an idea of their likely requirement at the forthcoming auction and generally attempt to gauge the feel of the market. In the meantime, the buyers have tasted their samples and formed their own valuations. On auction day the selling brokers sell off their catalogues and each lot is knocked down to the highest bidder. Where bids are not sufficient high, a selling broker would refuse the sale.

It is clear that the buyers and selling brokers are the two agents mainly involved in auction.

Cost of Production vs. Price: The average price of tea produced in the Nilgiris' District is generally much higher than tea from Darjeeling, Terai and Dooars, but this high price is usually more than offset by its high cost of production. In most cases, the Nilgiris variety fetched double the price of other varieties. Though the cost of production has been increasing, a sharp increase could be seen immediately after 1974 and 1979 when there were staggering rise in the oil prices and the subsequent rate of inflation.

Auction and Its Buyers: In the prevailing auction system, the scope of fetching more remunerative prices are drastically limited by a monophony situation, i.e. about 80% (65% in 1983) of the total product of the hills in our country is purchased by one party, the Soviet Union. The high concentration of buying power minimizes the extent of competitive bidding. Most of the managers are against this arrangement arising out of Indo-USSR Trade Agreements. They are also concerned about the rupee trade which deprives them of large amount of foreign exchange.

It is argued that the small number of large buyers regularly connive among themselves to keep prices low. They go for a tactic agreement to form a collusive monophony. This is usually done in two ways, viz. resigning from competition and the facility of dividing. In the first case, the bidders because of their pre-agreement start resigning from the bidding after a particular level thereby put a stop on the upward bidding. In the second case, a buyer is permitted to share a lot with a prescribed number of other buyers. This is a clear case of eliminating competition. They justify it, on the ground that often a buyer, particularly a small buyer, does not want the entire lot and would not bid for it at all unless the facility of dividing was available. The validity of this argument is weakened somewhat by the fact that many divisions are exclusively between the large buyers.

Though the fluctuation in prices challenges the authenticity of the first argument, the practice is prevalent and well known. Two measures are suggested to eliminate the abuse of dividing facility, viz. large buyers suitably defined could be prohibited from dividing with each other and the number of buyers who can share a lot could be reduced.

It seems that the transmission mechanism in the tea marketing is not at all perfect. The demand of tea of consumer countering is transmitted through buyers-exporters who operate at auction. Because of various factors like communication, lacking professionalism and inadequate advertisements, the original demand is not usually reflected in the auction which makes the auction prices lower. The fall in the number of buyers over the years is mainly because of changes in wholesale and retail tea marketing. Recently, because of the substantial increase in buying on Indian tea by government organization in East Europe and Middle East coupled with the reduction in the number of buyers have made the producers vulnerable to the dictates of buyers.

The intense involvement of brokers in the tea auction is another hazard for the tea produced by the TANTEA. These brokers get a few share or per cent of profit from both the sellers and buyers as commission besides kgs of each variety of tea as the sample for auction. They are invariably alleged to have resorted to surreptious activities while shouting auctions.

Brand Fraud: As a substitute for the regular availability of pure national packs, national tea promotion organization have permitted blenders the use of certain symbols to denote that a pack is of a predominantly, say, the Nilgiris variety, provided a certain per cent of tea in the pack is from TANTEA. Since there is no reliable way of establishing the per centage of tea of any particular area or country which is contained in any particular pack and monitoring is difficult, the concession is wide open to abuse ironically, at this trading stage only, it is alleged that every year considerable million kilo grams of mixed spurious stuff is sold under the charmed legend of Nilgiris' tea whereas the actual annual production does not exceed 12 million kilo grams. This stuff is sold both in domestic and international markets. This practice represents three things firstly there is a craze for Indian made tea, secondly, the real Indian made tea is not readily available to meet such a high demand and thirdly, the spurious blenders are having free time.

This further disproves the basic tenet of market mechanism in economics. In other words, on the one hand a clear trend is there for a high demand of Indian made tea and on the other hand the real Indian made tea finds it difficult to fetch a price even at par with cost of production. The basic flaw in the tea marketing is that the product being promoted is not sufficiently available. This suggests that the tea in the form in which consumers require must be readily available in the consuming market.

Non-auction Sales: In order to avoid all these disadvantages and malpractices in the auction system, the producers have developed their own marketing arrangements nearer the consuming centres. This has largely eliminated the profit of the middlemen, to the ultimate benefit of the consumer. The various promotional agencies have been suggesting the tea producers to be closer to the consumer in terms of marketing, cost and quality. Responding to this, these producers have developed their own consumer packs, retail outlets, advertising and sales promotion agencies and have provided consumer with a quality product at a reasonable price. All this has necessarily meant a reduction in the volume of tea in the auction which have in turn drastically reduced the profit margin of certain segment of the tea trade having a major vested interest in the auctions. Non-auction sale, sometimes described as private, ex-garden, ex-factory, ex-warehouse, forward contract have started to assume a larger dimension.

In order to review the marketing of tea, Government of India appointed Tandon Committee in 1978. This committee recommended the ex-garden sales with some safeguards because of its intrinsic advantages. Those stipulated safeguards were," (1) weak garden may be offered suitable financial assistance, tailor to meet their needs, (2) all gardens should inform a monitoring authority, say, the Tea Board, of their sales ex-garden, C and F of auctions and the prices at which they were made. The ex-garden prices should be compared with the auction prices to ensure that generally speaking they were on a par, after allowing for the difference in costs. Based on the experience of the Tea Board with the monitoring system, if it is found that the prices are comparable, the system can be allowed to continue as it is, but if it is discovered the ex-garden sales of comparable quantities in comparable period were significantly below the auction prices, the loopholes should be plugged. The monitoring should however be continued both to collect information and keep a continuous watch, (3) after a year of experience of the monitoring of the study, it would be also be interesting to see whether the comparative position of auctions and ex-garden sales has altered in favour of auctions or ex-garden sales. It is possible that once producers are made accountable for their ex-garden sales, some may prefer to deal through auctions in which case it would be best not to interfere with these who genuinely find it advantageous to sell ex-garden.

Unfortunately, the monitoring system is yet to be set up. However, out of non-auction sales the advantages to a producer lie in (1) an improved cash flow position, (2) a premium in price on account of the saving in expenditure which will be incurred in sending the teas to auction and (3) the development of a market, domestic or foreign for his own crop. Over the long run, having popularized his tea, he can except a premium in price and a preference for his tea.

In case of Nilgiris' tea, marketing problem could be solved only either by diversifying markets and reducing Soviet monopoly as a buyer or by creating an export agency based in the Nilgiris' District only. The tea companies of the Nilgiris' District can themselves initiate an auction based on their past experience of market of their crops.

The past experience reveals that Germany which generally buys second grading tea, pays much higher than what the Soviet Union pays for the first grade tea.

For the Government of Tamil Nadu and India

Lacking Advertisement and Promotion: The promotional strategy has to be renewed. Both generic and uninational promotions should be revitalized. The traditional tea buyer like UK who imports one-third of its total import from India can be induced to buy more orthodox by ensuring that the quality control followed in India fits into the strict quality factor control and regulation prevailing in UK. The quality factor is a major hindrance in selling Indian tea there. London auction centre should be utilized more vigorously mainly to (1) reduce the pressure on primary auctions, (2) to take advantage of higher prices sometimes anticipated in London relative to primary auction and (3) to keep certain markets continually available in London for fear that in their absence buyers will turn permanently to alternatives.

Need for Brand Promotion Scheme

The individual brand promotion scheme should be made more operational and popular. These various tea gardens belonging to different companies who fetch extraordinarily high prices in auction centres should be given ample scope to promote their brand directly in overseas country. In this context, Tea Board's brand promotion programme for values added tea is worth noting.

Under the scheme, a corpus is created. The tea companies intending to launch brand promotion in overseas markets will be required to prepare project reports, relative to the market in view and the brand it wants to promote. The companies will have to give their expenditure projections on a three year basis but apportioned on annual basis. While 50 per cent of the approved yearly expenditure will be the responsibility of the concerned companies, the other 50 per cent will be met by the Tea Board, which will release funds well in advance to facilitate launching of brand promotion scheme according to pre-determined schedules. Companies will have to repay the loan from the corpus and such repayment, in installment, will start, after three years, i.e. after the Brand Promotion Schemes has ceased to be in operation. The progress of the scheme is to be monitored once in every six months. The scheme will obviate the need for companies to permission of the RBI on year basis.

Besides this scheme, recently there are various marketing schemes including that to give a brand name of Ooty to only those blends which have 50% or more of Ooty tea in the mix. Tea Board's efforts for better marketing of Indian made tea had met with some success. It had persuaded both Poland and Iraq to fix one million kg of Indian made tea each in 1984.

4

Occupational Safety and Health in the Tea Plantation Sector in Sri Lanka, 1996-97

Background

There is an acute shortage of information relating to safety and health in the tea growing and manufacturing sector, though this is still a major foreign exchange contributor to the national economy in Sri Lanka. Many mechanical and chemical hazards exist in the plantations, where a large number of unskilled and semi-skilled workers are employed. Due to management and worker ignorance, negligent use of fertilizers and pest and weed controlling chemicals and bad work practices in some estate factories, serious hazards have been created and many accidents have occurred. About 15% of the total poisonings and deaths in Sri Lanka are caused due to occupational accidents due to the intake of harmful substances. The impact of these harmful substances that enter the environment is yet to be quantified.

Development Objective

The survey and the findings would assist in the on-going national effort in improving the standard of Occupational Safety and Health (OSH) in Sri Lanka. It could be used as information, or conclusions in order to create awareness of existing OSH problems and to find solutions, where necessary to enhance safety and health standards.

Immediate Objectives

1. The report is a compilation of OSH information and accident data from 161 tea growing and manufacturing estates. The findings would assist the member companies to reduce OSH and accident-related costs, by providing solutions to the vital aspects of safety that are highlighted in this study. The sample selected for this study represents different estates, which vary from size, number of employees, the degree of hazards, the level safety awareness, safety standards and number of accidents.
2. Another objective would be to provide information to other interested parties. The authorities responsible for safety and health find it difficult, or do not have the capacity, to monitor such information, especially after privatization. The availability of safety information with the EFC would assist the government and, perhaps even the ILO, in looking at these issues objectively and finding suitable remedies.
3. Another purpose is to attempt to link up with other agencies that are involved with OSH in Sri Lanka in order to exchange and inter-link information and resources relating to OSH on the plantations.
4. Lastly, the data would be used as a tool to eventually train management personnel, particularly superintendents, involved in OSH in the plantations. In turn they would be able to impart knowledge on proper OSH practices among estate workers in order to minimize hazards and prevent future accidents.

Methodology

Phase I of the project involved an extensive survey among the tea estates managed by 21 Plantation Management Companies, who are members of The Employer's Federation of Ceylon. The estates surveyed are located in the Central hills, Sabaragamuwa, Western, Uva and Southern provinces in Sri Lanka.

A comprehensive questionnaire seeking information on prevalent occupational safety and health standards and accident records for the year 1996 and for the first half of 1997 was designed for this purpose by the EFC.

The questionnaire was sent to 408 tea estates managed by 21 Plantation Management Companies in December '97. It sought information on the number of work-related accidents that occurred in the estate factory and the field, the nature of injury to the workman, the area of the anatomy to which the injury was caused, the cause of injury, the number of days of work lost due to work-related accidents, the number of victims, severity of the injury, amounts paid as medical costs or compensation, and, information on safety training, health and welfare (*Copy of questionnaire annexed*).

161 estates submitted completed responses. Thus, a 39% response was achieved at the end of the survey.

Based on some further suggestions by Dr. Ranjith De Alwis, Deputy Commissioner, Occupational Hygiene Division of the Department of Labour, and Safety and Health Consultant to the ILO, an additional questionnaire was sent in March '98, to the estates that responded to the initial questionnaire (*Copy of the additional questionnaire annexed*). This questionnaire sought information on accident records and investigation, types of fertilizer, insecticides and fungicides used, the number of workers involved in tasks such as spraying, use of personal protective equipment, and, safety and health training programmes.

It was envisaged that the responses could be obtained by April '98. However, due to an unforeseen postal delay of two months, all responses to the additional questionnaire were not received by the project completion date of 31 May 1998. Reminders were sent to the respondents requesting them to submit their completed responses once again. The final report was completed by 30 June 1998.

The responses indicate that, there is much enthusiasm in participating in projects such as this, and to share information on health and safety levels on the plantations. It is been very satisfactory to achieve a response rate of 39%, particularly considering the fact that many estates do not maintain or have up-to-date health and safety records.

It is also encouraging to note that a few estates surveyed have a very impressive safety record with no OSH problems or accidents being reported during the period covered by the survey.

Tea Plantations in Sri Lanka

The growing of tea in Sri Lanka commenced in 1867 and emerged as the major plantation crop after coffee plantations were destroyed by coffee leaf blight. In the beginning, a migrant labour force of nearly 150,000 persons was brought to the country from South India to be employed on the plantations. For a long period, the plantation sector was the primary sector that offered the highest level of regular employment. In 1953, the contribution of the plantation sector to total employment in the economy was 29%. In 1996, it had declined to 20%. In terms of providing a livelihood to people in the country, this sector is second only to the rice-growing sector.

Changes in Management and Ownership

As the tea sector experienced problems of management and profit making under State ownership, a restructuring program was initiated in 1992. Twenty-three regional plantation companies were formed. The management of the estates was handed over to private management companies on a profit-sharing basis for a five-year contract period. These management companies did not have a stake in the ownership and the management contracts were short termed. Hence, there was a disincentive to invest in capital expenditure, which was vital for the development of the sector.

In 1995, a major structural change took place, and shares in the regional plantation companies were sold to the private sector. It was anticipated that private sector participation would encourage investment in fertilizer application, replanting and investment in new plant and machinery.

Contribution to the National Economy

The tea industry has contributed immensely towards the foreign exchange earnings of the country and was the single largest foreign exchange earner for a considerable period of time. However, the tea sector, which played a dominant role in the economy in the past, has now shown a declining trend. The contribution to the GDP from the tea sector, which stood at around 8% in the early 1950s, had declined to 1.5% of the GDP by 1996.

Location of Tea Plantations

Tea grown in Sri Lanka is divided into two categories. Depending on the elevation of growth, tea is categorized as high grown and low grown. The area under tea plantations increased from 225,000 hectares in 1950 to the highest level of 245,000 hectares in 1981. However, it had declined to 188,000 hectares by 1996. Marginal tea lands have been used for other crops and housing. Tea growing was earlier concentrated in the mid elevations (600-1,200 meters) and higher elevations (1,200 meters and above). Tea growing has extended to low elevations (600 meters and below) gradually. The distribution of tea lands in Sri Lanka is mainly among the Central hills, Sabaragamuwa, Uva, Southern districts of Galle and Matara and in some areas of the southwestern slopes of the island.

The Sample

One hundred and sixty-one (161) tea estates were selected as the sample for the purpose of this study. These estates vary by land extent and location, people employed, amount of chemicals and fertilizers used in the fields, safety levels, accident statistics, and, safety awareness and training.

Table 4.1: Number of Estates Selected from each Planting Region and the Administrative District to which the Estate Belongs

District or Region	Province	No. of Estates Covered	% of Sample from Area
Dickoya	Central	1	0.62%
Hatton	Central	2	1.24%

District or Region	Province	No. of Estates Covered	% of Sample from Area
Kandy	Central	5	3.1%
Maskeliya	Central	2	1.24%
Matale	Central	4	2.4%
Nuwara Eliya	Central	42	26%
Kegalle	Sabaragamuwa	25	15.5%
Ratnapura	Sabaragamuwa	20	12.4%
Galle	Southern	7	4.3%
Matara	Southern	6	3.7%
Badulla	Uva	33	20.4%
Hanwella	Western	1	0.62%
Kalutara	Western	13	8%

The majority of the estates included were from the Central and Sabaragamuwa Provinces. A total of 56 (35%) estates were included from the Central Province, while, 45 (28%) estates were included from the Sabaragamuwa Province. 33 (20%) estates were from tea plantations in the Uva Province, 14 (9%) estates from the Western province, and 13 (8%) from the Southern Province.

Tea Production

The manufacture of tea increased from 136 million kilograms in 1948 to 258 million kilograms in 1996. A clear improvement in tea production was witnessed after the privatization of the industry. Productivity in the tea sector has also increased. The average yield has increased from about 650 kilograms per hectare in the early 1950s to about 1,500 kilograms per hectare in 1996. At present, Sri Lanka is the leading tea supplier to the world with an approximate market share of 21%.

Employment in the Tea Plantations

Of a total labour force of approximately 400,000, there are approximately 280,000 workers, including casual workers employed by the plantation management companies, who are members of The Employer's of Ceylon. This is about 70% total plantation labour in the country.

Employees Covered by the Survey

Approximately, 115,000 employees are employed in the 161 estates that were included in the survey, which is nearly 29% of the total workforce employed in the tea sector. The number of employees covered in the survey consisted of 51,175 (44.5%) male workers, 61,525 (53.5%) female workers and 2,070 (1.8%) child workers (children above the age of 14 years and up to 16 years).

Approximately, 102,350 (89%) of the total labour were employed in the fields, of which 42% are males, 56% are females and 1.8% are considered children. Nearly 7,590 (6.6%) of the total employees covered, were employed in the estate factory which carries out the entire manufacturing process of tea. Of this figure 62.5% were males and 36% were females. Nearly 2% were children.

Safety and Health in the Tea Plantations

Like in any other employment sector, workers in the tea plantations run an equal if not higher risk of being injured as a result of the type of work they do. The main risks posed are from unguarded machinery in the factory, exposures to fertilizers, pesticides and other agro-chemicals, and accidents caused as a result of the terrain in the fields. Most of the field workers are required to work on high altitudes and uneven terrain under wet weather conditions.

Many chemical hazards exist in the plantations. Although Sri Lanka does not manufacture chemicals, they are widely used in all economic activities today. About 200 varieties of pesticides are formulated in the country. Large quantities of pesticides and fertilizers are used in the agriculture sector, where 37% of the labour force was employed by the end of 1997. Occupational diseases resulting from exposure to chemicals are also under-reported or not reported at all, possibly due to poor diagnosis. From the large number of cases of acute pesticide poisoning it could be presumed that many thousands of cases of chronic poisoning are not even diagnosed. It appears to be obvious therefore that there is a need to take action in the field of chemical safety and prevention of major occupational diseases and accidents at a national level.

The high number of cases of pesticide poisoning clearly indicates that safety awareness in the use of chemicals is rather low. Sri Lanka being a primarily agriculture-based society lacks the necessary safety training and education. According to the Health Ministry's statistics on pesticide poisoning, in 1993 the number of reported deaths was 3477. This figure had declined to 1677 in 1995, which is a positive sign in the effort to increase safety levels in the agricultural sector.

In the plantation sector, large quantities of chemicals are used as fertilizers and pesticides. Many accidents have taken place among the users of these pesticides, who are mainly estate labourers and their families. Many different varieties of pesticides, weedicides and fertilizers are used in the plantations every day. The quantities used vary from estate to estate. These pesticides and fungicides, most often, are not transported and stored in a safe manner. Unauthorized or poorly trained persons are sometimes involved in preparation of pesticides. In the mixing of concentrate, safety precautions are often neglected by these persons. Measuring utensils and personal protective equipment are improperly used or not used at all, thereby causing serious exposure hazards. There are instances where entire communities have been affected due to fungicide sprays contaminating waterways and wells. There have also been instances of plantation workers being poisoned after consuming food in the fields that were contaminated by chemicals.

Government Agencies Responsible for Occupational Safety and Health in Sri Lanka

The Factories Division and the Occupational Hygiene Division of the Department of Labour are statutorily responsible for the implementation of Occupational Safety and Health Programmes in Sri Lanka. The main function of the Factories Division is the enforcement of the Factories Ordinance through inspection, advisory services and legal action where necessary. Its functions are regionalised, and, all factories operating within the regions are required to register, and report work-related accidents to the Factories Division.

The Labour Medical Office, which was established in 1945, gradually developed as the Division of Occupation of Hygiene. The main activities of this Division are to provide laboratory and advisory services on OSH, set standards, knowledge and education in OSH, research, and information services. The Division is also responsible in coordinating all national referral and research laboratories in occupational and environment hygiene, with special reference to industrial effluents, air pollution, agro-chemicals and statistical surveillance. It also provides advisory services on pollution control for ensuring safe and healthy workplaces and environments. The Hygiene Division is instrumental in defining national problems in workers health and hygiene, developing research and action programmes to counter such problems, establishing national OSH standards and organizing training activities.

Legislation in Sri Lanka Relating to Occupational Safety and Health and Occupational Hygiene

The principal Legislation in Sri Lanka relating to safety of workers is embodied in the Factories Ordinance Act No. 45 of 1942 and subsequent amendments. However, there are other pieces of Legislation that includes sections on welfare of employees, sanitation, safety and accident prevention to a certain extent. The payment of compensation to injured workers is defined in the Workmen's Compensation Ordinance Act No. 19 of 1934 and its subsequent amendments.

Safety and health legislation was first introduced in Sri Lanka in 1896 with the enactment of the Mines and Machinery Protection Ordinance No. 2. After four decades, basic legislation covering safety, health and welfare in factories was introduced in 1942. The Factories Division of the Department of Labour was set up in 1949 and the Factories Ordinance became operational in January 1950. However, the Factories Ordinance does not cover safety of field workers such as farmers in the Agricultural Sector, in which 38.9% of the working population of Sri Lanka are employed at present. Only industrial hazards are covered by the Ordinance. The Factories Inspectorate comprise a team of engineers, doctors and scientists attached to the Department of Labour who are in charge of enforcement of the Factories Ordinance. In addition to the Factories Ordinance there is the Shop and Office Employees Act, the Workmen's Compensation Ordinance, the Environment Act and the Control of Pesticide Act that cover safety and health of workers in Sri Lanka to a certain extent. The Environment Act and the Control of Pesticide Act mainly cover safety in the use of chemicals, and protection of users and the environment from harmful effects of chemicals.

The major causes of occupational accidents in Sri Lanka are due to mishandling of equipment, falling, being struck by flying objects in the work area, irregular use of personal safety devices by workers, and chemical exposures and poisoning, particularly in the agricultural sector.

The Factories Ordinance

The Factories Ordinance No. 45 of 1942, the subsequent Amendment Act No. 54 of 1961 and Law No. 12 of 1976 is the principal occupational safety and health legislation in the country. It makes provision for safety, health and welfare of workers in factories as defined under the Ordinance. It stipulates the minimum safety standards to be maintained by the employer. The Ordinance deals mainly with machine safety, welfare and safety precautions that should be taken by employers. The sections on health and welfare deal with cleanliness, work area and overcrowding, temperature, ventilation and lighting, sanitary conveniences, consumption of meals within restricted areas, lifting of weights, water for consumption, and first aid.

Rules relating to safety in the use of chemicals while at work are also found in this ordinance to some extent. The sections include maintenance of adequate ventilation and rendering harmless all fumes, dusts and other impurities that may be generated due to the use of chemical substances which could be harmful to the health of the worker; powers to direct medical supervision of a preventive nature, where the substances used at work may pose a risk of causing injury to the health of the employee; fencing of vessels containing dangerous substances; precautions to be taken with respect of explosives and inflammable gases, vapour and other substances, provision of exhaust ventilation and isolation of plant and equipment containing ammonia, chlorine, carbon dioxide and other asphyxiates or irritant gas and vapour; and, the supply of safety equipment including breathing apparatus for workers working in environments where the above substances may be present. The Ordinance also includes sections dealing with the notification of industrial accidents, dangerous occurrences and occupational diseases, and the requirement of authorized factory doctors to investigate and report on cases of injuries and deaths caused by exposure to dangerous substances.

The Shop and Office Employees' Act

In addition to the Factories Ordinance, the Shop and Office Employees' Act enacted in 1954 prescribes, inter alia, provision for the safe health of workers employed in shops and offices and, sets out requirements for adequate light, ventilation, sanitary conveniences and washing facilities at workplaces. This Act would cover all employees working in the offices maintained on the tea estates.

The Maternity Benefits Ordinance

The Maternity Benefits Ordinance, which is directly applicable to females working on estates, imposes certain restrictions with regard to employment of pregnant females on certain types of work that could be considered injurious to her, or to her child, and, with regard to termination of their services. The term 'injurious' is not defined clearly in the Act and should, therefore, be interpreted to include any work in the estate or factory of a heavy or arduous nature. The Ordinance also requires an employer of a female employee who is nursing a child under one year of age, to allow her two nursing intervals within the normal working day, at such time as she may require. The Medical Wants Ordinance that covers estate women workers, also prohibits dangerous or heavy work during pregnancy and after confinement on similar lines of the Maternity Benefits Ordinance.

The Workmen's Compensation Ordinance

The Workmen's Compensation Ordinance No. 19 of 1934, the Workmen's Compensation regulations in 1935 and the amendments thereafter provide for the payment of compensation to workmen who are injured in the course of their employment. The Amendment Act that became operative from 1 June '90, brought in drastic changes. The Act discusses in detail, the coverage of workmen, the amount of compensation payable, the distribution of compensation, procedures for recovery of compensation, surcharges in the event of failure to pay compensation, etc. It also lists the injuries deemed to result in permanent and partial disablement and the loss of earning capacity. It also contains a list of occupational diseases.

The Environmental Act

The Environmental Act No. 47 of 1980 and the Amendment Act No. 56 of 1988 has some provisions for safety in the use of chemicals. The National Environmental (Protection and Quality) Regulation No. 1 of 1990 requires all industrial concerns to obtain an environment protection license. This regulation prohibits the discharge, deposit or emission of waste into the environment that would cause pollution. The Central Environmental Authority (CEA) obtains information from industrialists about the chemicals used in their manufacturing processes, transport, handling and storage facilities and safety precautions in the use of chemicals. The CEA has drafted a new environmental law and is awaiting approval. The draft Act defines toxic substances that may have immediate, and long-term cumulative harmful effects on the environment and human life. With regard to industry, the Minister would be empowered to make regulations for guidelines for the use and possession of toxic substances, registration, manufacture, labelling, packaging, advertising of such substances, the control of imports and exports of toxic substances, distribution, collection, storage, transportation and handling of chemical substances, monitoring the effects of toxic substances and their residues on human and occupational health and the environment and the control of emissions or deposits into the environment, and establishing standard laboratories for the testing of toxic substances.

Control of Pesticides Act

The Control of Pesticides Act No. 33 of 1980 provides for the licensing of pesticides; to regulate the import, packaging, labelling, storage, formulation, transport, sale and use; for the appointment of a licensing authority; for the establishment of a pesticide formulary committee. This is the only law in Sri Lanka that deals with classification and labelling of chemicals that are used in the manufacturing of pesticides. Pesticides are classified according to the lethal dose values (LD 50). The labelling regulation specifies the identity of the contents, languages and size of the lettering, danger symbols and colours, precautions during handling, first aid and antidotes, etc.

As many deficiencies of this Act were identified, it was amended subsequently in 1994, bringing broader control measures. The amendment law required more information to be submitted in the application for registration of a pesticide. The validity of the registration license was restricted to a maximum period of three years and it was made a requirement that the label be sent for approval at the time of registration of the pesticide. Another important feature was the classification of different pesticides and the restriction of their uses. It was also made a requirement that a certificate for the sale of pesticides should be obtained.

Deaths due to pesticide poisoning were the fifth leading cause of death in Sri Lanka in 1994. Most of these cases of poisonings and deaths are due to intentional consumption in order to commit suicide. A small per centage of nearly 15% account for occupational causes and accidental intake. A large volume of weedicides and pesticides are used in the plantation sector where approximately 400,000 workers are employed. In most of these cases, chemical agents are released into the environment thereby causing land and water pollution. As large numbers of population are clustered within small regions using common living amenities the chances of chemical poisoning are far greater. In the tea estates, most of the workers do not use personal protective equipment when spraying pesticides or weedicides. Many reported cases have shown that the effect is caused whereby the chemical agent has direct contact with the skin. The worker pays less attention to his or her health, as the effect of the chemical is long term.

There are many instances where large numbers of workers have been hospitalized with acute poisoning due to chemicals used in the workplace. Most often the causative agent was a solvent used in an air-conditioned area, gradually building up in concentration within the air of the work environment subsequently causing poisoning.

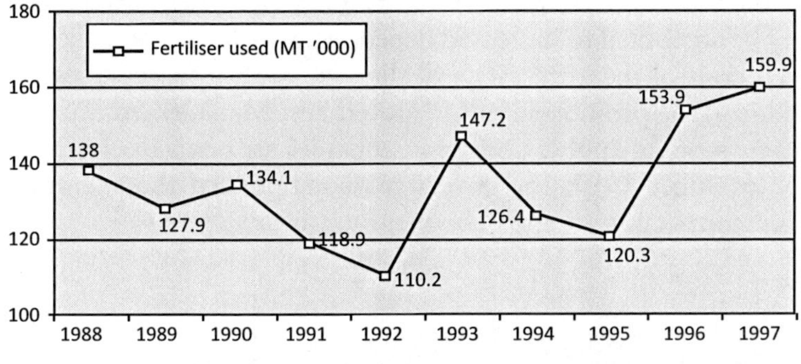

Fig. 4.1: Use of Fertilizer in Sri Lanka

There has been a considerable increase in the use of fertilizer in the agricultural sector in Sri Lanka Fertilizer used during 1997, was approximately 524,558 metric tons. Among the plantation crops, tea recorded the highest increase in fertilizer usage. In 1995 only 120,000 metric tons of fertilizer was used in the tea sector. By the end of 1997, 160,000 metric tons of fertilizer was used in tea production. This was approximately 6,000 metric tons more than the amount used in 1996, and 40,000 metric tons more than what was used in 1995. The improved prices for tea and the favourable weather conditions during the year contributed to enhanced fertilizer application by 4%. The fertilizer subsidy scheme also contributed to the increased use of fertilizer. The fertilizer subsidy scheme in respect of four major varieties of fertilizer, namely urea, sulphate of ammonia, muriate of potash and triple super phosphate continued in 1997. Urea is a major fertilizer used in the tea plantations. The graph indicates the amount of fertilizer utilized by the tea sector during the last decade. The usage of fertilizer has increased sharply after 1995.

Use of Agro-chemicals in Sri Lanka

According to provisional estimates provided by the Registrar of Pesticides, the total quantity of agro-chemicals (insecticides, weedicides and fungicides) sales in 1997, declined by 6% compared to the same figures of 1996. The quantity of weedicides, which account for about 50% of total agro-chemical sales, increased by 6% to 2,985 metric tons, while insecticide sales declined by 10% to 2,144 metric tons. The quantity of fungicide sales also declined by 31% to 579 metric tons. Increased sales of weedicides may be attributed to increased dependency by farmers on chemical weed control measures. The decline in sales of insecticides may be due to the promotion of Integrated Pest Management methods (where straight applications of insecticides are being discouraged). In November 1997, the government announced the exemption of customs duty on agro-chemical imports.

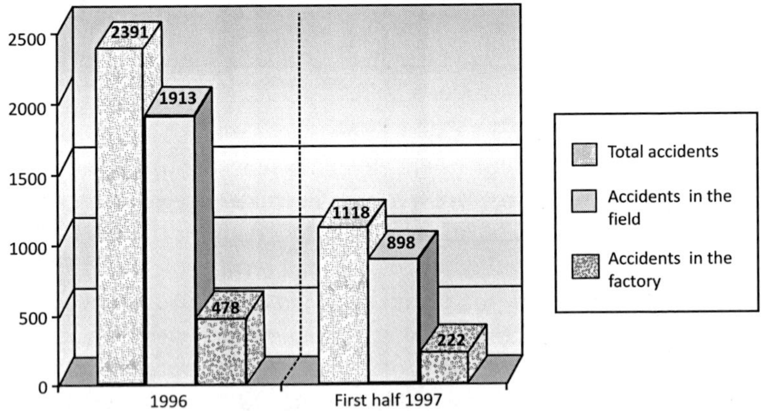

Fig. 4.2: Total Number of Accidents in the Plantation Fields and the Tea Factories

Accidents Reported from the Estates

There were a total of 2,391 accidents reported from the 161 estates during the year 1996. This included 478 accidents that occurred in the factory premises and 1,913 accidents that occurred in the field. The graph indicates the number of accidents that occurred on the plantations during 1996 and the first half of 1997.

A total of 1,118 accidents were reported during the first half of 1997, this included 222 accidents in the factory and 896 accidents in the field. It could be assumed that if the frequency of the number of accidents during the first six months continued for the second half of the year, a total of 2,236 accidents would occur by the end of 1997. This is approximately 7% less than the number of accidents that occurred in 1996. This projection indicates that the number of accidents in 1997 would be less than the number that occurred in 1996. This could be attributed to the fact that most employers in the plantation sector are now realizing the importance of safety and health of their employees and attempting to provide necessary training and precautionary measures.

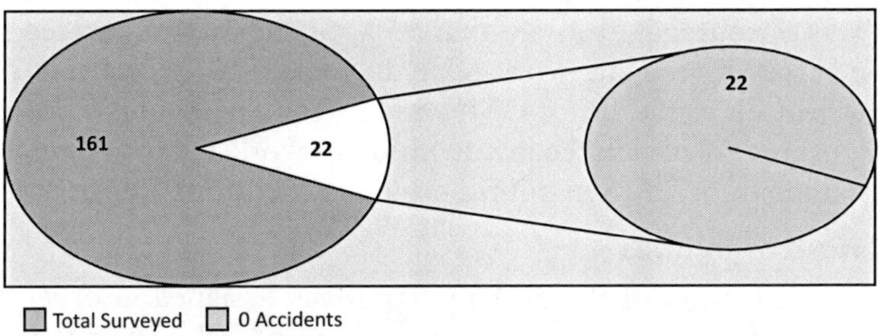

Fig. 4.3: Total Number of Zero Accidents in the Field or the Factory

Twenty-two (22) of the one hundred and sixty-one (161) estates surveyed reported zero (0) accidents in the field or factory during the entire year of 1996 and for the first half of 1997. This is 13.6% of the total number of estates covered by this survey. Fourteen (14) plantation companies managed at least one estate where no occupational accidents had taken place during the period covered by this survey. There were four estates of one plantation company where no accidents were reported during the period covered by the survey. There were five plantation companies with two estates each, where no accidents were reported during the period covered by the survey. There were eight plantation companies where no accidents were reported from one of their estates during the period covered. All these estates had safety training and awareness programmes implemented within their estates and employees had been given training in work safety.

Maintenance of Accident Records and Accident Investigation

Approximately, 97% of the respondents maintained records and had information on all occupational accidents that occurred on the estate, while 76% of the respondents maintained records of accidents that occurred in the estate factory as well. 86% of the respondents stated that they maintained records of all occupational hazards and accidents and 80% confirmed that they maintained records of accidents that required giving the worker more than three days leave.

Of the total number responding, 74% stated that they maintained records of cases where employees had suffered from some occupational disease. 81% of the respondents indicated that there was an Estate Medical Assistant available on the estate. It was encouraging to note that 95% of the estates covered in the survey investigate work-related accidents that occurred on the field or in the factory. This indicates that there is a lot of importance placed in the investigation of work-related accidents are done in order to minimize or eliminate future occurrences.

Nature of Injuries

This section of the questionnaire was designed in order to obtain information on the nature of injury. All accidents that were reported required hospitalization or specialized treatment of a medical practitioner.

Table 4.2: Most Common forms of Occupational Injuries that Occurred on the Tea Plantations during 1996 and the first Half of 1997

Type of Injury	Rank-1996	Rank-1997
Sprains/fractures and dislocations	1	1
Bruises and cuts	2	2

Type of Injury	Rank-1996	Rank-1997
Poisoning due to snake bites	3	3
Occupational dermatitis	4	4
Amputations	5	9
Burns	5	5
Chemical hazards/ exposures	5	8
Internal injuries	8	7
Respiratory injuries	8	6
Injuries to the nervous system	10	10
Noise-related injuries	11	11

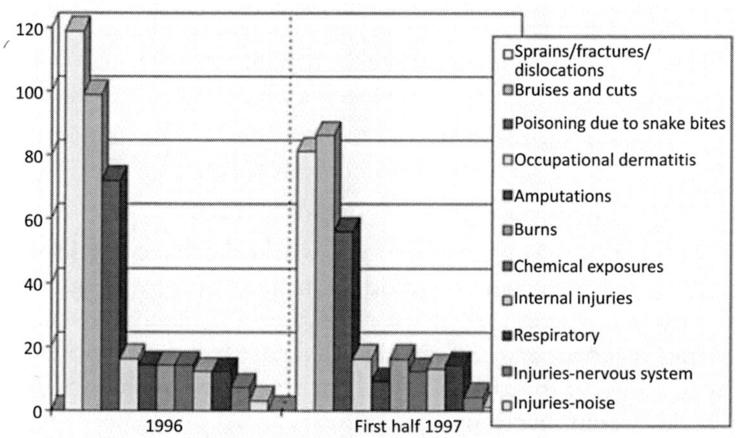

Fig. 4.4: Most Common Forms of Occupational Injuries that Occurred on the Tea Factories during 1996 and the First Half of 1997

Fractures, Sprains, and Dislocations

The most number of injuries caused on the plantations were either in the form of fractures, sprains or dislocation of limbs. In 1996, there were 119 cases reported. These included 59 sprain injuries, 40 cases of fractures and 20 cases of joint dislocations. During the first half of 1997, there were 81 cases reported, which included 37 sprain injuries, 27 cases of fractures and 17 cases of dislocations. The sprain injuries are a result of persons falling and this is common in the fields due to the uneven and rough terrain. The estate worker who is mostly female is required to carry a heavy load of plucked tea on their backs, which causes loss of balance when negotiating rough ground. Fractures and dislocations are a result of many serious falls that may require hospitalization for a long period. Fractures are also caused due to accidents occurring in the factory where heavy machinery is used in the process of manufacturing tea.

Bruises and Cuts

The second most frequent type of injuries that occur on plantations is due to cuts and bruises sustained. In 1996, a total number of 99 cases with serious bruises and lacerations were reported. This figure had already reached a high of 86 incidents by June 1997. The most common reasons for the high rate of injuries of his nature could be attributed to the following facts:

1. The improper use of a sharp cutting devises such as knives, shears, and mammoties, etc.
2. The non-use of protective foot wear.

In most of the above situations, workers are required to seek medical treatment which would mean that they are required to be away from work for at least a day. It also means that in the absence of necessary first aid and medical attention, workers are forced to use traditional methods of treatment, which may lead to serious complications.

Poisoning Due to Snake Bites

This is the third most common type injury caused to plantation workers. Sri Lanka being a tropical country is known to be the habitat for many venomous species of reptiles. In 1996, 72 cases, which required hospitalization or special medication due to snakebites, were reported. 60 cases reported by June 1997, required hospitalization. This form of poisoning is prevalent mainly in the fields, which have thick undergrowth, and due to the close proximity in which the tea plant is grown. In the plantations, workers are required to commence work early in the morning and in most cases under poor visibility conditions. Also the fact that many of them do not use protective footwear has contributed to the alarmingly high rate of snakebite incidents in Sri Lanka. The non-availability of necessary first aid and medical care in most instances has increased the risk of fatality in snakebite victims.

Occupational Dermatitis

Occupational dermatitis is also a common form of injury caused to workers on the plantations. In 1996, there were 16 instances where occupational dermatitis cases were reported. This figure had already reached 16 by June 1997. This indicates that the number of cases may double by the end of the year. Unless proper care and prevention is taken, this may result in a serious occupational problem among plantation workers in the future. The reasons for skin disease to be common among the estate workers is the lack of awareness in the use of pesticides and weedicides, the lack of proper sanitation facilities and the ignorance of the need to maintain high standards of personal hygiene. In most cases, pesticide and weedicide sprayers do no follow the required safety standards such as wearing protective gloves and masks. They are often clad in the same clothes during their working hours and thereafter at home until the end of the day and this causes serious skin exposure. Many of these workers do not obtain medical treatment for these skin irritations, which may spread rapidly among the other members of the community thereby causing epidemic situations.

Amputations

Amputations as a result of an injury were also common on the estates. There were 14 cases of amputations reported in 1996. This figure had reached nine cases by June 1997. Amputations result in a neglected injury of a serious fracture or cut. It is unfortunate, as an amputation done on an estate worker would mean loss of earnings either temporarily or permanently. Once again, it is the seriousness of the injury and the time taken between the injury and treatment, which result in an amputation.

It is only by increasing the level of medical care that one could reduce the number of incidences of this nature.

Burns

There were 14 cases of injuries resulting in burns in 1996. By June 1997, 16 such cases had been reported already. Burns are caused due negligent handling of chemicals and in some cases due to inadequate safety precautions when igniting fires.

Hospitalization Due to Chemical Exposure

Occupational injuries due to contact with chemical substances were prevalent in the estates surveyed. In 1996, there were 14 cases of hospitalization reported due chemical poisoning. By June 1997, there were 12 cases reported. However, the numbers exposed to chemical hazards were greater than the actual number of hospitalization cases. Chemical exposure figures are given under the title 'chemical exposure', elsewhere in this report. Many hazardous chemicals are found in different quantities in the various pesticides, weedicides and fertilizers used on the plantation. These are known to be of high toxicity and acute or chronic exposure would often lead to serious health complications. In the plantations, the most common form of exposure is through the skin or through oral ingestion contaminated food or water. In most of the estates surveyed, there are hardly any worthwhile OSH programmes on safety awareness and many workers do not know the importance of using personal protective equipment to safeguard against these chemical hazards.

Injuries to Internal Organs

In 1996, there were 12 cases reported where injuring occurred to internal organs due to occupational hazards. These include exposure to direct damage caused from a mechanical accident, fall, etc. This figure had already reached 13 cases by June 1997 and is expected to increase further by the end of the year. All these cases required hospitalization or long-term treatment.

Injuries to the Respiratory System

This could be directly linked to hazardous exposures where workers suffer from temporary or permanent lung disorders.

The nasal cavity and mouth are the major routes through which toxic substances enter the respiratory system of the body, and, is easily effected by gases, dust or fumes. There were 12 cases reported in 1996, from the estates that responded to the survey. By June 1997 there were 14 cases reported already. It is evident that the numbers of victims of respiratory disorders are increasing on the plantations. It is difficult to conclude whether these cases could be directly linked to the type of work they perform, as the effects may be long term. However, in cases where workers are involved in the preparation of pesticides or weedicides, or those who do spraying in the fields may be affected even in the short term. Inadequate personal protection and ignorance of the effects of their incorrect actions cause many a worker to suffer from respiratory problems.

Injuries to the Nervous System

The nervous system is highly sensitive to the hazardous effects of organic solvents. Organophosphate insecticides such as malathion and parathion that are used interfere severely with the functions of the nervous system leading to weakness and paralysis and sometimes death. There were seven cases of serious nervous system injuries that were reported in 1996 and there were four cases by June 1997.

Noise-related Injuries

There were three cases of injuries reported due to noise hazards in 1996. Long term exposure to high audio frequencies, which are above 90 dbh, may cause serious hearing disorders. The types of machinery that are used in the factories of the tea estates are known for the high level of noise. There was one case of noise related injuries reported in June 1997. Special personal protective equipment such as earmuffs or earplugs is not worn in many places thereby increasing the risk of injury.

Physical Location of the Injury

Information was also collected on the physical location to which occupational injuries or diseases were caused. The objective of this exercise was to find out whether the work-related injuries were particularly high in a specific part of the human body.

Eye Injuries

There were 319 eye injuries during the year 1996. These injuries ranged from minor irritations to major accidents, which required emergency surgery. The number of accidents resulting in injuries to the eyes of the workers remained high at the end of the first half of 1997 as well. There were 193 cases reported during this period. Injuries to the eyes were in the form of burns, chemical exposures, and cuts and bruises of the face. Based on the mid-year statistics available it could be assumed that the number of eye-related injuries would increase by the end of 1997.

Ear Injuries

In 1996, there were 120 cases where the ears of the workman were directly affected or injured due to the occupational injury. This figure had reached 62 by June 1997. The figures indicate that by the end of 1997, the number of ear injuries would remain the same as 1996. Though the number of occupational injuries remained low during the periods surveyed, the injuries could be due to other causes such as cuts and burns suffered to extensive areas of the face and head.

Facial Injuries

Injuries caused to the face of the workman also remained high during 1996. There were 155 reported cases involving injuries to the face. The figure had reached 89 by the end of June 1997.

Head Injuries

There was a high rate of incidence of head injuries caused to employees while at work. These ranged from minor external injuries such as bruises, cuts and burns to fractures and other serious injuries. Nonetheless in 90% of the cases the injuries were of a minor nature. In 1996, there were 232 head injuries reported from the estates. By June 1997, 131 such cases reported.

Neck Injuries

There were 64 cases of neck injuries reported in 1996. This figure had reached 44 by June 1997. In most cases, the injury is caused due to sprains and other muscular disorders suffered by the workmen who are involved in carrying heavy loads over their backs.

Back Injuries

Most back injuries are caused due to the heavy load of the tea basket saddled to the back being carried by the workman. This causes the spine to suffer extensively and in most cases result in severe back disorders which may have immediate or long-term effects. By the end of 1996, there were 101 cases of back problems reported. This had reached 58 by June 1997, which meant that the condition was not improving.

Injuries to the Torso

The classification under this category included injuries caused to the torso of the workman excluding the limbs, the back and internal organs. In 1996, there were 80 different cases of injuries reported and this had reached 46 cases by June 1997. Most of the injuries were caused due to falls suffered by the worker.

Injuries to Arms and Shoulders

Injuries caused in this category consisted of simple cuts, muscular disorders, fractures and amputations. More than 95% of the injuries were minor ones and did not require specialized treatment but were reported as minor accidents. In 1996, there were 262 accidents reported where the injury affected the arms or shoulder of the workman. By June 1997, 120 cases had been reported. The figures indicate the injuries caused to this part of the body are very common among plantation workers and are likely be high.

Injuries to Hands and Fingers

Like in the above category, work-related injuries caused to the adjoining part of the arm, i.e. the hands and fingers were very high among estate workers. In 1996 alone, there were 790 cases reported, most of which were caused due to cuts and bruises. In almost all the cases, the improper use of tools and sharp edged field tools were the main cause of the accident. By June 1997, injuries in this category already reached a high of 440 and, this is expected to increase by end of the year.

Feet and Toe Injuries

Occupational injuries caused to feet and toes of the worker were also high among plantation workers. The reasons attributed for the high rate of incidence is cuts and lacerations due to the improper manual use of tools and equipment, slips and falls, reptile and insect bites, and wounds caused due to the non-use of footwear. By the end of 1996, there were 591 injuries reported in this category and this had already reached 305 injuries by June 1997. Of the injuries suffered to the feet of the worker, injuries caused to the toe and surrounding area remained the highest. There were 680 cases where the toe or fingers were affected the most. This was during the year 1996. By mid-1997, there were 347 injuries reported where the toes and fingers were affected. Injuries caused to hips and feet are most frequent among plantation workers who work in the fields during most of their working hours.

Dermal Injuries

Injuries in this category ranged from occupational dermatitis to burn and bruises. The non-use or improper use of personal protective equipment and the exposure to hazardous material while at work were seen as the major causes of skin-related disorders. In most cases, the injuries resulted in accidental spillage, exposure during preparation and spraying of pesticides and weedicides, and improper handling and storage. The majority of work-related skin disorders prevalent among these workers are eczema, irritation and inflammation of the skin, which can have a non-allergic or allergic reaction after exposure to chemical substances. Statistics reveal that in 1996 there were 143 cases reported with some form of skin disorder. By June 1997, this figure had reached 67. In most of the cases, non-seeking of proper medical treatment, and the application of native treatment have aggravated the problem. Since plantation workers live in large communities and use common sanitary facilities, the chances of spreading skin-related disorders among others in the community are very high.

Other Injuries

There were only a few cases where injury was caused to other parts of body, which are not included here. There were 10 cases of occupational injuries reported in 1996. This figure had already reached 5 by June 1997. The findings of the survey clearly indicates that among plantation workers, the most vulnerable areas of the human body which are exposed to occupational hazards and prone to occupational injuries are, the upper half of the human body which includes the head, the back, limbs and fingers in the hands and feet. This could be attributed to the fact that estate workers are required to work in the fields for a major part of the working day and are required to use sharp-edged tools and equipment, carry heavy loads on their backs and walk bare foot on rugged slippery terrain. All these factors contribute greatly to increasing the chance of occupational accidents occurring. The nutritional level of the estate worker is also considered rather low. It has been found that the average calorie intake of an estate worker is lower than the necessary daily calorie intake of an average adult. This factor coupled with some extreme working conditions during the day certainly causes a drop in the level of physical tolerance of the worker, of whom the majority is females.

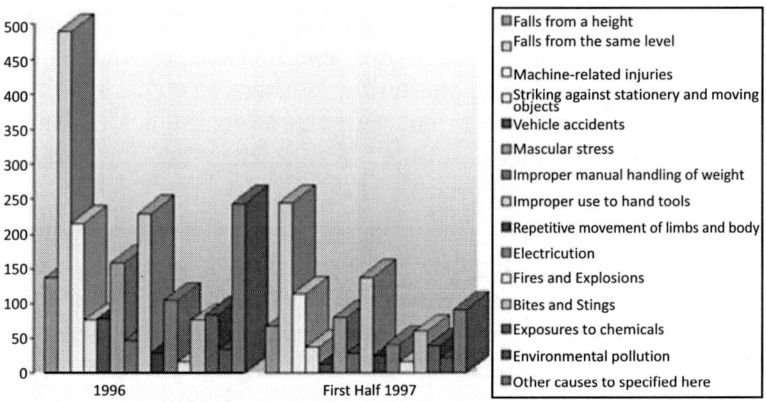

Fig. 4.5: Common Causes of Occupational Injuries

Falls from the Same Level

Slips and falls from the same level is the commonest form of accidents that occurred among plantation workers. This included people tripping and falling in the fields as a result of unseen obstructions such as roots and stone, unprotected drains and trenches, and stepping on loose earth. The reason for this being those workers are always ignorant of the immediate danger that may be caused from any small obstruction. In 1996, there were 490 such cases reported. By June 1997, there were 245 cases of injuries reported as a result of tripping and falling. This was approximately 50% of the incidences reported in 1996.

Falls from Heights

A common cause of work-related injury was caused as a result of employees accidentally slipping and falling from a height. In 1996, there were 137 cases of falls from heights being reported where injuries were caused. By the end of the first half of 1997, 67 cases were reported which is 49% of the total cases reported for 1996. The type of work performed by the estate worker, especially the plucking of tea on steep and rugged terrain, without any hand support in most instances have led to the high incidence of falls.

Mechanical Injuries

Machine-related and other mechanical injuries were considerably low among plantation workers when compared to the occupational injuries that were caused in the fields. This is mainly due to the fact that only a few workers are engaged full time in the production process in the factory.

One contributory factor to the rate of machine-related injuries in the estate factories is, the fairly old, semi-automated machinery. In 1996, there were 216 accidents reported from the estate factories. These included accidents that occurred consequent to workers getting their arms and fingers entangled in heavy machines such as grinders. Some of this equipment which consists of many drives and pulleys are unguarded or situated within close proximity to each other. Most of the factory layout plans are outdated and do not conform to present-day safety requirements. However, by end of June 1997, there were 114 mechanical accidents reported from the estates. This was 52.7% of the cases reported for 1996.

Striking Against Stationery or Moving Objects

This is another common form of injury that occurs in estate factories and store areas. In most situations, workers are hit by moving objects such as trolleys, which are used to transport tea chests from the factory to the stores, or injured by striking against machinery or tea packing chests. In 1996, there were 29 accidents where workers injured themselves after colliding with stationery objects. By June 1997, this figure had reached 14.

Among the causes identified, the improper storage of tea chests in the stores, the location of machinery and equipment, the absence of safety signs and safety markings of passage ways in the factory are prominent. Compared to the number accidents caused due to collision with stationery objects, accidents caused by workers striking against moving objects was high. 46 persons were injured after being hit by moving machine parts or trolleys in 1996. This figure had reached 23 cases by the end of June 1997. Accidents in this category are often caused due to the negligence of workers who are ignorant to the imminent dangers and hazards that may be created by their own actions.

Motor Accidents

There were 78 motor accidents in which workers were injured in 1996. This figure had reduced in 1997 and there were only 12 accidents reported by June 1997. This was only 15% of the accidents that occurred in 1996. The high elevations on which the tea estates are located in Sri Lanka and the poor surface conditions of estate roads have been the major cause of vehicle accidents. Nonetheless, carelessness of drivers of heavy transport vehicles has contributed to the aggravation of the problem.

Muscular Stress-related Injuries

Muscular stress is another common cause of occupational injury among plantation workers. The high volume of physical work performed by the estate labourer and the poor physical condition of the average estate worker has aggravated the situation further. There were 159 cases of work-related muscular stress reported in 1996. The figure had reached 80 by June 1997, which is 50% of the incidences that were reported in 1996. Though the effects may be long-term muscular stress-related injuries a serious occupational hazard on the plantations.

Improper Manual Handling of Loads

Among injuries caused to plantation workers due to incorrect manual handling of material the most common were sprains to the back, hands, legs and shoulders. Loading and unloading of heavy material such as fertilizer could be the cause of spine injuries in many cases. Many workers are unaware of the seriousness of their incorrect lifting actions until permanent damage is done to the spine. At the end of 1996, 46 cases of injuries in this category were reported. The number had reached 28 by June 1997, which is nearly 61% of the injuries reported for 1996 in this category.

Improper Use of Work Tools

Accidents due to the incorrect use or misuse of hand tools and power tools were very high among plantation workers. In 1996, there were 230 instances of improper use of work tools reported to the management. This figure had reached 138 by the end of June 1997, which was already 60% of the instances reported in 1996. Worker ignorance due to the lack of training in the safe use of these work tools was seen as the main cause for the high rate of accident occurrences. Accidents often resulted in cut abrasions to the worker, which required specialized treatment from a hospital.

Injuries Resulting in Repetitive Movement of Limbs and Torso

These injuries are linked to muscular stress-related injuries. Impairment is caused to joints and muscles as a result of continuous movement of the limbs and body. It is the direct effect of the extensive physical work to which the plantation worker is exposed each day. During 1996, there were 29 cases reported where victims were diagnosed with occupational injuries that may have been caused due irregular body movements. By June 1997, the condition had worsened and there were 24 cases reported.

Electrocution

Physical injuries caused due to electrocution were high among the estate workers. Injuries ranged from minor shocks to serious burns. No deaths were reported during the period covered in the survey. These accidents occur mainly in the estate factory and are caused due to the carelessness of workers in most cases. Electrical wiring systems and power lines in some factories may be obsolete and this may cause an accidental electrocution of a worker. In 1996, there were 105 instances of workers being electrocuted reported from the estates surveyed. This figure reached 41 by June 1997.

Fires and Explosions

Occupational injuries caused from fires and explosions were not high among the plantation workers. In 1996, only 15 cases of injuries due to fires were recorded. However, accidents due to fires and explosions had increased by June 1997, and there were already 24 cases reported.

Exposure to Chemical Hazards

The number of exposures to chemicals was moderately high among the estates surveyed. In 1996, there were 85 cases reported. By June 1997, 38 incidences of chemical exposures were notified to the estate managements. Most of these exposures were due agro-chemicals. The most common routes of absorption were through the skin (dermal absorption) and through the digestive tract (ingestion). Some of these exposure cases required hospitalization.

Environmental Pollution

It is encouraging to note that the hazards caused to workers due to the pollution of environment are low in Sri Lanka. There were only 34 cases reported in 1996, where the polluted environment had affected workers or their dependants' health conditions. In the majority of these instances, the pollution was caused due to the contamination of waterways as a result of pesticide spraying. By June 1997, there were 22 cases of hazards of environmental pollution reported.

Snake Bites and Insect Bites

This was a common occupational hazard among plantation workers who were engaged in fieldwork most of the day. In 1996, there were 95 instances reported where insect or snakebites during work had led to injury. About 78% of these cases had to seek specialized treatment. By June 1997, there were 60 instances reported. Accidents caused due to reptile and insect bites are in the rise and it would be necessary to address this hazard immediately.

There were also 244 instances where accidents were caused due to other means that were not specified as a cause in the study. Sometimes accidents occur as a result of workers clashing with each other. Occupational diseases come under this category. By June 1997, there were 92 such instances reported.

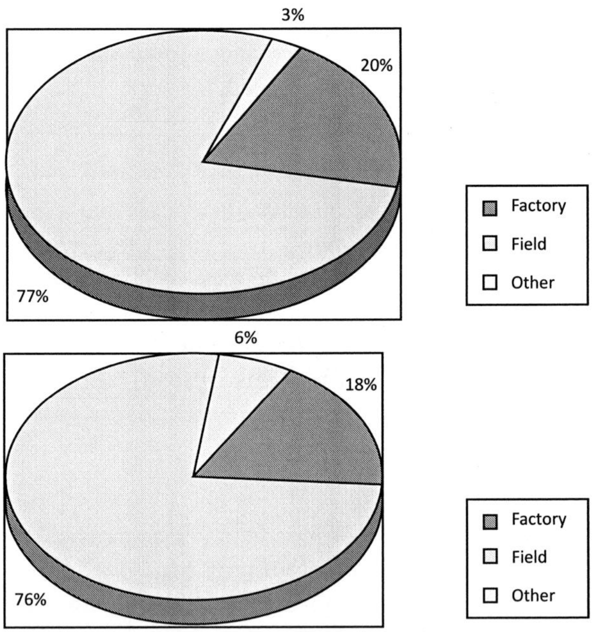

Fig. 4.6: Workdays Lost Due to Occupational Injuries

A total of 14,789 workdays were lost due to occupational injuries caused to workers during the year 1996. Of this figure 76% of the workdays lost were due to the injuries caused while doing fieldwork. Approximately, 18% of the workdays lost was due to accidents caused in the factory and subsequent absence. About 6% of the workdays were lost in 1996, due to absence from work as a result of an occupational injury caused in the estate office, stores or some other areas of the estate. There were a total of 2,391 accidents reported from the 161 estates during the year 1996, which meant that on an average every occupational injury resulted in approximately six workdays being lost to the estate.

By the end of June 1997, 8,195 workdays were lost due to occupational injuries. Of this figure 77% was due to absence of workers who sustained injuries in the fields. 20% of the workdays lost for the first half of the year was due to accidents caused in the estate factory, and approximately 3% of the workdays lost were due to injuries caused from accidents occurring in other areas of the estate. A total of 1,118 accidents were reported during the first half of 1997, which meant that on an average every occupational injury resulted in approximately seven workdays being lost to the estate. This indicates that the average loss of working time per accident has increased from six to seven days within the first six months of 1997.

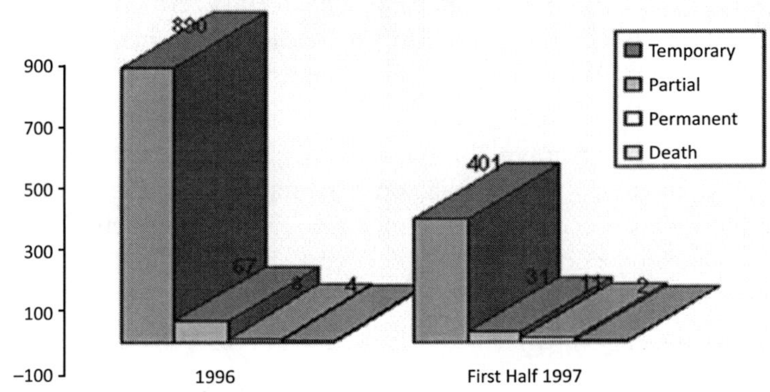

Fig. 4.7: Severity of Disability and Amount of Compensation Paid to Victims

Temporary Disability

There were 890 cases of occupational injuries that resulted in temporary disability in 1996. This meant that the workman was required to seek medical assistance for the injury. This figure had already reached 401 cases by the end of June 1997, which amounted to 45% of the total number of cases reported for 1996. A sum of ₹ 576,197/75 was paid out as some compensation to these victims in 1996. On an average each victim who suffered from temporary disability received a sum of ₹ 647.00. In 90% of the cases, this amount was paid as medical expenses and some payment for loss of earnings.

The Workmen's Compensation Ordinance provides for payment of compensation by the employer to a workman who sustains personal injury during work. Where the occupational injury is of a temporary nature the employer is required to pay wages to the employee during the first three days of absence from work due to the injury. The Workmen's Compensation Ordinance provides for 1/2 month's pay for absence beyond three days, computed according to the monthly wages of the employee.

Partial Disability

There were 67 reported cases in 1996, where the occupational injury had resulted in partial disability of the workman. This figure had reached 31 by June 1997. In 1996, a sum of ₹ 180,036/92 was paid out to these victims. An average of ₹ 2,687 was paid to each victim for medical treatment. A sum of ₹ 100,502 was paid among 31 victims, at an average of ₹ 3,242, by June 1997.

Compensation payment for partial disability is prescribed in the Workmen's Compensation Ordinance and the amount payable varies according to the monthly salary of the employee, nature of injury and the cause, the organ to which the injury was sustained and the per centage of loss of earning capacity lost.

Permanent Disability

There were eight reported cases where the injury caused permanent disability to the worker, which meant that there was a total loss of earnings thereafter. In this situation too, the Ordinance provides for compensation computed as specified in the preceding paragraph. A sum of ₹ 129,028 was paid among eight victims. On an average each person received a sum of

₹ 16,128 apart from the compensation receivable under the compensation Ordinance. By June 1997, there were 11 cases of permanent disability reported.

Death of Victim

From the 161 estates surveyed, there were four cases where the injuries had been fatal. A sum of ₹ 550,538 was paid, on an average of ₹ 137,634/50, to the dependants. By June 1997, there were two deaths reported and compensation amounting to ₹ 249,493 was paid to dependants of these victims at the rate of ₹ 124,746/50. The maximum compensation payable under the Workmen's Compensation Ordinance for injury resulting in permanent disability or death of a worker is fixed at ₹ 250,000.

Safety Committees

Safety committees are considered as the outset to having a successful safety and health programme in the workplace. The majority of the estates covered by the survey did not have a safety committee functioning on the estate. Of the 161 responses received, only 42 (25.9%) indicated that they had a safety committee. 106 (65.4%) of the respondents stated that they did not have such safety committees functioning. Thirteen of the respondents did not answer this question, therefore, it could be assumed that they do not have any safety committees set up within their estates. This is an important aspect of safety and health which has been overlooked by management in the plantations as well as in the commercial and industrial sector. A recent survey among 90 EFC member companies in the commercial and industrial sector revealed that only 22.5% had a safety committee set-up and functioning.

First Aid or Medical Facilities

Approximately, 136 (84%) of the respondents indicated that they have adequate first aid facilities available on the estates in the event of an emergency. Only 26 (16%) stated that they do not have first aid facilities within the estate. In most cases, the estate hospital or dispensary is located within a short distance from the factory. Accident victims are referred directly to these places in the event of an emergency. 138 (85.2%) stated that there was a dispensary or hospital within a one kilometer radius from the estate.

Training Workers on Safety

It is rather discouraging to note that only few estate management companies provide safety training for plantation workers. Only 44 (27%) of the respondents provide continuous safety training on a structured basis, and these were the estates on which very few accidents took place or no work-related accidents took place during the period covered by this study.

The training is predominantly in the area of chemical safety, where workers are trained in the safe use of pesticides, fungicides and fertilizer is done by many estates. Nearly 53% of the respondents stated that chemical safety training is provided to workers.

23% of the estates surveyed had conducted several programmes on OSH during the period covered by this study. Among the training programmes conducted, the focus was mostly on the safety in the use of tools and equipment, proper use of personal protective equipment, safe formulation and use of pesticides and weedicides and good housekeeping practices.

The following safety programmes are also conducted for plantation workers. Special safety training given to employees by the estate medical staff; training conducted by the Plantation Housing and Social Welfare Trust; safety, health and hygiene training conducted by health volunteers and Rural Farming Department personnel; and, personal protection awareness and chemical safety-training programmes conducted by suppliers of fertilizers and pesticides. Some non-governmental organizations also conduct safety-training programmes in the regions.

Accident Insurance Schemes

Due to the high rate of accidents that prevail on the plantations, most employers had secured accident insurance policies for their employees. Of the 161 responses, 131 (80.9%) stated that they do have such schemes in order to provide compensation in the event of any occupational hazards or accidents occurring.

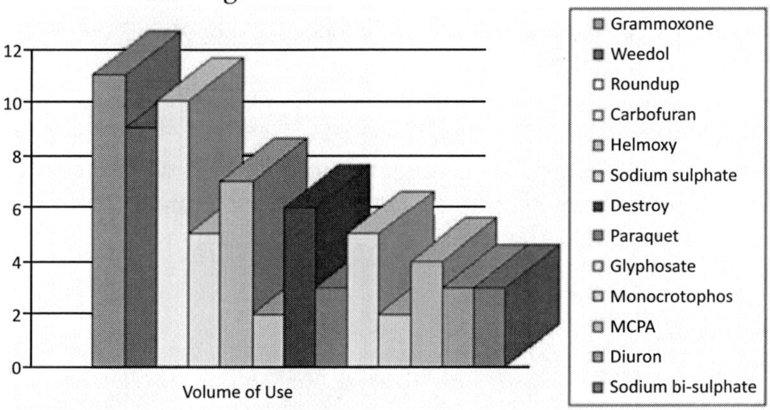

Fig. 4.8: Compensation in the Event of Any of the Following Occupational Hazards

Application of Weedicides

All the estates included in this study used these chemicals in high, low and moderate quantities. The quantity used depends on the cultivated land extent and the soil quality. Weedicides are commonly used on the tea plantations to destroy weeds and other unwanted plants that threaten the growth of the tea plant. Among the many weedicides and fungicides used the most widely used ones are indicated in the above chart. However, chemical agents such as gramoxone, destroy carbofuran, weedol, roundup are the most commonly used ones in Sri Lanka.

Fairly large quantities are used daily in the fields as they are known to destroy a variety of weeds and fungi that affect the tea plant. Other popular brands of weedicides in Sri Lanka are glyphosate, monocrotophos, MCPA, 2-4 DP and helmoxy.

These weedicides are found in powder and liquid form, and needs to be diluted to the necessary levels before they could be used.

Many workers are unaware of the risks to health at the point of preparation. Personal protective equipment is not used properly, therefore, leading to contamination either by inhalation of chemical dusts or dermal absorption of liquid formulas. Fungicides such as copper, diuron, sodium bi-suphate, oxichloride, parquet, and calixin are also used in low to moderate quantities in the plantations.

Chemicals such as rupepa, sodium sulphite, beloran, nexo bleach, caustic soda, sodium bisulphate, oxalic acid, formic acid, zinc oxide, sulphuric acid, ammonia solution and tamol are used widely in the estate factories. The volume used ranged from low to medium levels, depending on the size of the factory and the volume of production.

Application of Pesticides

The safe use of pesticides is determined by the care and attention given to precautionary measurers before, during and after application. In the plantations, the scale of operation, the area of application and the form in which the pesticide is applied is important. These pesticides are manufactured locally and are available in the local market under different trade names. In Sri Lanka, the control of Pesticides Act No. 33 of 1980, provides for the licensing of pesticides, the regulation of import, packing, labelling, storage, formulation, transport, sale and use thereof. This is the only law that deals with classification and labelling of chemicals and applies only to pesticides. The labelling regulation specifies the contents, languages and the size of the lettering, the danger symbols and colour codes, precautions to be taken in handling, first aid and antidote etc. However, most of the plantation workers are illiterate, therefore, cannot comprehend some of these precautions. It is vital that these employees are properly trained in the handling of chemicals. The most commonly used pesticides in the tea plantations are Bitertanol (Baycor), Copper Oxychloride (Helmoxy) Cobex, Bordox, Sulphate of Ammonia, Zinc, Fernoxone, Dolomite, Formic Acid, Methyl Bromide etc. The quantities used vary from low to moderate levels in 90% of the instances. In some large estates higher volumes are used in order to combat harmful fungi, pests and weeds.

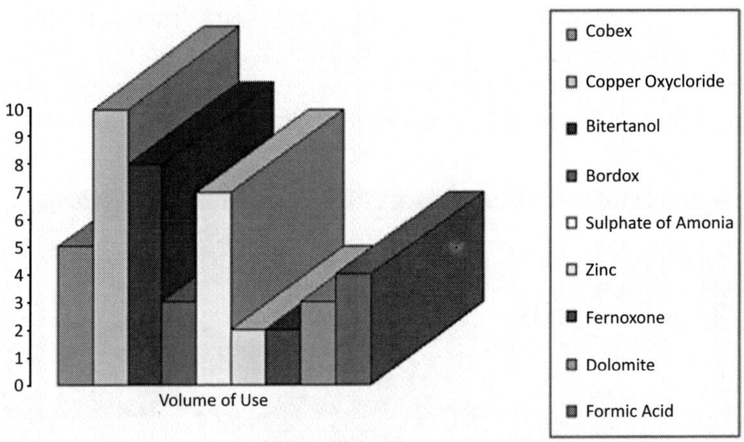

Fig. 4.9: Classification and Labeling of Chemicals with Regard to Pesticides

Fertilizers Used in the Tea Sector

A number of different fertilizers are widely used in the tea plantations in order to produce the maximum quantity of high quality teas. The volume of tea produced depends largely on the plant nutrients added to the soil. Therefore, the use of fertilizer in the tea sector has increased sharply over the years. The principal chemicals used for this purpose are nitrogen, phosphorous and potassium. The other elements needed in smaller quantities that are also vital to the growth of the tea plant include calcium, magnesium, sulphur, zinc and iron. Nitrogen is one of the micronutrients, and is needed in relatively large quantities.

The most widely used fertilizers are titled as the "U and T series". The "U series" includes manure mixtures titled U/230, U/280, U/300, U/625, U/709, U/625, etc. The "T series" includes manure mixtures titled T/65, T/250, T/875, T/1130, etc. These are a series of manure mixtures that include nitrogen, phosphorous pentaoxide, potassium oxide, and magnesium oxide. Other types of fertilizer used in tea growing are MCPA 60%, zinc sulphate, dolomite, epsom salt, urea, sulphate of ammonia, muriate of potash and kieserite.

All types of fertilizers mentioned above are used in moderate to high quantities depending on the extent of the cultivated land. Most of these fertilizers are very soluble in water, therefore, could dissolve in rainwater and get flushed down from the slopes of the plantation into waterways. Nitrates may also enter ground water and pollute it. Therefore, it is important that proper training in the use of fertilizer is given to employees who handle these material.

Storage Facilities

Planning and proper maintenance of storage areas is important in the plantations as large quantities of fertilizer and pesticides are stored within the estate. The hazards related to the fertilizers and pesticides can be grouped into storage, transport and application. Proper housekeeping is essential when working with dangerous substances to avoid any unwanted chemical reactions. Proper transport, loading and unloading procedures are also vital for safety. The survey revealed that 93% of estates do have proper storage facilities for the safe storage and distribution of fertilizer, pesticides and weedicides. It is encouraging to note that the estate managements have taken adequate steps to provide proper storage facilities, as the lack of proper storage may cause spillage and air exposure, which could be harmful to the workers, and to the environment.

Employees Engaged in the Application of Pesticides and Weedicides

Approximately, 4,784 employees are directly engaged in tasks such as preparation of fertilizer, pesticides, fungicides and spraying them in the fields. This is nearly 4.8% of the total workforce covered by this survey.

58% of the respondents stated that their employees who were engaged in jobs such as fertilizer mixing and pesticide spraying were rotated on the job from time to time. This is important as it is not advisable to engage an employee in tasks such as pesticide spraying and fertilizer preparation for long periods as the amount of exposure time to the chemical increases. Most of the superintendents have realized this fact, however, in 42% of the cases the employees are engaged in these jobs on a fixed basis.

68% of the respondents stated that employees who were engaged in the above tasks were trained in the safe use of chemicals. However, the rate of incidence of chemical exposures and related accidents indicate that negligence, and lack of proper awareness among estate workers are the main causes. 32% of the respondents stated that no special safety training has been given to these workers. In some cases, the suppliers themselves give employees some information on safety in the use of pesticides.

Use of Personal Protective Equipment (PPE)

Most agrochemicals used on the tea plantations and the machinery used in tea production and working conditions present a risk to the plantation worker. Engineering control measures could control some of these risks. However, the demographic conditions and the nature of work on the tea plantations make engineering control measures difficult. PPE, therefore, remains a necessary part of working with agrochemicals. The protection required would depend on the degree of hazard, the harmful effects of the agrochemical and the way in which it is prepared and used. In the tea plantations, proper eye and face protection, respiratory protection, protective gloves and working clothes are important when pesticides and fungicides are formulated or sprayed. In the estate factory, most of the machinery do not cater to present levels of safety standards. Therefore, personal protection and caution is vital for jobs such as machine operators. Only 60% of the respondents stated that PPE is provided to employees who are engaged in these tasks. Many employees do not use this equipment as they are not comfortable to use.

This shows that proper guidelines have not been observed when selecting the most suitable PPE for the job.

Safety Training for Estate Superintendents and Staff

Approximately, 69% of the respondents stated that no safety and health training or awareness was given to the estate superintendents and other staff. Only 31% of the superintendents indicated that the managing companies provided them with safety training. The type of training received were basic awareness building programmes. These were as follows:

1. Awareness programmes and safety demonstrations.
2. Information and awareness given by suppliers of personal protective equipment.
3. Training in the preparation and use of fertilizer and pesticides.
4. Special OSH training programmes organized by the plantation housing and welfare trust.
5. Training programmes on first aid.
6. OSH training organized by non-governmental organizations and health volunteers.
7. Special safety training programmes conducted by the National Institute of Plantation Management.

Current OSH Issues, and Future Recommendations for Improvement in the Plantations

The tea sector contributes greatly to the national economy. Unlike in other economic sectors, relatively difficult working conditions, illiterate and sometimes ignorant workers and hazardous work environments make occupational accidents and illnesses very common among the plantation worker. Workers have limited access to specialized advisory services and often young persons are employed on the estates making them more vulnerable to occupational hazards. The majority of estates do not have safety committees or a full time safety officer. In many cases, personal protective equipment are not worn by workers or not in proper working order. Fire drills are not conducted in factories and workers are not trained in fire fighting. Many employees are paid allowances for accepting to do tasks, which involve physical risks. These negative factors, in many instances, have been barriers to implement sound safety and health schemes.

It is also important to consider the differences among working people in Sri Lanka, and the effects the type of work they do has on their health. The main concern is that some workers in particular types of industry are more vulnerable than others. In the plantations, children help their parents on the estates to raise income levels of the family. Women form the major proportion of Sri Lanka's plantation labour force, and due regard should be paid to their dual role, family needs, and difference in educational levels, physique and mental capacities. The disabled and the older workers do not have the same mental and physical capacity for work as their younger and healthier counterparts. Their needs and capacities have to be taken into consideration when providing work. With the change in the demographic pattern in Sri Lanka a larger proportion of aged workers are expected by the next decade, and this will have to be considered in formulating safety and health programmes in Sri Lanka.

Therefore, it is necessary to integrate a clear occupational safety and health policy in national development plans. The national policy should include better structures for tripartite co-operation among government, employers and workers including a national tripartite consultative mechanism. There is also the need to review existing legislation relating to health and safety of workers. Safety and health legislation in Sri Lanka was first enacted in 1942, and does not cover all types of workers in all economic activities as specified by the International Convention on Occupational Safety and Health of the ILO.

The need for employers' organizations and trade unions to be more committed and organized to handle OSH issues should be emphasized. The national policy and program on OSH should include workplace level organization of health and safety activities involving both employers and workers. Although the employer is legally responsible for the safety and health in the workplace, the joint participation of employers and workers is necessary to deal with practical problems relating to occupational hazards within the workplace in a flexible manner. Training of new workers should include general principles of safety and health at work, as well as specific risks involved with every job. It would be useful to establish training for new workers and re-training existing employees. The training of trainers to train estate workers is of vital importance. Trainers should be taught about participatory methods of training. Though the Department of Labour, supported by the International Labour Organization (ILO) conducts many training programmes for factory inspectors and safety and health personnel, it is useful to involve employees at all job levels, in health and safety training, and, in handling disasters and disaster preparedness which is also becoming an important factor today.

Ready to use training material should be made available to every one who is concerned about human safety. Since occupational safety is a subject that requires specialized training, it would be useful to have properly structured training courses provided at national level. Since promotional activities play a vital role in encouraging occupational safety, objectives should be directed at securing national level commitment.

Conclusion

There are indications that the government is beginning to give high priority to workers' safety and health in order to reduce human suffering and enhance quality of work, work life and productivity. It is encouraging to note the State has declared an OSH week in early September of each year. The government is also attempting to address the problem of malnutrition and under nourishment among certain categories of workers. All vital factors in taking Sri Lanka towards a safer, healthier and productive nation by the 21st century.

5

Studies Conducted in Similar Plantations

Study Conducted in Coffee Plantations of Brazil

Context and contingency: the coffee crisis for conventional small-scale coffee farmers in Brazil. Watson, Kelly; Achinelli, Moira Laura. *The Geographical Journal*, 174 (Sep 2008): 223-34.

Brazil is the largest economy in Latin America and the world's leading producer and exporter of coffee. Smallholders are the predominant producers of Brazilian coffee and have been significantly impacted by post-ISI (import substitution industrialisation) neoliberal reforms that swept the nation's agricultural sector beginning in the 1980s. Coffee is one of the world's most valuable commodities and at least 25 million people around the world base their livelihoods on its production (ICO, 2006). The majority of these producers are small-scale farmers in the developing world, although the bulk of coffee consumption takes place in the United States and Europe (Daviron and Ponte, 2005).

Their research highlights the variable degree to which farmers cope with change and how farmer response differs due to specific national, regional, and local dynamics. The authors also emphasise that the ability of smallscale producers to withstand livelihood stress is influenced by the "access to, and command over, various forms of assets, capitals, services, knowledge and technology" (2006, 158). In a case study of coffee production within four separate Mexican states, Snyder (2001) demonstrates that the outcomes of neoliberal reform and globalisation differ not only between nations, but they also vary intra-nationally.

The findings of our case study are based on six months of combined fieldwork, daily interaction with a local non-governmental organisation, and unstructured and semi-structured interviews with farmers and their families, agricultural extension agents, community leaders and government officials.

The impacts of the coffee crisis are apparent throughout Brazil, where coffee is often grown in rural, isolated and poverty-stricken areas. Small-scale producers in these areas are most vulnerable to instability on the world coffee market, as their incomes are precariously tied to world coffee prices (Vakis et al., 2004). Largely unpredictable, price fluctuations leave farmers laden with risk. Many farmers are financially dependent solely upon coffee, dedicating their land, water, and labourto its production, while reserving few resources to grow subsistence crops or to diversify production.

Living Conditions

Rosário da Limeira is situated in an area of 117 km^2, with a few wealthy landowners, and many small-scale coffee farmers working private landholdings of 9 ha or less. Inequitable land tenure is a source of significant conflict throughout Brazil (Simmons, 2004; Wolford, 2005). The land used for coffee production in Minas Gerais is primarily divided into small, private land holdings; however, 20% of landowners are in possession of 60% of the total land area (Le Breton, 1998). Further, while fazendas (land holdings larger than 100 ha) represent only 3% of total land area, these lands are often the most favourable areas, with access to roads and water sources, and most importantly without steep elevation inclines.

Small-scale farmers generally occupy marginal lands, often growing coffee on steep slopes (Plate 1). Small-scale farmers in Rosário da Limeira live in simple homes which they often build themselves and they have very few possessions. Literacy rates in the municipio are the lowest in Minas Gerais, and only 66% of farmers have completed primary school (FAEMG, 1996). Most homes lack electricity and running water. The roads are unpaved; children attend school in one-room classes with mixed age groups; and most families do not have their own means of transportation. Some families share a horse and cart to meet their transportation needs. Entire families work the land—preparing the soil, planting and tending the coffee trees, harvesting, and occasionally basic processing. Relatives and friends contribute, especially during the harvest. In addition to farm labour, women cook the meals and take care of the home and children. Children generally work drying coffee beans, and this labouris often an impediment to educational opportunities.

Work and Wages

Many farmers share time between work on their own land and wage-earning work on fazendas. The large landowners pay at the same or just above Brazilian minimum wage (FAEMG, 1996) and, in some cases, this 'extra' work may bring in more income than the farmers' own plantations. Yet, in interviews, farmers often spoke of the importance and pride of having one's own farm. In addition to extra pay as seasonal workers, small-scale producers also rely on large landowners to provide basic farming and harvesting equipment. Large landowners, in turn, depend on the farmers as cheap sources of labour and coffee. This relationship limits the amount of time and labour which small-scale farmers can devote to the management of their own land in the face of rapid land degradation.

Study Conducted in Bolivian Sugar Cane Plantations

Children and youths account for half of the eight million people living in Bolivia. The ILO and UNICEF estimated that the sugar cane harvest mobilises almost 10,000 children and adolescents (2006:26). The National Institute of Statistics (INE) and UNICEF estimate that 2,540 children work in the sugar cane harvest (zafra) in Santa Cruz (2004:47); OASI, ILO and AECI report 2,619 youths participating in the zafra of Tarija (2006:22). In Bermejo, in 2004, there were 2,349 children and adolescents of whom 1,315 were of school-going age (Guevara, 2004:4).

Sugar cane is a significant agricultural crop and an important export earner: 30% of the product is exported. The raw sugar cane is processed into sugar and alcohol in large processing plants called ingenios. In contrast with the increasing production of sugar cane during the past few years, there have been a decreasing number of harvesters, or zafreros. According to directors and employees of different NGOs such as OASI and LABOR, the decrease has been from 30,000 harvesters in Santa Cruz in the 1980s to fewer than 10,000 harvesters today, and some sources even suggest that there are only 5,500 zafreros left, including wives, children and cuartas (assistants of harvesters) (Universidad Autónoma 'Juan Misael Saracho', 2005).

About 60% of the sugar cane harvesters are temporary migrants. Employers in the sugar cane harvest use a system of advance payments and debt creation to recruit and retain workers. Intermediaries and subcontractors are used to find workers in other regions of the country. They travel into, for example, Tarija and Potosí in the Bolivian highlands, which have large populations of poor, indigenous people (Sharma, 2006:3). The new zafreros are contracted in March and are paid a loan in advance. Once the workers have taken advances, they are obliged to work for that subcontractor and do not have the option of giving the money back, or finding work with someone else who might pay more. This system involving advanced payments through intermediaries is known as enganche, debt bondage. When the zafreros start working in April, they have to pay off their advances first before they can start earning money. They usually get paid every two weeks, but some employers pay their harvesters only at the end of the zafra, in an attempt to prevent people from leaving before the end of the harvest.

Research Setting

The research was conducted among large plantations (>50 ha) in two sugar cane regions in Bolivia: north of the city of Santa Cruz and in the southern part of the Tarija department (Bermejo). In both regions, the sugar cane harvest starts in May and ends in November.

Living Conditions

In Santa Cruz as well as in Bermejo, the living conditions of children and their families are precarious. Some plantation owners try to improve the living conditions but others, mostly the ones operating in remote zones and/or having small pieces of land and little financial resources, offer their harvesters only the most basic living conditions. Although conditions appear to have been improving, there still is much to be desired. Campamento Los Limones (Santa Cruz) has around 50 families and some 30 single men (adolescents and adults). For 4-6 months, they sleep in a well-constructed building that separates the families from the solteros (single men). The solteros sleep in bunk beds in a separate wing of the building. A family is allocated about 2 × 2 m by the contractor.

The zafrero, his wife and his children all sleep together in one bed. Families try to create some privacy by hanging sheets between their own bed and their neighbours'. But obviously, as all families sleep in the same big room, privacy is rare. The wives of the zafreros cook in a covered kitchen area. The camp has a communal space, the comedor, where people can share their meals. On rainy days and Sundays, families spend time together on their beds or sit in the comedor. As an exception, Los Limones has showers and actual toilets. The primary school closest to the Los Limones camp is about 1.5 km away, and transport of the 30-40 school-going children is arranged by the plantation owner. The children attend the regular school system.

Health Status

In this camp, children don't fall ill very often; when they do they mostly suffer from diarrhoea. The plantation owner makes sure there are medicines for the people who get sick and medical attention for the ones who get injured. This is an exceptional situation, resulting in the UNICEF representative in Santa Cruz to name the Los Limones camp a 'model camp'.

Campamento Los Elechos (Santa Cruz) is a mobile camp that houses about 40 zafreros. The families and single men construct their own tents; sanitary facilities are lacking. The work in the zafra takes only about four weeks. Upon completion, the harvesters leave Los Elechos and rebuild their camp near another plantation. The tents are open at both front and back ends; animals, like cows, can easily enter and plunder the food reserves. During the night, it can get very cold, and, during the day, it is extremely hot. The families construct their own beds. There are no cooking facilities and the women build wood fires on the ground. The primary school closest to Los Elechos is also about 1.5 km away from the camp. It actually is not much of a school: it functions only for 2½ days/week. Most families who work here do not have, or do not bring, school-aged children to the camp. Their children are generally much younger. There is no health centre close to the campamento in Los Elechos. The little children contract diseases related to the unhygienic conditions in the camp, like diarrhoea, and are often malnourished, which can lead to anaemia.

Housing Conditions

Campamento El Lapacho (Bermejo) houses about 20 zafreros, most of whom have come with their families. The families sleep in brick structures consisting of 3 × 3 m rooms that are shared by two families, and in which they construct their own beds. The single men and their cuartas (helpers) share rooms with two or three other people. It has about ten school-aged migrant children. The school lies at 1.5 km from the camp. Every morning, the children walk to school and attend classes until lunch time. During the zafra, the teachers become very busy with the extra pupils and their needs; migrant children are at a lower educational level and must do extra work to catch up with the local children. When the males move to another camp, the children of El Lapacho stay in the camp, together with some of the women who stay behind to take care of the children who then can continue in the same school. However, some parents are unwilling to use this solution and take their children along to a next camp where there might be no school. Hygienic conditions are very poor: there is no bathing area, no sanitation and children walk around in dirty clothes and with dirty hands and faces. The area is infested with mosquitoes, and so everyone is covered with bites.

Work Operations in the Sugar Cane Harvest

The year-round maintenance of sugar cane plantations (fertilisation, etc.) is usually done by a few permanent labourers. When the crop is fully grown, roughly between April and November, more labour force is required for the harvest. After the sugar cane has been harvested, it is de-topped and stacked into piles; then it is loaded onto a flatbed truck and brought to the ingenio to be further processed into sugar or alcohol. In Bermejo, most of the loading is still done manually, but in Santa Cruz, more and more plantation owners have started using mechanical loaders in recent years.

In addition to mechanisation, a new burning technique has also made the zafra less labour intensive. By setting entire plantations alight excess leaves and weeds are burned, leaving just the stalks behind, making cutting a lot easier. It also serves as protection from animals such as snakes, but the smoke caused by the enormous fires has obvious implications for air quality and causes respiratory problems, especially among children. The burning technique also results in less child labour: young children are no longer needed to help peel the leaves from the stalks or to weed between the crops. Adolescent boys of 14 and older already work as contracted harvesters. The work they do is the same as that of adults. They earn a salary of between 1,000 and 4,000 Bolivianos (100-400) a month, depending on the volume they manage to cut. They engage in setting the plantations alight, cutting down the sugar cane using a machete, de-topping the stalks, then stacking them into piles, which weigh between 40 and 50 kg. The stacks are then lifted onto their shoulder, and walked towards the flatbed truck where the loader has to climb a wooden ladder to the top of the other piles and deposit his own. This work is extremely heavy, and no younger children are involved.

Educational Opportunities of Workers' Children

In Bermejo, the zafreros often bring their own cuartas. These helpers are normally the zafrero's own wife, child, neighbour or other relative. Cuartas help with cutting, stacking and peeling. They don't generally participate with loading the sugar cane, which is done manually in Bermejo, as this work is too heavy for them (if it is a woman or child). Cuartas can themselves also hire helpers, often their own children. Children below the age of 14 rarely participate in the sugar cane harvest in Santa Cruz. The burning technique and mechanisation has led to fewer children working on the plantations. Parents try to leave all their children at home in the care of family members, so that home and school life are disturbed as little as possible. Unfortunately, adequate childcare is not always available, and so still too often, the youngest non-school-going children are brought along to the camps and plantations. These children accompany their mothers all day long and help them with some chores, like fetching water and cleaning, or just playing at their side.

Children and adolescents aged 12-17, girls as well as boys who are still in school, in Santa Cruz as well as in Bermejo, help their parents as cuartas in the sugar cane harvest after school, in the weekends and/or during holidays. These children participate in the different harvesting activities according to their age and sex. School going children of 11 and 12 years old participate in the same activities as older permanent helpers like cutting, de-topping and stacking sugar cane, after classes or on non-school days. In Bermejo, some of these children (only boys) also participate in the extremely heavy task of manually loading sugar cane onto the flatbed trucks.

Employment of Children and Adolescents in the Plantations

Usually children and youths working as cuartas earn a salary between 300 and 800 Bolivianos (€30-80) per month, but especially the ones who work with their family members tend to be unaware of their earnings and might not even earn anything at all. Helping out family members is perceived as family work for which minors don't need to be rewarded individually. Doña Delia, who also lives in the Porcelana camp in Bermejo, for example, told me that her 14-year-old son Daniel works as a cuarta with his father and doesn't receive a salary: "If he needs anything like clothes or something, he gets it from us, but we don't pay him. We just don't have enough money".

In Bermejo, like in Santa Cruz, women and adolescent girls do the household chores in the camps, even though they may work as cuartas too. Girls are never hired as full-time contracted harvesters because the work is considered too heavy for women. Women in the sugar cane harvest are expected to run the household and related activities. Zafreros who are not accompanied by their wives may bring along a female cuarta to cook and wash his clothes, in addition to her tasks in the harvest. Girls usually accompany their brothers to work as cuarta, or both of them work as cuartas, but the sister is the one who cooks and washes. The solteros need someone to cook for them. A pensionista is such a person; she gets money from a group of men to do groceries and cook for them. Girls from 14 years onwards, for example, 15-year-old Nina, are hired to do this work.

Social Position

The pensionistas' work is hard; they have to get up early to cook for others, they have to go on errands when others have a day off, they have to cook large amounts on a simple wood fire out in the open, they have to work in a subservient position relative to their male clients and must have a strong character to survive within the machismo environment. The zafreros work in clusters of two or four people and are paid as a group, according to the amount of cane that they have cut; this is normally about 17 or 18 Bolivianos (€1.70/1.80) per tonne of cut sugar cane. Experienced, very hard-working zafreros can possibly cut about 8 t/day, but young inexperienced harvesters might cut only 2 t.

Deductions Made from the Wages

Even though many deductions are made from their salary (advance, food costs, travel expenses, etc.), the adolescents earn more than they would at home; unfortunately, it is not enough to last them the rest of the year. The rest of the year they work their own land, or in other sectors such as construction, mining or agriculture, elsewhere in Bolivia or in Argentina. Although a small group of adolescents only works at the plantations during school holidays, most adolescents in Santa Cruz work six days a week, throughout the zafra.

Daily Routine Work

On working days, they get up at 4:00 am and have a cup of tea and a piece of bread. Around 4:30 am, the group of zafreros heads to the field, either walking or driven by their contractor on the wagon behind the tractor, and start cutting the sugar cane at sunrise. The adolescents work all morning without any real breaks; they only stop every once in a while to drink some water, smoke a cigarette, chew coca leaves and sharpen their machetes. At noon, the pensionista will have lunch ready, which she will either bring to the field or serve at the camp. The lunch breaks take an hour to an hour and a half. After the lunch break, the harvesters work the whole afternoon. Around 5/6 pm, they stop working and return to the campamento, have dinner and socialise until 8 or 9 pm, at which point everybody goes to sleep. Sometimes though, the loading machine is available only in the middle of the night and the zafreros will get up to use it.

Occupational Risks and Health Problems

In addition to the long hours and the high workload, the adolescents are exposed to an extreme climate with high temperatures. All workers try to protect themselves from the heat by wearing hats, drinking a lot of water and starting work very early. However, when a lot of work has to be done, they work through the hottest hours as well.

Because of the heat, the zafreros would prefer to work in sleeveless shirts, but the sugar cane leaves are sharp, thus protective layers are needed. Most adolescent zafreros work on sandals made from car tires, which leave their feet exposed to injuries. Even though cutting sugar cane all day causes hands to blister, none of the adolescent workers use gloves. A 16-year-old boy argued: "I think it doesn't help to put on gloves: they don't help because they get holes within one day's work. I prefer to just get hard skin on my hands".

Cuartas work six days a week. Female cuartas have to get up before the others to prepare breakfast. After breakfast, the zafreros and their cuartas head to the fields. Although most children help on days that they don't have school—accompanying their parents, combining their work with rest and play—quite a large number work full-time.

The plantation workers, and their children, live in a very unhealthy environment. Both children who work at the plantations and those who simply accompany their parents, are exposed to leishmaniasis, tuberculosis, scabies and lice, which is mainly on account of the overcrowded accommodations with poor hygiene and sanitation. The heat exacerbates the presence of insects and the general weak state of health and malnourishment make children more vulnerable to infections. According to 20-year-old Valentina, one of the harvester's wives in Santa Cruz, many accidents and illnesses occur because of the working and living conditions.

The work they do is very strenuous and risky, but not many serious incidents were reported. They appear to have become accustomed to serious accidents and do not consider them noteworthy or requiring medical treatment. Many children and adolescents who work as cuartas in the zafra reported machete cuts. As the machetes are sharpened several times a day, the cuts in the hands, arms, feet or legs tend to be deep. Nelson (8), a school-going child in Trementinal who helps his parents at the sugar cane plantations during the afternoon after school, recalls: "Once when I was working with my mother, I cut myself in the leg. It wasn't very bad but it hurt a lot and a lot of blood came out of the wound. They put something around it, but it kept hurting for many days. The machete was very sharp". Although cuts on hands, arms, feet or legs are common, few children are brought into health centres to seek treatment. Reaching a doctor or a health centre is difficult, and wounds are expected to heal themselves anyway.

Work Operations

Cutting, de-topping, stacking and loading sugar cane are heavy tasks, extreme tiredness is the most prevalent consequence of the work. Especially in the last months of the harvest, the workers complain about their bodies becoming weaker and they feel more tired and want to return to their homes. Many acknowledge ten children on Bolivian Sugar Cane Plantations 201 that the work physically wears them out. Francisco (15), from the Okinawa camp in Santa Cruz, complained: "I am really tired of the work and I have become much thinner since I came to the harvest; the heavy work really makes one lose weight". Mesquil (16) commented on how hard he found the work: "I didn't think that the work would be so hard. It is so hot and I am thirsty all the time. The first very day, my arm and my back started hurting". After a week of work, his hands had been completely rubbed raw and were covered with open blisters. Mesquil considered leaving after a few days, but he changed his mind and tries to ignore health implications for economic reasons: "Although the work is exhausting and my hands hurt, I am thinking of staying at least the whole month to earn a bit of money".

Educational Status of Children

When boys are about 14-15 years old, they are considered old enough to contribute to the family income. If they work fulltime, they have usually only finished primary school until the fifth grade. Only some of them have started secondary school, but dropped out before finishing. They usually, like Hector (15), do not perceive further study as a real option because they cannot afford the enrolment fees or book costs: "I finished eigth grade last year and then I quit going to school. I would still like to continue studying in high school but there is no money in my family for me to study. Maybe I'll have to pay for it myself". Some, however, dislike working in the sugar cane harvest so much that ten children on Bolivian Sugar Cane Plantations 203 their wish of continuing to study has grown stronger. Most adolescents like the fact that they have started to earn money or simply don't feel like studying anymore. Uriel (15), in the Campo Grande camp in Bermejo, is a good example of many boys who don't desire going back to school because they have become used to working and earning money for themselves or their families.

For children of school-going age (6-12), the zafra can be quite impacting. It either means that they travel with their parents to the zafra region where they try to find a school and work outside school hours and in the weekends, or that they stay in their hometowns to continue classes and wait for their parents to come home. This can take as long as six months if their parents stay for the whole zafra period. Either option can be emotionally and educationally disrupting.

Conclusion

Children who migrate to the sugar cane regions, despite some recent improvements, live with their families in overcrowded camps with generally poor living and hygiene conditions. The conditions in which the children and adolescents work are harsh. The climate is extreme, and the work is exhausting and hazardous. Few zafreros use protective clothing during their work. Adolescents from the age of 14 onwards engage in all harvest-related activities such as burning, cutting, de-topping and (in Bermejo) loading. They work six days a week, cutting the sugar cane with a machete, from early in the morning until the end of the afternoon, and earn between three and four a day. All zafreros and cuartas, including the younger children, suffer from machete cuts, abrasions, blisters, heat exhaustion, insect, spider or snake bites, backaches and even broken bones. Health centres are often far away from the camps, and so wounds or other health problems are left to heal themselves.

In Bermejo most of the children under 12 help their parents cut sugar cane with a machete, even if they attend school during the weekdays. Although children under 12 do not work in Santa Cruz, they nevertheless suffer from the miserable living conditions in the camps.

Although most school-going children attend school near the camps, the migration is disruptive to their education. Sometimes, children are left at home with relatives, or parents stop travelling to the zafra when their children start attending school, but when parents have no such choice, they bring their young children, either school-going or not, with them to the camps. Some families even move to several camps during one zafra season and each time the child has to adapt to a new situation and education suffers. Participation in the zafra familiarises adolescents with earning money and they often drop out of education as a result. A majority of the adolescents do not consider further schooling an option. For many adolescent zafreros, working in the zafra marks a transition period into adulthood. Although most adolescents have finished primary school, they quickly turn to work, as their hometowns rarely offer secondary education.

Different strategies have been implemented in the various sugar cane regions of Santa Cruz and Bermejo, aiming to eradicate child labour from the sector. In general, all the separate interventions have their own specific impact on the problem of child labour, and substantial progress has been made, particularly with regards to young children, but the impact on adolescents is still lacking. There is certainly not one type of intervention that would work best; a combination of complementary strategies is needed. The strategy of raising awareness about labour rights appeared to be an important one in stimulating harvesters to struggle for their own rights and understand the importance of education. The reasons for youths to participate in the sugar cane harvest vary among the different age groups, and so interventions have to be tailored to suit the needs of each group. Because school-going children work during non-school days or periods, projects to eradicate child labour among school-going children in the sector should focus on finding other pastimes for children during these periods.

The most difficult group to reach directly remains the group of adolescents who work as cuartas or contracted harvesters. Because their motive to work in the harvest is economic, the alternative requires income generation as well. Despite improvements, the harvesters rarely mentioned having been part of a project to improve living and working conditions and/or projects against child labour. Projects may have been in operation, but people may not have been actively involved and they thus do not seem to recollect. Yet, the incidence of child labour seems to have decreased. To what extent the different projects actually have reduced the number of children participating in the sugar cane harvest is hard to measure, because patterns tend to change slowly and projects often lack continuity. A decrease also may have been caused by other intervening factors.

As long as children continue to be present at the plantations, there is a danger of them becoming involved in child labour activities or living in an unsuitable environment. In order to make sure that the risks of such involvement are reduced, it would be better if children were not physically present in this sector at all.

6
Conclusion

The tea mania enthralled the minds of European planters who have fancied to become rich overnight, started tea plantation in the Nilgiris' District, Tamil Nadu even in most inaccessible part of the district. A large number of indentured labourers were brought from the southern districts of Tamil Nadu and more importantly from Ceylon and put them in different areas of the Nilgiris' District which were full of jungles and wild animals where no human being can think of living for a day. These labourers became the victims of circumstances and started their plantation work under the threat of European planters. Many labourers died due to malaria, kalazar, etc. Many escaped and died on the way. Those who stayed back in the garden tried to adjust themselves in new plantation environment and gradually settled there. With the passage of time, they forgot old memories of their ancestral places and began to develop a new human environment amidst multi-ethnic and multi-linguistic groups of the people drawn from different parts of the country.

They were compelled to settle in different labour lines where different groups of people were forced to live together. After a few decades these indentured labourers were metamorphosed in the plantation environment and a new life began and a new milieu emerged.

Exploitation at Workplace: It is known to everyone concerned with tea plantation that tea bushes were brought from other places in a most dignified way by the distinguished persons while the labourers were brought from other places in a most undignified way and that too by mischievous and dishonest persons. During the initial period, local labourers were recruited but the nature of tea plantation did not suit their temperament and they considered it below their status and dignity. But the expansion of tea plantation went on rapidly and requirement of labour was fulfilled by importation of labour from outside the province of Madras. The labourers immigrated to the Nilgiris' District, Tamil Nadu were from plain districts of Tamil Nadu, Kerala, Karnataka, Andhra Pradhesh and eastern and northern provinces of Sri Lanka. They were poverty-stricken, petty agriculturists or landless agricultural labourers. After their arrival in the tea gardens, all hopes and aspirations were shattered by the blow of misfortune. They were not habituated of doing plantation work and that too in unfavourable environment. From the day they put their feet in the soil of tea plantation, they started planning to run away from the garden and many lost their lives in process of desertion. Some made adjustment with plantation life.

Migration to tea plantation in the Tamil Nadu was basically different from the migration of labour from village to urban and industrial centres because the former was family based being encouraged by the planters in order to stabilise resident labour. The tea garden labourers are socio-economically backward. The tea garden labourers are virtually living in the land of isolation having no interaction with the outsiders. They have lost their linguistic chauvinism and have adopted the language of the local indigenous people. Educationally, they are poor and their cultural advancement is restricted to the garden environment. Their economic backwardness stand as a formidable obstacle on their progress.

The tea industry in the Nilgiris' District, Tamil Nadu has offered bread to immigrant labourers as well as the people of the concerned district. The industry has provided employment opportunity to many unemployed youths. It has also helped in early growth of urbanization in the hilly town. Due to tea industry large number of business, shops, diversified variety stores, workshops, etc. have come into existence, which has provided employment to shelter less persons. The subsistence economy has been changed into wage economy. The impact of the tea industry in socio-economic and political activities of the people of Tamil Nadu is also great since people from most of the districts of Tamil Nadu have found their permanent abode in the Nilgiris' District. The management of tea industry is a Herculean task. The agro-based industry depends upon the immigrant labourers. In the early period every dependent members of the immigrant labour used to get easy employment in the garden but his employment has become acute in every garden and the management is in trouble to solve the unemployment problem of the dependant of the labourers. Various Acts and regulations have checked the tyrannical administration of the tea garden managers. The labourers and their trade union organizations are active in pressurizing the management for fulfillment of various demands like increase in wages, bonus and other fringe benefits.

On many occasions, strikes and gherao of managers have become the order of the day. Many managers have been physically assaulted by the agitated labourers. Besides, the extremists in the hilly areas, though late, have raised their ugly heads and have created panic throughout the tea gardens of Tamil Nadu. They are extorting money and harassing the field staff. The healthy plantation environment has been polluted now.

The last but not less important point which deserves attention is the cause of sickness of tea gardens. There are various factors contributing to this. The primary reason of sickness of a garden is bad management. Management does not want to wipe out bad tea plants for some immediate gain which ultimately leads to loss of production. Slowly and slowly, the uneconomic old plants should be replaced by new ones. In any garden, there are good plantations as well as some old and bad ones giving little yield, but the average yield is not uneconomic. The old plantations should be replaced by new plantations so that in the long run when the good plantations will become old and turn uneconomic, the new plantation will make up the loss and sustain the tea garden to be economically available. This requires investment of a part of the profit. Owing to frequent change of hands, the new owner wants to have quick profit and is reluctant to invest in a share of it. Lack of investment increases the liability and through years due to cumulative effect a tea garden cannot bear the liabilities and become sick.

Many gardens do not possess necessary materials and equipments so that the pest, etc. could be controlled at an early stage of attack. Drought in some years inflicts heavy loss in production, shock of which cannot be absorbed in many cases.

Proper care and attention are to be paid for gearing up the economic availability of the tea gardens in India because this is not only an industrial sector earning foreign exchange but also employing a large number of poor labourers who have left behind their homes and came in search of a few morsels of food.

The solution of the problems of the tea plantation workers in Tamil Nadu depends upon several factors, namely first, the improvement of the general level of culture among the masses, which will enable them to take advantage of the industrial opportunities on the one hand, and to guard themselves against exploitation and undue advantages by employers on the other; second, the establishment of public employment bureaus for giving impartial advice on industrial opportunities and for helping in securing employment abroad; third, a cheap transportation system, for helping the emigration of the working people from the places of residence to those of work—the work of transportation may be conveniently combined with that of employment; and fourth, the betterment of the conditions of work and life on plantations themselves, by legislation or otherwise, so as to make them more attractive to the prospective workers.

Role of the Stakeholders: The solution of the problem depends upon four agencies, namely: (1) intelligent public opinion, (2) progressive legislation by the State, (3) enlightened self-interest of the employers, and (4) concerted action of the workers through 'genuine' trade unions. The greatest dynamic force in modern society is justice. It is public opinion or the national will that can enforce the incorporation of this ideal into social and legislative institutions.

While the legislative measures and welfare work already referred to might ameliorate the recruiting, working and living conditions, the real solution of the problem lies in elevating the social, political and industrial status of the Indian masses. It is their colossal ignorance, abject poverty and utter helplessness which have made them subject to exploitation. These can be removed only in the following ways, namely first, the introduction of free and compulsory education, both general and vocational; second, the removal of all barriers to social equality, e.g. the caste system and untouchability; third, the granting of universal suffrage to all men and women; and fourth, the development of industrial enterprise and creation of new industrial opportunities, where men and women, as intelligent, efficient and independent labourers, can find employment and can freely make a favourable bargain for their own welfare as well as that of society of which they are a part.

References

Books

Arbuthnot, J.C. *Report on the Conditions of Tea Garden Labour in the Dooars of Bengal, in Madras and in Ceylon*, Shillong, Assam Government Press, 1904.

Abu-Lughod, Lila. *Writing against Culture in Recapturing Anthropology: Working in the Present*, ed. Richard Fox: Santa Fe, N.M.: School of American Research Press, 1991.

Agrawal, A. Introduction: Women, work and migration in Asia. In A. Agrawal (Ed.), *Migrant Women and Work* (Vol. 4, pp. 21-45). New Delhi: Sage Publications, 2006.

Banerji, Sara. *The Tea Planter's Daughter*, Arrow Books, London, 1988.

Bandarage, Ashoka. *Colonialism in Sri Lanka: The Political Economy of the Kandyan Highlands 1983-86,* Mountain Publishers, New York, 1990.

Barker, George M. *A Tea Planter's Life in Assam,* Bengal Secretariat Press, Calcutta, 1884.

Bhowmik, S. *Class Formation in the Plantation System*, People's Publishing House, New Delhi, 1981.

Bohning, W.R. *Studies in International Labour Migration.* London: The Macmillan Press Ltd., London, 1984.

Chatterjee, Piya. "A State of Work: Women and Politics on Plantation Front-lines." In *Frontline Ferninisms: Women, War and Resistance*, ed. M. Waller and J. Rycenga. Garland Press New York, 2000.

Chatopadhyaya, H.I. *Indians in Sri Lanka,* O.L.S. Publishers Pvt. Ltd., Calcutta, 1979.

Cotton, Henry. *Indian and Home Memories*, Fisher Unwin Press, London, 1911.

Craton, Michael. *Searching the Invisible Man: Slaves and Plantation Lift in Jamaica*, Harvard University Press, Cambridge, 1978.

Das, Amal Kumar, and H.N. Banerjee. *The Impact of the Tea Industry on the Lift of Tribals of West Bengal*, Tribal Welfare Department, Government of West Bengal, Calcutta, 1964.

Das Gupta, Manas. *Labour and Trade Union Movements in Tea Plantations of Terai: Problems of Class Formation*, North Bengal University, Bagdogra, 1992.

Das Gupta, Manas. *On the Problems of Development of North Bengal: A Background Report,* Department of Economics, North Bengal University, Bagdogra, 1991.

Das, R.K. *Plantation Labour in India*, Prabasi Press, Calcutta, 1931.

Dasgupta, Pranab Kumar. *Maintenance of Ethnic Boundaries in the Tea Gardens of North Bengal and Assam*, North Bengal University, Bagdogra, 1984.

Deepak K. Mishra, Vandana Upadhyay and Atul Sarma, *Unfolding Crisis in Assam Tea Plantations*, Avantika Printers Private Limited, New Delhi, 2012.

Enquiry into the Cost and Standard of Living by Plantation Workers in Assam and Bengal, Government of India, Ministry of Labour, Published by Manager of Publications, New Delhi, 1948.

Elizabeth Kaniampady, *State of Women.*

Francis, T.R. *The Young Tea Planter's Companion: A Practical Treatise on the Management of a Tea Garden in Assam,* London, 1886.

Griffiths, Percival. *The History of the Indian Tea Industry,* Weidenfeldta Press, London, 1962.

Jain, R.K. *South Indians on the Plantation Frontier in Malaya,* Yale University Press, New Hagen, 1970.

Jam, Shobhi Jam, Shobhita. *Sexual Equality: Workers in an Asian Plantation System*, Sterling Publications, New Delhi, 1988.

Jayewardene, Chandra. *Conflict and Solidarity in a Guyanese Plantation*, Althone Press, London, 1963.

Iar Ali Khan. *Impact of Tea Plantation Industries on the Life of Tribal Labourers,* Anthropological Survey' of India, Government of India, New Delhi, 1983.

Karotem, S. Prel and B. Datta Ray. *Labour Welfare in Tea Plantations: An Assessment of the Plantation Labour Act in the Tea Garden Labour in North Eastern India*, Vendrame Institute, Shillong, 1990.

Khan, I.A. and D. Biswas. *Problems and Prospects of Darjeeling Tea Industry,* The International Press, New Delhi, 1990.

Kurian, Rachel. *Women Workers in the Sri Lankan Plantation Sector: Historical and Contemporary Analyses*, International Labour Office, Geneva, 1982.

Labaree, Benjamin W. *The Boston Tea Party*, Northeastern Press, Boston, 1979.

Lal, Brij. *Kunti's Cry: Indentured Women on Fiji Plantations Indian Economic and Social History Review*, Northeastern Press, Boston, 1985.

Moliapatra, Prabhu Prasad. "Class Conflict and Agrarian Regimes in Chhotanagpur, 1860-1950." *The Indian Economic and Social History, Review* 2.8, No. I (1991): 1-42.

Nalini, R. *Social Work and the Work Place,* Concept Publishing Company Pvt. Ltd., New Delhi, 2011.

Oddvar, Hollup. *Bonded Labour: Caste and Cultural Identity among Tamil Plantation Workers in Sri Lanka,* Sterling Publishers Pvt. Ltd., New Delhi, 1994.

Raman, Vasantili. *Child Labour in the Tea Plantations of North Eastern India*, UNICEF and Ministry of Labour and Social Welfare, New Delhi, 1991.

Ramsden, A.R. *Assam Planter: Tea Planting and Hunting in the Assam Jungle,* Althone Press, London, 1945.

Recldock, Rhoda, and Jair Shobhita, *Women Plantation Workers: International Experiences,* New York University Press, New York, 1998.

Sarkar, R.L. and Mahendra L. Lama, *Tea Plantation Workers in the Eastern Himalayas—A Study on wages, Employment and Living Standards*, Atma Ram and Sons, New Delhi, 1986.

Sharma, K.R. *Industrial Labour in India,* Atlantic Publishers and Distributors, New Delhi, 1997.

Kumar, Purnedu. *State and Society in North-East India—A Study of Immigrant Tea Plantation*, Regency Publications, New Delhi, 2006

Dasgupta, Pranab Kumar and Khan, I.A. *Impact of Tea Plantation Industry on the Life of Tribal Labourers*, Anthropological Survey of India, Government of India, Calcutta, 1983.

Report of the Assam Labour Enquiry Committee, 1906, Office of the Superintendent of Government Printing Press, Calcutta, 1906.

Report on the Survey of Labour Conditions in Tea Plantations and Tea Factories in India, 1961-1962, Shimla: Ministry of Labour, 1966.

Rajan, S. and Prabhat Kumar, *Historical Overview of International Migration*, Rawat Publications, New Delhi, 1996.

Teraj (West Bengal, 1984). Alipore: Superintendent of Government Printing, 1952.

Purcell, A.A. and J. Hallsworth. *Report on Labour Conditions in India. British Trade Union Congress Delegation to India, November 1927-March 1928,* Trade Union Congress General Council, London, 1928.

Phukan, Umananda *The Ex-tea Garden Labour Population in Assam*, N.L Publishers, Gauhati, 1983.

Journals

Adas, Michael. "From Foot dragging to Flight: The Evasive History of Peasant Avoidance Protest in South and South East Asia." *Journal of Peasant Studies,* 13, 110. 2 (January 1982): 64-86.

"A Workers' Cooperative in Tea", *Assam Review and Tea News*, 78, I.L.O. 9 (November 1989): 21-28.

Aggarwal, Ravina. "Shadow Work: Women in the Workplace in Ladakh, India," *Anthropology of Work Review*, 16, Nos. 1-2 (1991): 33-38.

Chatterjee, Suranjan, and R. Dasgupta. "Tea Labour in Assam: Recruitment and Government Policy." *Economic and Political Weekly* (special number, 1981): 1861-1868.

Athukorala, P. (1990). "International contract migration and reintegration of return migrants: The experience of Sri Lanka." *International Migration Review*, 24(2), 323-46.

Bandarage, Asoka. "The Establishment and Consolidation of the Plantation Economy in Sri Lanka." Bulletin of Concerned Asian Scholars 14, no. (1982):2-22.

Barbora, Sanjay. "Struggles in the Tea Plantations of Assam: Then and Now", *Revolutionary Democracy*, 5, No. 1 (April 1999): 41-46.

Beckford, George. "Caribbean Peasantry in the Confines of the Plantation Mode of Production." *International Social Science Journal*, 37, No. 3 (1985):401-19.

Behal, Rana P. "The Emergence of a Plantation Economy: Assam Tea Industry in the Nineteenth Century. Occasional Papers on History and Society", New Delhi: Nehru Memorial Museum and Library, 198$.1947." *Bengal Capital History Journal*, I (July-December 19/4): 30-78.

Behal, Rana P., and Prabhu Mohapatra. "Tea and Money versus Human Life': The Rise and Fall of the Indenture System *in the Assam Tea Plantations*, 1840-1908." *Journal of Peasant Studies*, Nos. 2-3 (1992): 142-71.

Bhowmik, Sharit. "Plantation Labour Act and Child Labour", *Economic and Political Weekly* (October 17, 1992): 2287-89.

Chatterjee, *D.N. Family Welfare Education Project: Study of Savings on Account of an Averted Birth. Binnaguri,* Doar Branch of Indian Tea Association, Bengal Secretariat Press Calcutta, 1960.

Clawen, A. (2002). "Female labour migration to Bangkok: Transforming rural-urban interactions and social networks through globalization". *Asia-Pacific Population Journal*, 17(3), 53-78.

Deb, K. *Impact of Plantations on the Agrarian Structure of the Brahrnaputra Valley,* Calcutta, Centre for Studies in the Social Sciences, 1979.

Dooars Branch of the Indian Tea Association. Annual Reports 1908. Baseline Survey Report for ILO/UNFPA/1TA Project: IND/80/ PO—Family Welfare Education in Tea Plantations. Binnaguri: DBITA, 1991. Training Course in Health and Family Welfare for Welfare Officers in Tea Plantations. In collaboration with the International Labour Organization. Bangkok: Labour and Population Team for Asia and Pacific (LA PTAP), 1990.

Enquiry into the Living Conditions of the Tea Plantation Workers in Darjeeling, *Economic and Political Weekly*, 20, No. 30 (July 27, 1935): PE42-52.

"From Peasants and Tribesmen to Plantation Workers." *Economic and Political Weekly*, 2, No. 4 (January 25, 1986): PE2.

John, J., S. Lahiri and A. Nanda. "The Plight of 'Unfree' Tea Workers." *Labour File: A Monthly Journal of Labor and Economic Affairs*, 5, 1105. 7-9 (July-September 1999): 1.

"Rise and Fall of Free Emigration in Asian Tea Plantation, C882.-1908." Paper presented to Workshop on Capitalist Plantations in Colonial Asia. Center for Asian Studies Amsterdam, September 26-29, 7990.

"Recruitment and Migration Policy in Tea Plantations in West Bengal." Bulletin of the Cultural Research Institute 15, Nos. 1-2 (1981): 23-33.

"Secure this Excellent Class of Labor: Gender and Labor Recruitment for British Indian Tea Plantations." Bulletin of Concerned Asian Scholars (1995): 43-56.

"Tebhaga Movement in Doars: Some Issues Regarding Ethnicity and Plantation Labour in North-East India." *Economic and Political Weekly*, 20, No. 13 (March 30, 1985): 538-541. "Wages of Tea Garden Workers in West Bengal." *Economic and Political Weekly*, 27, No. 40 (October 2; 1982): 1600-01.

"Tea Talk: Measures of Labor in the Discourse of Sri Lanka's Estate Tamils." Paper presented at Conference on Plantation Labour in Colonial Ceylon.

"The Gorkhaland Agitation in Darjeeling: Some Political and Economic Dimensions." Special lecture 9, Centre for Himalayan Studies, University of North Bengal, Bagdogra, March 1988.

Web Sites

www.springerlink.com/content/6799162w1040104/fittest/.pdf, 04/02/2014 3:20 p.m www.springerlink.com/content/m186003104372160/futtext/.pdf, 14/02/2014 1:10 p.m

www.springerlink.com/content/151244225742477 8/futtext/.pdf, 21/02/2014 5:40 p.m

www.springerlink.com/content/G65417086q008667/futtext/.pdf, 23/03/2014 4:15 p.m

+www.springerlink.com/content/35n035138q8x257/futtext/.pdf, 05/04/2014 1150 a.m

www.springerlink.com/content/U86wpr4663gu1276/futtext/.pdf, 16/05/2013 10:20 a.m

www.springerlink.com/content/W457028176103355/futtext/.pdf, 19/05/2013 6:20 p.m

www.springerlink.com/content/5122473776120 4t0/futtext/.pdf, 21/06/2013 2:20 p.m

w.w.w.springerlink.com/content/w1040104/futtext/.pdf, 29/07/2012 3:20 p.m

www.dgft.gov.ins 07/04/2013 10:10am

Asian Migration News 1–15 March (2007a). Govt. bans overseas employment of mothers with young children. http://www.smc.org.ph/amnews/amn070315/amn070315.htm. 16/04/2007 12:30 p.m

Asian Migration News 1–15 April (2007b). Ban on the migration of mothers with children unfair: MFA. http://www.smc.org.ph/amnews/amn070430/southasia/srilanka070430.htm. 08/09/2007 03:20 p.m

Asian Migration News 1–30 May (2007c). Govt. reconsiders ban on overseas employment of young mothers. http://www.smc.org.ph/amnews/amn070515/amn070515.htm. 08/06/2007 08:10 p.m

Asian Migration News 1–31 August (2008). New National Labour Policy. http://www.smc.org.ph/amnews/amn0808/amn0808.htm. 12/12/2008 05:00 p.m.